STREETS
OF LONDON

*The Official
Biography of
Ralph McTell*

Chris Hockenhull

First Published in 1997 by
NORTHDOWN PUBLISHING LIMITED
PO Box 49, Bordon
Hants GU35 0AF

British Library Cataloguing-in-Publication Data
A catalogue for this book is available from the British Library

ISBN 1900711 02 8

Edited by John Tobler

Designed by Simon Joslin

Also available from Northdown Publishing:
Rhinos, Winos & Lunatics! The Legend Of Man by Deke Leonard
Down By The Jetty – The Dr Feelgood Story by Tony Moon

PICTURE CREDITS

Photographs in this book have been reproduced courtesy of the Ralph McTell and Chris Hockenhull archives. Thanks are also due to: Dany Gignoux, Topic Records, Henry Bartlett, Jo Lustig, Tony Russell/Redferns, Bruce May (Music Management), Christopher Ridley/Radio Times, Michael Putland, Mogens Eskildsen, Barry Plummer. Granada TV, David Gahr, Ian Burgess, Mike Diamond.

While every effort has been made to trace the owners of photographs used, this has sometimes proved impossible: such copyright owners are invited to contact the publishers.

Contents

A word from Billy…

Ralph McTell is everything that I aspire to be.

Not only is he a brilliant songwriter, wonderful singer and an exceptionally gifted musician but he achieves all of this with unassuming dignity and charm.

Is it any wonder that I have a profound love and respect for Ralph and his work and value his friendship greatly?

This is not only a book about my hero but about a national treasure.

Billy Connolly!

By May 1971, I was 15 years of age. I had recently caught the music bug and was on a seemingly one-dimensional quest to compare every singer-songwriter's work to that of Bob Dylan, who I had in my mind as the benchmark for anybody who wrote a song. And they were never going to do it as well as he. Therefore, it was a shock for me to be actually persuaded by my girlfriend of the time to not just listen to but actually pay to go and see one of these 'wannabes' in Liverpool.

I'd never heard of the bloke before, although I did actually know two of the songs. His name was Ralph McTell and the other of those two songs was called 'First And Last Man' – I think I'd seen the Spinners do it on the television.

That night changed my opinions a lot. Here was the most intimate act I'd ever heard. With each song, I felt varying emotions, ranging from laughter, sadness, optimism and hope as the night wore on. Ever since then, the work of Ralph McTell has stayed very close to me and his songs have remained one of the few constant things in my life of many changes.

Acknowledgments

The purpose of this story is for you to share in the life and songs of Ralph McTell in the hope that it will help to demonstrate that there is a lot behind this very gifted artist. If you think he's only written one major song, it may lay that myth once and for all and 'Make you change your mind'.

I would like to express my gratitude to the following for sharing their memories:

Martin Allcock, Mick Bartlett, Iris Bentley (RIP), Vernon Burford, Pete Chalkley, Nanci Griffith, Carolyn Hester, Bert Jansch, Johnny 'Jonah' Jones, Raymond 'Wizz' Jones, Jo Lustig, Mick McDonagh, Jacqui McShee, Bruce May, Nanna May, Winifred May, Christy Moore, Alan O'Leary, Dave Pegg, Arthur Taylor and Danny Thompson.

To Fraser Massey, for his excellent (but sadly unpublished) second McTell interview for *ZigZag* magazine which was a great source of information, my thanks from afar.

For expert help all the times the computer(s) wouldn't do as I asked, I thank Ben Heal and Adam (you should have gone to Dixon's) Redpath.

To Beryl Higgins who I can blame for persuading me to go hear RMcT at Liverpool University.

To Sylvia and Annie Hockenhull. Also my friends who have seen this project from the beginning and have helped me through.

To John Tobler – I consider it an honour to know such a nice fellow who has helped and cajoled me when I needed it most.

To Ralph McTell who will know what I mean when I thank him for being there at times when I was most grateful for his friendship. To the wonderful May family – I thank you all.

And finally to the long suffering Janet Grant, who has helped enormously in terms of support throughout the time she has known me while I have been writing this story. Thanks and love don't seem enough, but I send them to you all the same.

I would especially like to dedicate this, my first book, to the courage, dignity and memory of Iris Bentley, who it was a great pleasure to meet, and who devoted her life to the cause of her late brother when she herself was terminally suffering.

"To the homeless and abused"

Chris Hockenhull
Merseyside, 1997

Spring 1975. The plane ride from London had been uneventful. Magazines read through. Books glanced at while not taking anything in that the pages offered. Various attempts at sleeping had been broken by a sporadic awakening, with all sorts of images running through the mind. Sure, one had often travelled alone before. It was all part of the game. But this time it was different. This wasn't another tour. There was to be no-one waiting at the airport. There was no itinerary. No plan to follow through. It was a journey of escape. Running from home.

Soon the lights of Los Angeles came into sight below. There lay another world which would not know the traveller and would therefore not wish to make his acquaintance or ask anything of him. But this was the reason for the journey. This was to be a resting point.

Hotel rooms around the world tend to look identical. The only difference between one and the other is the mood or state of mind of its occupier on entry, which can alter the scene and feel in the room. Here in the room at the motel on Sepulveda Boulevard, the emptiness jumped out as the guest walked through the door. With excess baggage in his mind as his only companion and the deafening sound of silence to listen to, the door was shut behind him. Ahead lay uncertainty.

Behind were a thousand memories. Of childhood, travel, fame, friends, family. Here in Los Angeles were a million faces who did not care about the traveller. Nor had he come to see them. Just how had it all come to this? Was this really the way it was all meant to be? Where would the journey lead to? Where did it all begin?

Introduction: The Traveller

Chapter

1 *War Baby*

" **I** hate a song that makes you think you're not any good. I hate a song that makes you think that you're just born to lose. Bound to lose. No good to nobody. No good for nothin'. Because you're either too old or too young or too fat or too slim or too ugly or too this or too that. Songs that run you down or songs that poke fun at you on account of your bad luck or your hard travelling. I'm out to fight those kinds of songs to my very last breath of air and my last drop of blood.

"I'm out to sing songs that will prove to you that it's your world and that if it has hit you pretty hard and knocked you for a dozen loops, no matter how hard it's run you down and rolled over you, no matter what colour, what size you are, how you're built, I'm out to sing the songs that make you take pride in yourself and your work. And the songs I sing are made up for the most part by all sorts of folks just about like you."

Those words were spoken by Woody Guthrie on WNEW Radio in New York City on 3 December 1944. Guthrie, the hard-travellin' songwriter of the dustbowl and depression days of the 1930s who was to become an influence on countless aspiring musicians (including Bob Dylan), would not have known of the events occurring in the life of one family thousands of miles away in England that very day. For in the county of Kent, yet another 'war baby' was about to emerge into an uncertain world.

The Second World War continued as 1944 drew to its conclusion. Six months on from the Normandy invasion, Allied forces were progressing across Europe towards Berlin. Yet despite their ever-increasing foothold in Europe, Britain was plagued by air raids from German rockets, or 'doodlebugs' as they were more commonly known, and there seemed little change for most ordinary people from the previous five years of air-raid sirens, bomb-damaged cities and rationing. However, life still had to continue amid the uncertainty and fear – as it did in the lives of Winifred and Frank May.

Winifred Iris Moss was born in Hammersmith, West London, in 1916. At the end of the First World War in 1918, she had moved from the city to the town of Brackley in Northamptonshire: "Before the outbreak of war in 1914, my father had been a butler and valet and had travelled abroad with his employers. He joined up in 1916 and, after the war, returned to England to find that his employer had died and there was no longer any work for him.

"However he had been left £200 in the will, so this enabled him to buy a house in Brackley. When I left school, I too went into service and became a children's nanny. However, when war was imminent again in 1939, my employers decided to emigrate to Rhodesia, but I didn't want to go so I went to live with my sister Olive in Banbury, Oxfordshire."

Frank May, too, was in service, though only for a short while before the outbreak of the Second World War, working mainly as an odd-job man and then later as a chauffeur for Lord Charnel. His father had worked in the gardens of the Archbishop of Canterbury in Addington, Surrey, and Frank had been baptised by the Archbishop. Later on, Frank too became a gardener and worked on the estate of the composer Ralph Vaughan Williams. He had been a volunteer soldier since the age of 15 and, after joining the regular army, was already stationed in the Middle East when war broke out.

Meanwhile, back in England, Winifred was working at a chemist's shop in Banbury; because there were no clinics, the shop was almost a creche for the new-born of the town. "I would dole out the orange juice and weigh the babies, basically continuing my nanny role. I really was in my element there."

After they met, Winifred Moss and Frank May embarked on a most unique courtship. They did not see each other for several years after they became engaged, corresponding by letter while Frank was away serving in the army. Aside from her day job at the chemist's, Winifred was serving in the auxiliary fire service, and was on duty the night Coventry was blitzed. By 1943, Frank May was in Palestine as part of the British 8th Army, the 'Desert Rats', and, while he was home on leave in November of that year, he and Winifred were married before he returned to his regiment.

When Winifred learnt she was expecting their first child, she decided to move back nearer to London: "I had a friend in West Wickham, near Croydon, who knew of a flat that was available so I decided to take it. Just before I was due to give birth, I went off into Croydon one day with a huge suitcase to collect a pile of nappies that I'd been saving my coupons for. When I was walking back to the flat, one of the doodlebugs came over and landed just up the road. The force of it knocked me flying! Fortunately, I landed on top of the suitcase, but I was really worried about the baby and was hoping no harm had come to it."

Winifred and Frank's first child was born at the hospital in Farnborough, Kent, on 3 December 1944. A boy, they named him Ralph after Frank's love of the music of his one-time employer Ralph Vaughan Williams. Frank was given one week's compassionate leave before returning to his regiment once more.

"I remember one night while Frank was home and Ralph was in his cot," Winifred recalls. "The sirens sounded and I heard the doodlebug's drone, then that deadly silence fell before the explosion. Frank and I were hanging out of the window to see where it had landed. Ralph was fast asleep through it all. Frank's mother had given me this huge petticoat she had cut down the middle to wrap Ralph in during the air raids, and we'd both go under the stairs until it was all over."

The christening card for Ralph May.

The May family left the flat in West Wickham when Ralph was ten months old, and moved to a basement flat at the Waldrons, a large Georgian family home converted into flats to help ease the chronic housing shortage. Winifred continued to work as, with her husband still away, times were difficult financially. Upstairs lived a young couple, she a frail girl from Lancashire, he a soft-spoken Irishman.

Kevin and Marjorie Connaughton were to become much valued neighbours to the Mays, as Winifred May recalls: "Marjorie Connaughton was always a very delicate girl. She had been very ill due to a hole in the heart and, despite being sterilised, had somehow become pregnant and gave birth with some difficulty to their daughter, Josie. I would often take Josie for a few hours to give Marjorie a break as she suffered from blackouts and needed time to recover. Josie probably lived with us as much as she did with her parents. Kevin was a driver for the Co-Op."

Life continued, with Winifred making the best of it for herself and baby Ralph. VE Day, the end of the war in Europe, came in May 1945, although Frank remained on active duty for some time. Months before, he had been sent home on leave, but was almost immediately recalled as part of a force being sent to Anzio. By this time, he was suffering from the experience of war and, after seven years of action, felt he could cope no more, and decided to go AWOL. He was eventually caught by the military police, who gave him a rough time. After a period in captivity at the military prison in Colchester barracks, he eventually returned to civilian life as a car mechanic.

Winifred May: "I have a photo of Ralph taken on VE Day when he was only five months old. For some reason, he'd had a big red mark in the shape of a 'V' on his forehead when he was born, and it was still there. Everybody would look at him and say 'Oh look, it's the victory baby'." A second child was born in 1946, another son named Bruce. However, things changed drastically for Winifred and her two small children a year later, when Frank walked out on them.

"He left us to go off with somebody else," his wife remembers. "I had absolutely no warning of it at all. I had no idea there was somebody else. Times had been quite happy until then, although with Frank being away a lot it hadn't been easy to get a normal family life started.

"The war, I believe, had a lot to answer for. It seemed to be going on everywhere, families splitting up, though you never think it's going to happen to you. I carried on working at the chemist's shop where I remained for 17 years. I think, despite him only being two and a half years old, Ralph kind of understood what had happened, although Bruce wouldn't have. I remember Ralph saying to me quite soon after Frank left us, 'I'll look after you, Mummy'. I guess he'd got used to Frank being away all his short life."

Ralph: "For me, my father leaving was a very traumatic thing to deal with, and I can remember it most vividly. The last time I ever saw him I was about six years old, and I went into a rage, telling him never to come back, thinking I was defending my mum, who always got upset about him, and he never did come back. I always had a dream that one day I would catch up with him, face him man to man and ask him just why he felt the need to walk away from us, although I was denied this as he was killed in an accident when I was in my early teens.

"One day, this woman came to our front door and asked if my mother was in: I just *knew* she was the woman my father had lived with, and I was right. She needed some papers signing or something. She had a heart to heart with my mum, went away and never appeared again, and that was the end of that. But the feeling of needing a father figure to look up to stayed very close to me until my late teens."

Following his release from military custody, Frank May had changed a great deal. While he had always had a fiery temper, he was now often in trouble with the law. He would go missing for varying lengths of time, doing odd jobs. After abandoning

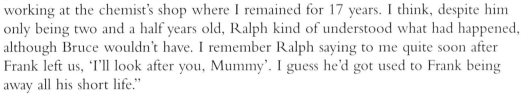

his wife and their two boys, he had settled in a village called Laughton, near Brighton, and was working in a butcher's shop.

One day he was working in the cold store when he came into contact with a defrosting device he had rigged up and was electrocuted. The May family only learned about his death when a neighbour saw an article in the *News Of The World* about a Frank May who had an accident in this manner. His age was the same and his wife came to the conclusion that it must be the same man. Throughout the following years, his father's leaving disturbed Ralph greatly.

Many years later, he decided to try and see the area where his father had settled for himself: "I drove out there alone and found the village, and decided to take a look around. I could find no butcher's shop there, but I went into a sweetshop where I got talking to the woman working there.

"I enquired about my father's death, not saying why I was asking, and I couldn't believe it when the woman told me the accident had happened in that same shop: the butcher's was now the sweetshop where I was standing. That was a very eerie experience."

Radio, celery and Sunday tea
It is nicer here, just us three
And I know he won't come again
There is no need to explain.
('Daddy's Here', 1968)

With no father of his own, Ralph began to look up to other children's fathers, in particular Kevin Connaughton. Ralph: "He was a wonderful man, always smiling. I guess he'd come over from Ireland after the war looking for work, as many others had. He would go out for a drink on a Saturday night and get into the odd scrape, but would always try to give Bruce and me what little spare time he could find.

"He made us a soap-box cart, which gave us endless hours of fun. I remember him buying an old motorcycle which he seemed to be forever trying to repair in the yard, tinkering around with it until dark some nights. And he almost became a figure of fun trying to get it to work, until one night there was this blue sheet of flame…he'd done the impossible and got it to work at last."

I remember when you built us a soap-box cart
With the wheels from a pram and a plank out in the yard
And you gave us a bit of string but we steered it with our feet
Oh boy, it was the best one on the street.
('Mr Connaughton', 1980)

At the age of five, Ralph suffered a serious accident. Winifred May: "I had to go to work. Bruce was in nursery, and Mrs Leisk, a neighbour, was going to collect Ralph from school and look after him until I returned home from work. It got to 6pm and they weren't back, then there was a knock at the door. It was the police to tell me there had been an accident and that Ralph was in Croydon General Hospital. I got there and he was laid out in quite a bad state."

Mrs Leisk, her daughter and Ralph had been in the high street in Croydon and while the children were looking in a sweetshop window, a furniture lorry came by driven by a driver under the influence of alcohol; as it swung past, it collided with the window, showering glass all over Ralph, cutting both legs from his groin to his knees. When the ambulance came, the crew, seeing how much blood he had lost, thought he was going to die. Indeed, Ralph can still remember a hospital orderly telling a colleague the boy wasn't going to make it.

He had countless blood transfusions and was on the danger list for about a week before his mother was allowed to see him: after that initial visit, she was not permitted to visit him again for the entire 13-week period of his hospitalisation. Winifred May: "I used to go every night and take him a few sweets, which I later learned he was never given. There was a kindly nurse who would bring Ralph out on to the balcony, and that was the only time I ever got to see him.

"When he did come out, he was in a dreadful state with his nerves; the surgeon told me that if he hadn't been so young he'd have probably lost both legs. He has terrible scars. He could have had skin grafts, but he never bothered – thank goodness he wasn't a girl, as he'd have never have been able to be a ballet dancer!"

Ralph emerged from the whole event severely traumatised. Bruce May: "Though I don't recall it myself, my mother told me in later years of the state Ralph was in following the accident. His nerves were totally shot, and he suffered from all sorts of infections. When he came home, he was always asking for someone called Anne, and it turned out that she was the nurse who would bring him to the window so mother could see him. She was Irish and had left such a mark on Ralph that when he came home he was speaking in an Irish accent!"

Following the accident, Mrs May sent Ralph to Banbury for a period of convalescence at his grandparents'. The scents and smells around their home at 63 Banbury Road still stick in his mind, and his troubled dreams evaporated while he was in the countryside.

The house in Banbury always seemed to smell of paraffin and coal, of old age itself. There were always used tea leaves and potato peelings on the fire and they would literally keep the heat out of the room. There was no new-fangled television, nor even a radio. The heavy loud tick of the clock on the mantelpiece. The smell of grandad's Woodbines. Gas masks still hung on the kitchen wall 'just in case'. But outside in the coal-shed on the wall was a most wondrous item: a German officer's helmet from the First World War.

Ralph used to sneak in and hold the helmet in his hands, thinking of heroic deeds. Hanging in the house was a photograph of his grandfather in his army uniform taken in 1916. Ralph often wondered just how he had obtained the helmet. Did he wrestle it from the German with his bare hands after his bullets were spent…or did he get it from a fellow soldier in exchange for cleaning his kit? He never did find out how it had been acquired. Years later, their grandfather bequeathed the helmet to Ralph and Bruce, but by then it was mouldy and rusty and its strap had perished. The eagle's crest had fallen off into a box containing some of Ralph's father's tools. Everything was lost years later when the family moved house.

It was about this time that Winifred May got the first inclination of her eldest offspring having some sort of musical ability: "There was a big store in Croydon called Kennards and I would take Ralph and Bruce to see Father Christmas there. The present he gave Ralph was a mouth organ made out of plastic, and he took to it immediately, learning to play a tune called 'Hot Cross Buns' which impressed us all.

"My father could play the harmonica, and he taught him to play 'Sally Ran Round The Jampot' and was very encouraging towards

Ralph's efforts. When my sister Olive came, he never wanted her to see him play it so he'd go behind this old screen: we'd peer over and watch without him knowing."

Like many children, young Ralph May developed a vivid sense of imagination, mainly because his family were from a desperately poor background. In particular, he was fascinated by magic and his mother would obtain Victorian conjuring manuals for him from Croydon library which he would read avidly, and attempt to learn tricks that would impress his family and friends.

"He was always making things," says Winifred May. "My father had given him an old horsehair bow which he'd use to try and get sounds from various things. He also gave him a one-string fiddle which he'd made out of a broom pole and a cigar box which he used to play for hours on end. We couldn't afford a TV set, so Ralph made one out of a cornflake packet, with cotton reels for the buttons and pictures he drew. He tried to get them to move on the screen, and he'd lose his temper when he couldn't get the thing to work like he wanted it to. In our basement at the Waldrons, there was this little room and all you could fit in it was a cot, so Ralph made it into a haunted house. He'd also put on puppet shows for the children and charge them a penny each to watch – but all that he made would go into a collection box for a good cause. He was always doing things like that."

Ralph: "It is pointless to say that those early days were hard because they were hard for everybody. What I remember was that there were few cars, so the street became a huge adventure playground for us all. Looking back, I don't feel it was a deprived childhood. I had a very rich childhood in many, many ways."

> I was a cowboy, back in the alley
> Me and my six gun, kept law on the prairie
> I remember my first horse well, he was lean but a fast one
> We travelled miles together, until he got stolen
> And the sheriff said get early to bed
> And always keep your hat screwed on real tight
> Case you get in a fight
> Well that's one of the tricks that you must employ
> If you want to be a cowboy.
> **("When I Was A Cowboy", 1972)**

The situation Mrs May and her two boys had been left in could be described as nothing less than desperate. There were very few luxuries to be had, and no money or state support was available. There was no hot food, and Mrs May, a proud and dignified lady, attempted to do her best to keep her young family together by scrubbing doorsteps and taking in ironing. Toys and games for Ralph and his brother had to be invented for themselves.

Bruce remembers the way Ralph's ability to create his own amusement rubbed off on other children. "Because of this, he was never short of friends. He invented games and adventures inspired by things he'd read or seen at the Saturday-morning picture shows and because of this was always able to bring other children into his world. I remember hanging around the street corner waiting for our mother to come home from work, but Ralph always seemed to be invited back to someone's house to play after school."

For Ralph and Bruce, one escape from their poor lifestyle came when they spent their summer holidays with Aunt Olive and Uncle Reg in Banbury in Oxfordshire. Out in the country, away from urban Croydon, was another world where imaginations could run riot from dawn till dusk in the safety of the countryside.

Chapter
2 Croydon Childhood

Country boys catch tadpoles, dive into water
Made shy by their laughter we wandered down stream
And summer rolled o'er us with no complications
'Cept thinking of Mamma sometimes in dreams.
('Barges', 1972)

Formal education for Ralph was in a school which laid a heavy emphasis on religious studies and was staffed by many teachers belonging to various Brethren groups. Only a few of the children were Brethren. The first school he attended, St Peter's, was originally a church school that eventually merged with Howards, an ordinary primary school with a high pass rate for the 11-Plus examination.

It was a very strict school, which McTell remembers as pretty terrifying: he was caned at the age of six for writing a rude word. "Years later, I was sent a letter from the school as they had discovered that I was an ex-pupil, and they wanted me to speak to their present pupils about my memories. I had to tell them that I just couldn't, as my personal memories were not particularly happy."

During his education, Ralph, in common with many small children, learnt about Jesus and the Gospel stories. These would have a considerable effect on him. "While I wouldn't describe my mother as being a religious woman, she had begun helping out at the local Sunday School, and I guess I drifted into it that way. She was very morally correct, and my brother and I learnt right from wrong from a very early age, but she used to go to a non-denominational church where there was lots of singing: I think she got a lot of comfort from that in the years after my father left home.

"The churches were all packed in the postwar years. She encouraged Bruce and me to go to Sunday school. While I had lots of friends, I had lonely thoughts, and having a belief in something gave me a lot of comfort. I think around the age of ten or twelve, you become aware of your own mortality and you start to move from childhood to the teen years; I read the Bible and prayed every night up to about the age of twelve.

"I suppose once you have had religious feelings of some sort, they don't ever entirely go and, though I don't have the same beliefs today, I would like to think I have some kind of spirituality. There is a lot about the Christian faith that I like, and I feel the basic rules are pretty good – though maybe not the way they have been interpreted."

In those childhood days, there was another influence on Ralph's ideas on religion. "At the top of the road by the Waldrons was a huge house where an artist named Cicely Mary Barker lived," Winifred remembers. "She was famous for her pictures of flowers and her flower fairy pictures were all based on her studies of children. Just before one Christmas, she asked me if I would let Ralph pose for her, which I did, and her picture of Ralph looking in at Jesus in the manger became her Christmas card for that year. After the trauma he went through following his accident, he never really wanted to attend the church that much.

"There was this big figure of Jesus on the cross outside St Andrews church, and when we'd go past it, he'd always look at it and ask 'Mummy, why is Jesus on the cross?' and I'd say that people had been very cruel to him, which seemed to make him reluctant to go in anymore.

"Miss Barker had painted lots of murals in St Andrew's church, and one day she called and asked why we had stopped going. I told her that Ralph had become terribly frightened about Jesus on the cross and the cruelty he suffered, and she brought me a beautiful book for him that her sister had written of Bible stories, hoping it would make him think, but he never went back.

"He liked the Sunday school at Mint Walk that he and Bruce went to. It was a little hut painted green and brown, and that is where he met Mrs Adlam, who told them about guardian angels and made the Bible stories come alive for them all. He became very interested in the choir, and I still have this image of him years later in the church in his cassock, wearing his big white-soled blue bumper shoes with luminous socks shining out: I remember thinking 'Oh Lord, he's not mine!'."

Lily Adlam.

Sundays occasionally
We were invited back for tea
And bread with jam and cream
Made Sundays seem a dream
In the dingy mission hall
Mrs Adlam praying
And down the street back home
All our mates were playing
With Mrs Adlam's angels everywhere
And we thought we saw a halo in her hair.
('Mrs Adlam's Angels', 1968)

In 1952, an event occurred in Croydon, not far from where the May family lived, that would reverberate around the whole of Britain and remain in Ralph's memory throughout his life. On the evening of 2 November, two boys, Christopher Craig (aged 16) and Derek Bentley (aged 19) were spotted on the rooftop of Barlow and Parker's confectioner's warehouse in Tamworth Road. The police were called to the scene and were able to take Bentley into custody. However, Craig had a gun, which he fired and shot PC Sidney Miles dead.

As a result, following a rather swift trial, Derek Bentley was found guilty and was sentenced to be hanged, yet the killer, Craig, did not hang because he was too young to be sentenced to death – Bentley, an epileptic with an IQ of 66 and a mental age of nine, went to the gallows despite a nationwide campaign for him to be pardoned for a crime everyone conceded he did not commit. Ralph: "I can remember it all so vividly, as if it was only yesterday. The newspapers were full of it and everybody was talking about it.

"It was only seven years since the end of the war and there was a general fear about gangs of youths mugging people, plus the fact that it was a policeman who had been shot. Even as a young boy, I knew that Bentley hadn't killed anybody, yet he was hanged. Now you don't get over something like that because, no matter who I'd talk to, no adults were able to give me a satisfactory answer as to why Derek was hanged. I used to live very close to where the shooting took place, and every time I walked down Tamworth Road I used to look at the building and think… There is no doubt that a terrible injustice had taken place, and the government of the time did very little to save his life.

"It was unbelievable that from the incident in November, his execution was in January – two months! That incident was never to leave me."

> Oh you men on our behalf who sanctioned that boy's death
> There's still one thing left to do
> You can pardon Derek Bentley who never took a life
> For Derek Bentley cannot pardon you.
> **('Bentley And Craig', 1982)**

There were other family links to the event, as Winifred recalls: "I was working at the chemist's shop. At the time, Iris Bentley was working in a shop opposite ours, and she and Derek used to come in quite a bit. I remember one day a rather flash-looking young man coming into the shop. Mr Strong, the dispenser, called me to one side and said 'That's Craig's older brother. He's just out of clink too. They're all no good, that lot.' Ralph used to ask me a lot about what was going to happen to Derek after the incident: it bothered him a lot."

Would-be musician Wizz Jones, who would enter Ralph's life years later, also has good reason to remember the case. "The police felt that they needed to do something constructive for the youth of the community after what had happened. So they opened a boys' club there, which I went to, and every year they put on a show. I saw this young guy playing a guitar who absolutely knocked me out, and I immediately wanted to be just like him. So I learnt the guitar and the first gig me and my little skiffle group, the Wranglers, did was at the club: the MC who announced us that night was a guy who turned out to become the comedian Roy Hudd! So I indirectly owe my start, somewhat oddly, to the Bentley case, and Roy Hudd too."

By 1957, the May family had left the Waldrons and moved to 17a Miller Road, off Factory Lane in Croydon, which was then the largest town in Surrey and had a true identity and culture of its own. Bombs had caused much destruction there during the Second World War. It had an airport that would remain the official airport of London until closed in 1959. It had its own big town hall with a bell that rang out loudly, and large department stores in which you could get lost. Kennards, a particular favourite for Ralph, had men demonstrating magic tricks, a small zoo and a horse-riding display in the basement!

There were many parks and recreation grounds throughout the area, as well as the bomb sites which still hadn't been cleared. Two theatres that had regular entertainment, a busy market full of colour and vigour, pigeon racing which brought its characters along with it, and a boxing tradition of its own. With its fogs, streetlamps and busy pubs it was a stimulating place to live in. Ralph and Bruce were never bored there, and Croydon offered them many compensations for the poverty in which they lived.

By this time, Ralph was attending John Ruskin Grammar School, where he was streamed for University entrance. He didn't settle well and his disinterest led to him often being at the centre of mischief. One such incident involved the unsuspecting Mr Robshaw, who taught French. He was renowned for writing reams of words on the blackboard from the moment he walked into class, at such a speed that it was hard for the pupils to keep pace with him.

To stem the flow, Ralph painstakingly hollowed out a piece of chalk, in which he placed a matchstick. The 'loaded' stick was placed close to the blackboard ready for to use. True to form, Mr Robshaw burst into class and was soon writing away when the chalk suddenly exploded, the flash and the sulphurous odour which filled the classroom resulting in muffled expletives. Ralph owned up and was ordered to remain after class. "He said to me 'May, how the *devil* did you do that? I've never had that done to me before. Well done. Now that was bloody dangerous. Don't ever do that again'. I couldn't believe I got away with it."

Throughout his schooldays, Ralph had been friendly with Vernon Burford. Virtually inseparable, like many other lads of their age, they bonded in a gang they formed. Weekends spent at Saturday-morning picture shows and attempting to emulate their heroes like Flash Gordon and Hopalong Cassidy made life one big adventure. "Ralph and I spent all our childhood and teenage years in the same schools," Burford recalls, "so I had always been used to having him around and naturally thought that I would always have him around.

"This group of us at school hung around together: the collective noun that was used was 'gang', but I like to think we were a little more refined than that – although looking back now, I'm not so sure that we were. But you know how it is at that age, you're all best mates together in a 'gang'. You're part of the gang, and the gang is part of you. It gives you a strength and an identity, it needs protecting, you are part of it or you are not."

However, at this time Ralph was developing his own thoughts and ideals like most normal boys of that age. Rock'n'roll was everywhere, and like many before him, Ralph was completely knocked out with 'Heartbreak Hotel' by Elvis Presley. "I must have played it twenty times continuously after my cousin played it to me and I went to sleep trying to sing like Elvis. It was funny, but the way Elvis sang I thought he had a stutter. It was only years later that I learned it was the echo!"

The skiffle boom had also hit England: the trusty harmonica was swapped for a ukulele and, with the aid of the 'George Formby Method', McTell learnt 'Don't You Rock Me Daddy-O'. His first band, formed at school, performed at the second year's Christmas party. By 1960, religion too had been replaced by a newly-found interest in socialism. There seemed too many distractions in his life, mainly brought on by a sheer hatred of his schooldays.

"I can't tell you how much I loathed going to school. I used to get a sick feeling in my stomach as I went through the gates and felt so distant from everyone there, pupils and teachers alike. Part of this was to do with the fact that I came from such a poor background despite my mother's best efforts. Although we were working class, we weren't *ignorant* working class. There had always been books in the house and she always read to Bruce and me – and, because she had been in service, she read us the books she'd had to read to other children. Despite having no money and living in a slum, we had values other kids didn't.

"By the time I went to grammar school, I had all second-hand clothes. I had a second-hand jacket and trousers, but somehow mum had got the money to buy a school badge. I had two poplin shirts that were new and were my pride and joy: mum used to wash one each day so I always had a clean shirt every day. But I was so aware of other kids having money and us not having anything that I just felt so different. We were the poor relations to everyone else. I felt totally outclassed there."

As a way out, McTell, at the age of 15, decided to leave school and join the army. He was to see the organisation as another way to fulfil his quest of belonging to something with a structure to it. Like many other disheartened youngsters, Ralph had been taken in by the almost glamorous recruiting messages used by the army. He saw it as a chance to redeem himself, fit in with other boys of his own age and no longer feel an outsider.

His application was enthusiastically received, as it was rare for grammar-school boys to apply, but matters would not turn out the way both Ralph and his mother had hoped.

Junior Private Ray May 23783801.

The adverts in the papers solicit soldiers for the Army
But they never tell you nothing about the girls in the garrison towns
Like how they will mistreat you and how old friends will see you
When you trade your name for a number and a uniform of brown
When you pick up a gun
And you say goodbye to Mamma
And away from home you run.
('Pick Up A Gun', 1971)

"I believe we were both conned into it," says Winifred. "They came to the house to see us and, with him being at grammar school, their line was that if you join the army you can still continue with your studies and earn your degree that way. Soon after he joined, he realised that it was nothing like what we had been told."

While Ralph had felt an outsider in school, he became even more isolated among his fellow recruits of the Queen's Surrey Regiment Junior Leaders Battalion at the Plummer Barracks in Plymouth: "I'm not trying to say how clever I was, but I realised there was no-one else there who had the same standard of education. I used to write letters home for three other boys because they couldn't read or write. I did find a couple of other lads as time went on who I could share some common ground with.

"There was a lad named Robert Edward Weller who was known as Sam because everybody had to have a nickname (Ralph, incidentally, was known in the army as Ray May) and he got his from a character in *Pickwick Papers* called Sam Weller. It amazed me how a working-class lad like Sam could know about Dickens and a grammar-school boy like me didn't.

"I always liked the name Sam because of Sam Weller so much that I named my first child after him. I always remembered his address in Gravesend and many years later I mentioned this story during an interview for a local Gravesend newspaper. They picked up on this, ran it in the paper and we met for the first time since the

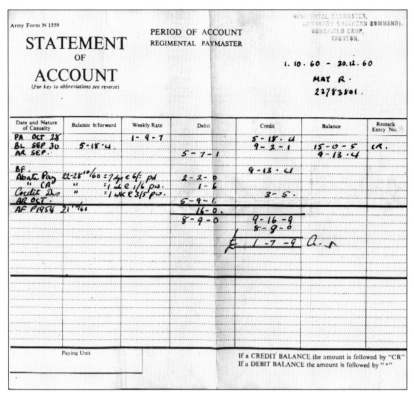

army. He said to me 'Ralph? Ralph? But your name was *Ray...*' I never saw him again."

Ralph's decision to join the army had shocked his friends to a point where they felt let down. Vernon Burford: "Ralph always had a passion for a uniform, and I firmly believe that it was the uniform, not the 'Your country needs you' ideology that made him join up. It shocked all of us in our little 'gang'. Here's this valuable gang member, great fun, always been around, believing (I thought) in the words 'Your gang needs you'.

"And then suddenly, because he had stomped around the playground a bit in an Army Training Corps uniform and played around with real guns, he got this idea that he might like the 'big gang' better, and that all of us were somehow a bit too childish. So you see, when he went into the army, I felt that he had let us all down."

Moving on from Plymouth to Oswestry, Shropshire, the harshness of army life began to unfold. The young recruits were brutalised from the moment they arrived and, like so many others, Ralph became a victim of the initiation ceremony known as a kangaroo court.

"One day we were cleaning our kit and somebody came to attention next to me and said 'Junior Private May. You are charged with being a recruit. How do you plead?' They marched me up to a desk and they had a court-martial set up. I was *shaking*. Even though I hated it there, I'd not hurt anyone, and tried to get on with everyone. I had to march to the 'court', they found me guilty and gave me a right slapping about, banging my head on the bed and putting lighted matches on my chest.

"They pretended to put a hot iron on my back, although they didn't actually plug it in, but the coldness of it makes you think you are being burnt as you're so terrified. I did hear of other boys this was done to who would scream and blisters would actually appear on their backs. They cut my hair off at the front and I had this big square cut out on my head. My mate Alan got tied up with straps and they gave him a real beating. I was asked by officers what had happened to me, and all you say is 'Nothing. Fell over, Sir'. They all knew it went on, but you don't complain."

Back home, his mother was well aware through his letters that Ralph wanted out of the army. "Though recruits were only 15 years of age, they were very hard on them. In fact, two of the other boys committed suicide and, as a result of the following investigation, major reforms were brought into place within the battalion. He was so unhappy in there, but I wasn't in much of a position to do anything about it. His Uncle Reg used to say to me 'Oh leave him in there. It'll do him good', but I thought 'No, if he's that unhappy, I'll borrow the money and try to buy him out'."

Ralph explained to his officers on his third day that he was unhappy and wished to leave, but was basically told that there was no chance, and that he'd have to get on with it; besides, all boys felt this way at first and soon got used to the way of life.

"I witnessed and heard abuse, from recruits and officers alike, that I had never known of before. The Sergeant would just verbally abuse the lads. They would break those lads down to nothing, and then build up again. The plot was to take away the individual and build up the soldier. But because I had made known my intentions to leave, I was a marked man and had to watch myself carefully.

"I was with a lad from Ireland, and in those days the Irish would join up at 14 and do their basic training before going back to join the Free State Army. He told me he could get me over to Ireland and into the IRA, which I'd heard of, although it wasn't active. I had a route planned and kind of threatened my mum by saying 'Look, if you don't raise the money, mum, I'm gone and away, over the wall. There's a railway line at the back of the camp'. I said to Sam Weller: 'I can't handle it anymore, Sam. I'm cracking up. I'll go crazy if I stay here any longer'. I had stopped washing, as I had just lost interest in myself.

"Sam warned me to watch out, as I was liable to be given a regimental scrubbing where they put you in a cold bath, use a yardbrush on you and tear off all your skin. When I left there were seven lads in there who had attempted suicide, and six months after I got out, two of them had sadly succeeded. I remember years later, when I was in Greece, I read *Borstal Boy* by Brendan Behan and thinking it was a holiday compared to the things we had to go through. I admit that when I came out after six months, I was leaner, faster and fitter and I was no longer a kid – though I wouldn't say I was a man. But my God, I saw things and learnt things I didn't know existed before."

Eventually, his mother scraped up the £50 she needed to end his nightmare. Winifred: "He promised me that he'd somehow pay me back for buying him out. And he did, by getting himself a job as a gardener at weekends, earning £2, of which he'd give me one." Returning home, Ralph, by his own admission, half-heartedly resumed his education, enrolling at Croydon Technical College where he obtained three GCE 'O' levels and an 'A' level for Art.

Vernon Burford: "Gradually, our gang broke up. Schooldays were over, and real life started. I met Terri, whom I eventually married, and while she wasn't terribly impressed with the gang, she put up with it. I always said to Terri that Ralph would be famous one day. I could tell that he was a natural with music and could get a tune out of anything!

"We heard with glee that Ralph was coming out of the army and reckoned that he would be in touch pretty soon…but we never heard from him. Those were happy but busy days, when the need to earn a living and build a future is more important than the past. The gang finally was no more, and Ralph never did reappear."

Chapter
3 Beat Generation

Ralph's time at college marked an important milestone in his development. Music began to exert an influence on him, as did the ever-changing cultures in which he found himself. "Around the age of 16 I fell in with a group of people who considered themselves to be beatniks and were trying to copy the American Beat generation of the 1950s. They had read the works of Corso, Ferlinghetti, Kerouac and Ginsberg, and listened to jazz, and I was amazed and was just soaking up all this stuff as an impressionable 16 year old would.

"Although I tried to read some of this stuff, I just didn't have a clue until somebody gave me *On The Road* by Jack Kerouac, which just amazed me; having read it, I thought that anything was possible. One night while I was at the technical college, I had been to the jazz club and somebody put on an EP with a picture of a train on the cover, and this guy doing a spoken introduction: 'Oakland is just across the bay from San Francisco. That's where Jesse Fuller lives.'

Legendary American troubadour Woody Guthrie.

"The EP was by Jack Elliott and it had 'San Francisco Bay Blues' and a couple of talking blues on it as well; there was something about the sound of his guitar and his voice that sounded so authentic that it just grabbed me. I took the EP home and, like everybody after the skiffle era, I had a £5 guitar, an Egmond plywood job. I don't know how I did it, but I worked out the chords of the songs for myself, so that by the end of the week, I'd bought myself a better guitar for £15 and away I went.

"I embarked on a voyage of acoustic music with Woody Guthrie, Jesse Fuller and a host of black players, who just opened up new horizons for me. Somebody heard me play and said 'I know a guy who plays that stuff', and his name was Max Faulkner. I showed him this A7 chord in 'San Francisco Bay Blues' that he just couldn't get, so he traded it for an E minor! The only thing left to fuse it all together was to get the sleeping bag out and, with the guitar, head off on the road."

Max Faulkner was also to be responsible for introducing another fellow with similar tastes in music to Ralph. Mick Bartlett: "It was at an old pub in Croydon called the Whitgift Arms (acknowledged on the sleeve of 'My Side Of Your Window'), which was frequented by some wonderful local characters: it became our regular meeting place. Ralph was learning guitar on a beaten-up specimen that was virtually impossible to play. Max taught him some 'licks', mainly 'flat picking', and he was very keen to learn. I possessed a growing record collection, mainly folk, blues and jazz. We became firm friends, and I spent a lot of time at Ralph's house playing my records. I remember getting hold of an EP of Alexis Korner and Davey Graham which knocked us both out, and he spent hours learning the tune 'Anji' until he got it right."

Having met like-minded spirits, Ralph started to embrace this new-found culture, which was a million miles away from his experience in the army. Regular forays into Soho in central London again opened up new worlds: there, among the maze of pubs, were poets and beatniks and all sorts of interesting people the likes of which they had never come across before. Seeing someone playing a 12-string guitar for the first time in his life was another eye-opener for the starry-eyed adventurer.

Soon the desire to ride the rails and travel, playing music, was to become a reality, though not quite in the same romantic way Jack Elliott and Woody Guthrie had experienced. With a new group of friends regularly meeting at the Whitgift, Ralph, Mick Bartlett and others would go off at weekends in search of music and good times.

One trip to the Birmingham Jazz Festival has stayed in Bartlett's memory. "We'd hitched to the festival and had a great day – but, come nightfall, it was absolutely thundering down with rain and there was no sleeping accommodation to be found. We wandered around, soggy and despondent, searching for shelter, until I spotted a lorry parked in a driveway. We decided to kip underneath and scoot off early the following morning. Inevitably we didn't make it, and were roused by a young girl asking if we'd like some tea!

"I had visions of the police arriving, and being yanked off as vagrants, but quite the reverse. The family were brilliant, taking us in and drying our clothes and feeding us bacon sandwiches, before sending us on our way with hot sweet tea in lemonade bottles. As we hit the road my lasting memory was of the whole family lined up, waving us farewell. That little incident typified the different attitude that existed in those days."

Poole, in Dorset, was another point of call for McTell. He went there with another friend, Tony Dickinson, and they shacked up with some local beatniks in a flat in Poole High Street. The group contained such diverse people as Pepe the potter and an author called Dick. Mick Bartlett (better known as 'Henry', for reasons to be explained later) visited to join in the fun, and they obtained work as Hoffman Pressers at a local laundry. McTell and Bartlett, along with two other guys, then rented a house for the winter in Southborne, near Bournemouth. As they were all penniless, the need to work in order to maintain their bohemian lifestyle became a priority, especially as the winter was beginning to bite hard.

By day Ralph worked at a local laundry and then at the Metal Box Company steel factory by night, while continuing to explore as much music as he could. But this was an era of near full employment and, while trying his hand at as much music as he could find, McTell also found work in many places. "Among other things, I was a waiter for a morning, which was the shortest job I ever had, timber yards, kitchen porter in a hotel in Bournemouth, building sites, factories, anything. I'd work for as long as I wanted to, and then move somewhere else."

With the boom in acoustic music and the ever-growing 'folk revival', everybody seemed to be in a position to influence one another; also, by 1962, records were being imported from America at a rate where new influences were available on an almost daily basis. Soon, many folk and blues clubs were opening, and these places just had to be investigated. At weekends they would all go off to Eel Pie Island, a haven for musicians of the London blues scene.

"One day we were there, and standing nearby was Eric Clapton, who was at that time really making a name for himself with the Bluesbreakers. So Henry goes over to him and says 'What's all this nicking all these Elmore James riffs then?', because he knew all about blues music and people didn't generally know about the old black musicians then. And Eric looks around and replies 'Ssh. Nobody else knows that. Don't spread it around'. It's funny, but years later, when Eric did his 'Unplugged' album, his repertoire struck a chord with me, as many of those songs were what we were all doing back in those days. We all had the same repertoire, as that was what was available to us white lads in England at that time."

Bartlett organised himself a club in a Croydon coffee bar called Under The Olive Tree. On the ground floor was a jukebox containing records by Muddy Waters, Big Bill Broonzy, Woody Guthrie and Howlin' Wolf, among others. Downstairs was a small dance floor where, on several nights of the week, DJ Dave King played records not even the BBC had acquired, which added still further to the place's undoubted importance.

It was here Ralph first met Wizz Jones. "I had first seen Wizz on Brighton beach in 1960, during what were known as the 'Brighton Raves'. Everybody would pile out of Ken Colyer's Jazz Club, jump on the milk train and go down to Brighton. All the beatniks were there sitting on the beach wrapped in blankets, trying to appear 'interesting', while getting windswept. I could hear this music and I remember seeing this bloke with really long hair playing this guitar which was held together with glue! Someone said 'This bloke's called Wizz' in very reverential tones."

Wizz Jones didn't remember that occasion: "The first time I recall ever seeing Ralph was when I was a resident at the Olive Tree doing Sunday-afternoon sessions. His brother Bruce used to work behind the coffee bar. It was a great meeting place for all musicians into blues and folk music. Loads of top folk and blues artists would drop in like Long John Baldry, Bert Jansch and Alex Campbell. Eric Clapton and the rest of the Yardbirds were often there, too. Ralph was just starting out then. I remember he was extremely shy and very nervous. He'd do the odd spot playing one or two Woody Guthrie songs."

Also among the clientele of the Olive Tree were two performers who would go on to become legends in the folk-music world in years to come. Martin Carthy: "I remember that first time we met – that Sunday afternoon. I remember this very lanky bloke standing up and playing guitar and singing. The next I heard of him was when he came back to London from Cornwall and he was taking the folk-club scene by storm."

Jacqui McShee, who would become a founder member of Pentangle, was another Sunday-afternoon visitor: "I first saw him play there late '62 /early '63, and my sister Pam and I had started to do some singing with him. He struck me as being ever so keen on all things musical and loved playing. He was a very popular young man who was very much in demand at parties where those who could would bring instruments and play and sing. I remember that, at one time, Ralph was working on a building site and was illegally driving a dumper truck around which he managed to fall out of and break his leg! It didn't stop him playing – he turned up with his leg in plaster only to fall down the steep back stairs, ending up at the bottom in a heap. He still went on and played, though!"

In the dingy rooms of the Olive Tree, beatnik types would meet and talk music and poetry. There one day Ralph came across a youth who would also become an important influence upon him – Martin Sole, better known as Tubs. He was ideally suited to the apprentice beatnik lifestyle but aimed to find enlightenment by sleeping, chasing women and getting drunk as often and as cheaply as possible. He did have a passing interest in acoustic music and would be found constantly performing his version of Big Bill Broonzy's 'Hey Hey' to anyone who would listen. Tubs and Ralph hit it off: the two became best buddies and continued to explore life in Croydon and beyond together.

Jacqui McShee recalled one night of mayhem that involved Tubs and Ralph. "I'd been playing at the Scot's Hoose in Cambridge Circus with Chris Ayliffe. John Renbourn was also on the bill, and Ralph came along with Tubs, who was driving this van he'd got from somewhere. When we came to go home, we found the police had towed the van away and we'd have to pay a fine. So Ralph, Chris and myself decided to go down to Leicester Square and do a bit of busking to earn enough to get the van back. It was going well when two drunks appeared and started to get

rather abusive. For some reason, they were carrying with them one of those old-fashioned ashtrays on a pole, which they were waving around rather menacingly.

"Ralph eventually lost his patience, put his guitar down and asked me to get out of the way as he didn't want anything to happen to me. It was then I noticed that Chris had retreated around the corner, leaving Ralph alone with the two drunks. Ralph took a swing at one of them and just as a fight was about to break out the police arrived.

"It turned out the two drunks were reporters who had been at some reception, got drunk and walked out with the big ashtray. So the police carted them off, and left us to continue! Eventually we got enough money, and got the van back from the police. That should have been the end of it, but Tubs dropped everybody off at various places and, as I lived furthest away, I was the last to get home. However, the night was rounded off by the van being involved in an accident from which I still have the scars to remind me of that eventful evening."

Henry Bartlett had later started up another club at the Buck's Head in Mitcham with Wizz Jones and

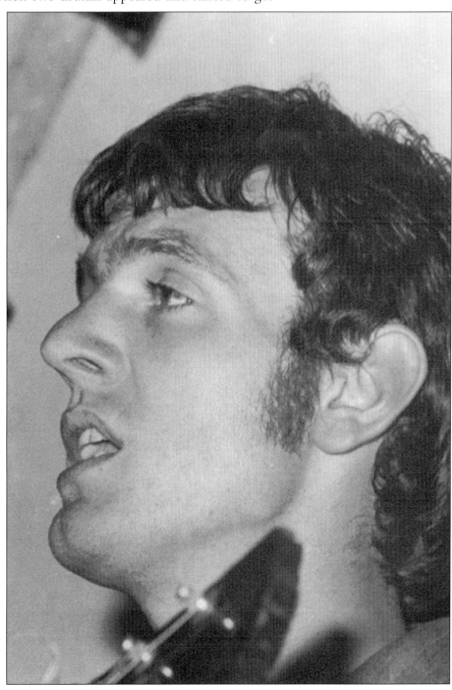

Ralph as resident players along with various weekly guests. He had also managed to secure Ralph May's first proper gig at Green Street Green in Kent. Bartlett: "The journey there was a nightmare. It was the beginning of Ralph's now legendary pre-show tension, with him being what I can describe as 'seriously nervous', and with me losing my way, which didn't help matters.

"We were snapping at each other and barely speaking a word when we arrived. However, he went down really well and gained a great deal of self-confidence. From what I can remember, what he did that night were some Woody Guthrie and Jesse Fuller songs: 'Working On The Railroad', 'San Francisco Bay Blues', and of course 'Anji'."

Another friendship born in the Whitgift Arms, in the shadow of Croydon Gasworks, was with another musician, Pete Chalkley, who was a member of a bluegrass band called the Hickory Nuts. They were probably the most experienced musicians Ralph had met up to that point, having appeared on BBC-TV with the Rolling Stones, and played at the 100 Club in London's Oxford Street with Sonny Terry and Brownie McGhee.

Pete Chalkley: "The music relied more on energy than skill, and our disrespect spared almost no-one. The pundits and agents reckoned the Hickory Nuts should move out of the world of folk music and into the world of pop. We even had press write-ups about having a following that was little short of Beatlemania. We began to be signed up for gigs which were quite unsuitable, yet which proved to be a

An early poster, also appearing on the back of Ralph's second album.

24

great source of experience. I guess I first saw Ralph at the Whitgift, where he would often be found sitting in a corner in the public bar, shyly picking away on his Harmony Sovereign guitar. After hours, we would end up at the Olive Tree. It was there that he was probably led astray by the band."

When Ralph joined, the Hickory Nuts comprised Ray Tassie on mandolin, guitar and banjo, Mike Ward-Lewis on double bass and Pete Chalkley on banjo and fiddle. To Ralph, who had hitherto played mainly Guthrie and Dylan songs as well as blues and ragtime (styles which required subtle finger-picking), the frenetic flat-picking pace and simple chord changes (G, C, D7) of bluegrass came as something of a shock. The inane words of the songs often provoked laughter from Ralph and the band – usually at the most inappropriate times. Nevertheless, he joined the band, and the new-look Hickory Nuts took to the road for a small tour of England.

In one week the itinerary included Sheffield one night, Bognor Regis the next, Accrington the next, then back down south for the Fairfield Halls in Croydon, back the next day to Manchester, and finally Didcot in Berkshire. Pete Chalkley: "The trouble was that, legally, only Mike could drive, although the other three were learning. As with many people who are teaching someone else to drive, it was less harrowing for Mike to drive than to be responsible for a learner. It wasn't made easier by the fact that Ray liked driving on the pavement, and Ralph couldn't help driving with two wheels over the centre line of the road."

The first gig for the Hickory Nuts was a prestigious one at Sheffield University, where the hall was about 150 feet long with a stage at one end and the audience of about a dozen people at the other! There was no amplification and, as Ralph had only been in the band a few days, the repertoire was pretty thin. Yet the contract said they were to play for two hours! Pete Chalkley takes up the story:

"Our six numbers took about 20 minutes, after which the band were left staring at each other, dumbstruck and in sheer panic. The only answer was almost unheard-of in the history of musical entertainment: repeat the first six numbers, then let Ralph take the strain from there on and hope for the best. So he played a few songs of his own, plus 'San Francisco Bay Blues', 'Alberta' and a few Blind Blake numbers, which the crowd loved – if you can call a dozen people a crowd. By then, the total time taken was about 35 minutes, which still left nearly an hour and a half to go. Inevitably, the result was disastrous. One by one, the audience politely left the hall, leaving the band playing to itself."

If that was bad, the gig at Accrington Stanley Football Club certainly piled on the agony. Once again, the band had to make a death-defying dash to get up to Lancashire in three hours. Once there, they found that the venue had been arranged like a night club, ready for dining and dancing. By 9.30pm, the band still outnumbered the audience, yet the club manager insisted the show must go on.

Pete Chalkley: "After the first couple of warm-up numbers, the loudest sound that could be heard was the clanging of the fruit machines occupied by all four members of the audience. Later, three other couples arrived and left within 20 minutes, but only after they had recouped their entrance fee by beating hell out of the one-armed bandits."

From here on, things should have got better. Next was a gig at Didcot Folk Club, which was frequented by workers from the Advanced Weapons Research Authority at nearby Harwell. After the grief they had suffered thus far on the tour, the omens looked good, as the club had placed a ten-foot poster of the Hickory Nuts on the main wall. On a warm, balmy evening, they found an audience in receptive mood. What could be better? Pete Chalkley: "The problem here was that this was one of the first folk clubs to have installed a sound system. Unfortunately, it continually buzzed and crackled all evening. Never mind the lack of audio technology, we thought it was all down to the audience being radioactive!"

The ultimate low point in Ralph McTell's career in the Hickory Nuts came in Birmingham when, after a gig, a curry and more pints than it was safe to drink in three months, the band were in no fit state to drive back to London. In the early hours of the morning, the only option was to find a quiet street where they could park the van, try to settle down in the back among the instruments and other debris, and go to sleep. Pete Chalkley: "After five hours of groaning and grunting and creating all sorts of curry-induced smells in the confined space of a Morris J4 van without any open windows, we awoke to a beautiful spring morning.

"As soon as we fell out of the back doors of the van, we realised that we had parked in Birmingham's equivalent of Mayfair, with all its prim young secretaries tripping smartly to work past the van. Ralph McTell and the band from hell had arrived in Birmingham. Having drunk and eaten the night's takings, we then discovered that we had run out of petrol. There was only one answer: busking!

"Things did eventually get better, and we started to make some good sounds together. The most notable occasion was probably a performance at the Fairfield Halls in Croydon in November 1964, for which our fee was 12 guineas between us, with the most expensive seats being 12/6d! But certainly Ralph went through a baptism of fire during the time he was with the Hickory Nuts, and gained a considerable amount of experience playing in public. Yet all of us knew that because of his commitment, spontaneous humour, and above all, his 'touch' on the strings, he would make his mark. To paraphrase one of his songs, 'He never knew he'd make it, but we knew he would somehow'."

Jacquard Folk Club,
MISCHIEF TAVERN, FYE BRIDGE
TONIGHT — We present the Old Timey
HICKORY NUTS
Resident Group — THE JACQUARDS
Club opens 7.30   Session 8-10.30
"PRIVATE EYE" on sale

WEDNESDAY, FEBRUARY 24th
We present in concert at THE STUART
HALL, NORWICH, the country's leading
traditional group, stars of TV, radio and
records
The Ian Campbell Folk Group
Tickets available from club, or George
Wortley Ltd., Charing Cross, Norwich. Postal
applications with s.a.e. and party bookings
to Secretary, 48, William Street, Norwich.
Tel. 22053.
JACQUARD TOP FOLK PRESENTATION

Chapter
4 On The Road

R alph's travels had, initially, been to various jazz and blues festivals around England until, in 1961, he took off for Europe for the first time armed only with a guitar and a pocketful of dreams. The last few years had been an ever growing realisation that there was an open road out there that needed exploring, gleaned from the musicians and writers that he devoured with such a passion. The enormous appeal of going those few miles across the English Channel to encounter different cultures grew stronger by the day. Teaming up with Max Faulkner, the original intention was to make it to Greece, but Munich in Germany was as far as Ralph managed.

"We'd decided that we'd hitch to Greece," Bartlett recalls, "setting off in pairs, Ralph with Max and myself and a girl called June. We arranged to meet at Hadrian's Arch in Athens. June and I arrived, and dutifully went to the Arch every day for two weeks, but to no avail. Seven weeks later, when we eventually returned, it turned out they hadn't made it as far as we did. They'd pitched camp on a foggy night only to wake up on the central reservation of a motorway, which influenced Ralph's decision to return home."

Nevertheless, Ralph and Max decided to have another go at getting further into Europe. "Max's forte was the Carter Family and Lester Flatt-type guitar playing," Ralph remembers. "He used a big Levin, and sang in a high tenor voice. I could flat-pick as well, and we got on well. We were supposed to go with another guy called Beau Dickinson, who we'd meet in Munich, and take a trail to Greece. Beau was notoriously unreliable, but we waited in Munich for a few days, which wasn't easy as I'd only brought £5 with me. I was living off the sausage stand at the station and sleeping in a doorway down the road."

With the money nearly exhausted, Ralph decided it was time to move on. The idea of Greece was becoming an impossibility and morale was sinking fast. Despite being only away from home a mere month, Ralph had started to endure poor health through being unable to feed himself properly. France became the alternative route, as it was said to be easier to live on the streets and earn a living. Ralph got to Paris, but the trip was over for the time being and they returned to England. Regardless of this latest setback, the seeds of travel and the yearning for freedom on the road had been sown and, undeterred, Ralph hit the road once more the following year.

Busking with Olaf on the Ponte Vecchio, Florence, 1964.

STREETS OF LONDON

Despite having the confidence to travel, he was still not fully certain of his ability to play on the streets, although he again took his guitar – as well as a new travelling companion, his girlfriend of the past two years named Jill, to Spain. "Jill was quite a stunning girl, blonde, slim and tall, who caught the eyes of all the blokes. I never realised the purgatory that poor girl went through with fellows always making passes at her. One night, while we were sleeping out in the woods, these two Algerian guys came along and literally tried to steal her. They were carrying her away when she woke me, and one of them had a knife at my neck. I was trapped in my sleeping bag absolutely unable to do anything... Fortunately, we got away, but we were so close to both being killed that night."

They both made it safely back to England, only to part when Jill went off to America. While she was away, Ralph went to RG Jones, a studio in Morden, South London, armed with his 6 and 12-string guitars, and made his very first recording for £20. He recorded four tracks: Bob Dylan's 'Girl From The North Country', 'The Bells Of Rhymney', 'Dry Bone Rag' and 'I Love My Baby'.

While Jill was still away, he received a letter from a Norwegian seaman named Olaf, whom he'd previously met on the road in Genoa. The letter informed Ralph that "there is work to be done and money to be made," so the guitar was packed again and off he went. By now, Ralph had gained in confidence and the two played together. "Olaf was a strummer, not very good, but he had plenty of bottle... I got a bit resentful in the end as he couldn't play that well but I was still splitting the money with him. We met a couple of girls who bottled (collected the money) for us, and they hitchhiked with us as far as Istanbul."

But ill-health hit, just as before, and the dysentery that nearly killed Olaf also afflicted Ralph soon afterwards. "We were in this dreadful place called the Gulhane Hotel, where the water was filthy. The poor fellow couldn't eat, and if he had a drink of water it would just go straight through him. Then I got sick, too, so I decided that I would move on when I recovered and maybe see Olaf in Milan or somewhere, but just get out of this awful place."

Hitchhiking through Yugoslavia, Ralph literally walked for days on end and eventually made it to Greece.

> *And once I walked a million miles*
> *All the way to Yugoslavia*
> *And carried you all of the way*
> *For where I was then there you are.*
> **('Heron Song', 1973)**

With no money, desperate measures had to be taken which resulted in him having to sell some of his blood in order to survive. But that, too, had its problems. "I was still ill, and when I went to give blood my pressure wasn't high enough. There was this bloke there who was saying 'as socialists, we should not be selling our blood. These guys are gangsters who will sell it off to the highest bidder. I am going to give my blood for nothing, and I want all you guys to do the same.'

"My face fell, as I was sick and had no money and I had to forget my principles and go on in. As they wouldn't take it, I went back outside where it was about ninety degrees and ran around the block to get some steam up! They knew I was desperate and eventually took a pint from me. I went back to the place where I was staying and was out cold for two days."

Arriving in Milan, he was loaned £10 by a kind stranger to get back to England. On his return, he found Jill had also returned. Yet while they had been apart, both their lives had changed. After a few days together, Jill had to visit her parents in Bournemouth – but in those days Ralph had realised their relationship was dying before his eyes. They set off on the journey together, but Ralph got only halfway there before deciding to leave the train and return home. He knew it was all over.

> *I took a little day trip, found myself in France*
> *Heard that stuff about the Paris girls*
> *And I thought I'd take a chance.*
> **('Take It Easy', 1974)**

Back home, the winter was setting in and Ralph was unsettled, having returned home to Croydon to find that little had changed. The lure of life on the road and music still pulled hard. He found work in a timber yard in Mitcham, where he met another of Tubs' pals called Bunny Doyle. One day, while working in the pouring rain in the yard, it was agreed that it was better to be wet and damp in Paris than Mitcham. Two days later Ralph and Bunny were in Paris.

Soon they were established in the beatnik Hotel Du Commerce on the Rue de la Montagne St Genevieve on Paris' left bank, a low-rent area that leads to the Pantheon. To call the hotel run down was putting it mildly – it was 'managed' by a colourful character known as Madame Mattutzi. The toilet walls had notices in English and French about not dismembering children and flushing them away, as it tended to block the drains!

But Madame Mattutzi took a liking to the young English lads and would invite Ralph and Bunny in for a drink some nights, pouring them glasses of an unnamed but lethal liquid that left them quite literally bewildered. Ralph shared the ground floor with Bunny and two prostitutes who were so ugly they could only work late at night. Having arrived with only £5 in his pocket, Ralph needed to earn some money quickly.

> *Madame Mattutzi she ran a cheap hotel*
> *On the Rue de la Montagne St Genevieve*
> *And me and my buddy, we're doing quite well*
> *Playing the streets of the Latin Quarter.*
> **('Rue De La Montagne St Genevieve', 1978, still unreleased)**

Standing on the Rue des Ecoles, Bunny announced their game plan. Two cinemas where people queued up each day was to be their pitch, while playing the likes of 'Rolling In My Sweet Baby's Arms' and 'San Francisco Bay Blues' was, he figured, the way to earn some money.

With nerves jangling, they would go up and down the line of people, slowly working their way back to the front of the queue as they finished their final number, when it was time to get the hat out and collect the money just as the cinema doors opened and people started to move. The takings were beyond their wildest dreams, enabling them to eat, drink and – most importantly of all – pay for their board and lodging.

> *Brigitte Bardot she made a film in this hotel*
> *On the Rue De La Montagne St Genevieve*
> *Madame Mattutzi says it was right here in my room*
> *She's a terrible liar I know*
> *But I want to believe her.*

STREETS OF LONDON

Returning home for a brief visit for Christmas, it was back out to Paris in early 1966. The weather was even colder, but they continued to work the streets with their small but effective repertoire. Tubs had also arrived in Ralph's absence, bringing with him another friend, Robin Best who, while wanting to earn a living with them, couldn't play a single note! After a brief attempt to teach him how to play a collapsible bass guitar he'd brought with him, it was decided that Bestie's talents lay in collecting the money up and down the cinema queues. Using rather demanding methods, their takings increased considerably.

Snowbound streets and a seemingly constant drop in temperature made life difficult. The streets were filled with others who had dreams, but were finding the reality of winter far harsher than they had imagined. Ralph: "We would troop off back to the Commerce at the end of an evening and we'd regularly see guys sleeping over the hot-air gratings above the Metro with their boots under their heads so they wouldn't be stolen. Occasionally, we would leave some small change in a shoe if it was visible.

"We became on passing terms with some of the old winos up at the Place Contrescarpe. We were all stunned to learn one night that one of them had frozen to death on the street the previous evening. A couple of days later, turning left out of the hotel, I noticed a pile of snow about a metre high begin to move, and two people emerged from under a blanket and brushed the snow off themselves. I began to form the idea of a song about the poor people of Paris, but that had been done before. Maybe Paris boulevards or Paris streets – I put the idea on hold for a while, but it never left me."

> *In the winter of '65 it snowed so cold*
> *That it froze on the streets of the Latin Quarter*
> *But she gave us a little drink and a paraffin stove*
> *We got the steamiest little room*
> *In this whole hotel.*

As the spring approached the temperature thankfully started to rise again. The intrepid foursome had their pitch established, but one had to guard it with some force in order to protect it as everywhere, it seemed, there were conjurers, fire eaters, sword-swallowers and magicians. Outside a cafe on St Germain Des Pres, one elderly entertainer playing a flute caught Ralph's attention. While he played, a mouse would run along the instrument giving the appearance that it was dancing, and the unusual nature of this act enabled the old man to collect a bit of change. One day Ralph watched the old man's pre-show preparations and saw him dip the mouse into a glass of cold water. With a combination of fear and cold, the mouse would give the impression of warming itself over the finger-holes!

Paris was awash with all sorts of nationalities, helped by the number of buskers arriving in their droves and the locals were becoming a little put out. As a result, the French government decided to get tough on the newcomers to Paris, viewing them more as beggars than entertainers, and the authorities embarked on a purge to clear the streets. One of the measures taken was to put police in plain clothes in the cinema queues. One day, Ralph was playing on the Rue Medecins when a stranger jumped out of the queue and approached him. However, much to Ralph's surprise, he wasn't a policeman but a newly-arrived American who decided that what Ralph was doing seemed more interesting than the movie. His name was Gary Petersen.

Having just turned 21, he had inherited a trust fund from his wealthy father and with it had purchased a Gibson Les Paul, a vintage 1941 Martin D 28 and – with his new bride, Melinda – a pair of one-way tickets to Paris. Petersen had managed to avoid the draft in America and had left California to go to New York where he had studied guitar with the legendary Rev Gary Davis and renowned jazz player Les Spann. The occasion was to have an important effect upon Ralph.

"That night in his hotel room, I heard the best live guitar playing I had ever heard in my life. Among my friends, I was regarded as pretty good, but in Gary's company I was a rank beginner. His classical ragtime playing was sensational: my jaw literally dropped at the things he could do and it stayed dropped. The boys got me to play my bits of Blind Boy Fuller and 'Anji', and although Gary was complimentary, I knew he was out of my class.

"He not only had a remarkable set of ears but he also understood music in an intellectual way. The fact he'd sat at the feet of Rev Gary Davis meant that he was in touch with a living thread to the past. There was a great anticipation whenever I got to play with him. Each time I learnt something new, and through him I learnt how to play ragtime properly."

Ralph wasn't able to demonstrate his ever-developing finger guitar style out on the streets due to the noise, but instead belted out his Guthrie and blues numbers with harmonica, achieving a fair degree of success. One day, Tubs said to him "Ralph, I've got two girls bottling for me. One's an American Indian and the other's from Norway. You can borrow one of them." The young student from Norway became Ralph's bottler. Her name was Nanna.

Martin 'Tubs' Sole (centre in denim) and Robin Best (behind in cap) in Paris, 1966.

Chapter
5
Nanna's Song

Born in Oslo in 1943, Nanna Stein was one of three children born into a middle-class family. Her father was a survey engineer and her mother worked as his secretary. Like many other girls of her age in the 1960s, she was attracted by French culture, language, fashions and film stars like Jean-Paul Belmondo. At 19, she decided to investigate France for herself and, accompanied by a friend and with the support of her parents, embarked on her own adventure.

"I set off to Montpellier in the south of France and enrolled on a three-month college course to learn the French language and history. Beyond that, I had no other plans, and following the course, I got a job in Paris as an au pair with an American/Chinese family. I was meeting other girls all the time who themselves were away from home for the first time and gained confidence through my freedom."

While in Paris, Nanna met and became engaged to an American serviceman called Bill and moved in with him. However, a year later, they decided to split up for a while; Nanna moved in with three girls to an apartment in the Latin quarter. At this time, she had a great interest in jazz, but no particular leaning towards folk music, although this would inevitably change. "I was in a cafe bar one day with my two friends, Eve and Karen, when these two guys started chatting us up. It was Tubs and Robin Best. They were playing the streets and asked if we'd be interested in collecting the money for them.

"Tubs told me one day that they had this friend in England who was a great guitar player. If he came back they would be able to earn even more money. Some time later, in a cafe, I was introduced to this tall guy. My first impression was of a scrubbed face, and he was shy and very polite."

Ralph: "I first saw Nanna standing outside the big bar at the end of Rue des Ecoles. She was wearing a very green coat and black suede boots that were too wide for her slim legs."

> *Ice cream and candy bars*
> *A Paris moon and Paris stars*
> *Can you count the times*
> *That we heard the chimes*
> *Of Notre Dame across the Seine*
> *To remind us sadly once again*
> *Time, just like the river, was swiftly passing by?*
> **('Nanna's Song', 1967)**

Female company made a pleasant change, although Ralph felt he made very little impression on either of the girls. Nanna's fiancé was quite fanatical about her and, having witnessed his father shooting his mother, could be both sinister and unpredictable. Even so, Ralph and Nanna's friendship grew and grew, despite the fact that Nanna was too gentle a person ever to be the best bottler on the streets. The shy boy from Croydon was beginning to fall for the slim Norwegian girl.

Around this time, Ralph had met a German by the name of Bernhard Grey and, seeing that Tubs was more and more going off and doing his own thing, the pair began to play the streets together. Meanwhile, word had got to Bill about Nanna's friendship with Ralph and he was said to be extremely angry. Since Bernhard was planning to visit Brussels for a few days, this seemed an ideal excuse for Ralph to leave Paris and allow matters to calm down.

On their arrival in Brussels, Bernhard deposited Ralph in the Cafe Welkom and vanished for the next two days, leaving him to survive on his own. Sitting around listening to endless groups of students, he heard a name spoken several times that caught his attention: "Among all the chatter, they mentioned Derroll Adams a number of times. I thought it must be the same fellow I'd heard of, and amazingly it was. It turned out that Adams lived in Brussels and they could arrange for me to meet him."

In the early 1960s, Derroll Adams had recorded an album with Jack Elliott, 'The Ramblin' Boys', that had exerted a tremendous influence on all those following the Woody Guthrie tradition. Ralph longed to tell him how much he and Max Faulkner had idolised Adams and Elliott years before. Having obtained directions to where Adams lived, Ralph went in search of his hero. He nervously knocked and waited.

Nanna outside the infamous caravan in Cornwall with borrowed 12-string, summer 1966.

"I wasn't prepared for the sight of the man who arrived on the doorstep and carefully stepped down to the pavement. He was very unsteady and I babbled on about how pleased I was to meet him and how great an influence his music had been on me.

"Derroll appeared not too interested in all this and instead motioned that we go to the bar where I'd been the day before. I asked him what he would like to drink and I ordered his usual, a whisky and coke. I was shocked when I was given a quarter-bottle of whisky and a small bottle of coke. His hands were trembling and I had to help him get the top off the bottle. Halfway down the bottle he began to talk. Three-quarters of the way down, he started to take an interest in me. Eventually, after much persuasion, he picked up his banjo which had appeared from somewhere and started to play it.

"For me, it was a moment of pure joy – and, as I just happened to have my guitar with me, I asked if I could play along. As time went by, I managed to persuade him to busk with me in a couple of places nearby which he reluctantly agreed to do. It was and still is a proud moment for me when I recall the fact that I worked a few bars with the great man. Unfortunately, to this day, Derroll can't recall any of it!"

Ralph returned to Paris high on his latest adventure, leaving Bernhard behind. He had missed Nanna a great deal and was eager to see her once again. As time went by, they began to spend more time together until eventually Nanna broke off her engagement and moved in with Ralph.

Naturally, Bill was livid at this news and vowed to take revenge on the English guitar player who had 'stolen' his intended. Ralph takes up the story. "One night, we were in this place called Le Bombarde, having a drink, and someone said 'Watch out. Bill's in here, he's got a knife in his boot and he's after you.' I was terrified, I have to admit.

"So I went up to him and said 'Look, this has happened and I don't know what to say to you' and said to Nanna that it would be best if she talked to him. So she went outside with him. I can remember it very clearly: there were two other

Ralph in Croydon's Wandle Park, 1967.

Americans there and suddenly one of them shouted, 'Look out, he's got a knife.' He pulled this knife on Nanna, knocked her to the ground and was kicking her. In the mad rush to the door I got pushed behind it and couldn't get out. This other guy came out into the street and tackled Bill around the waist: the two of them ended up going through a restaurant window, which caved in.

"Bill and this bloke landed on a table where people were eating, the table broke and this woman had her leg broken. There was glass everywhere. By this time I was in on it and I had Bill's arm up his back. He said to me `You're dead' or words to that effect! The military charged him, but he was out on the street within 24 hours looking to kill both of us. So Nanna moved in with me. You'd see him stalking the streets. It was a really scary time. I used to sleep with a lump of wood under my pillow."

Remember the room without any view
Frightened of meeting someone that we knew?
No farewells or how do you dos
In the Grande Affaire.
('Grande Affaire', 1974)

One day, when Ralph was playing the queues with Bernhard, a small Frenchman stepped out of the line and asked McTell if he could play guitar finger-style. Bernhard translated the eager Frenchman's questions: would Ralph like a job off the streets? Would he call at the address on this visiting card the following morning?

After finishing their 'show', Bernhard, Nanna and Ralph went to a nearby bar to divide that day's takings. Bernhard was looking at the card and announced: "Ralph, they want you to play an audition at L'Olympia my friend!" The following day, the trio arrived at the theatre to a scene of chaos with musicians and stage-hands milling about. Among them, Ralph noticed a gangly French lad of about his own age nervously watching what was going on. His name was Antoine, and he was known as 'the French Bob Dylan'.

The trouble with Antoine was that he couldn't play guitar so the plan was that he would have Ralph, Bernhard and a young French musician sitting behind him and playing, dressed in evening suits. Ralph was the only one whose playing was audible – the other two were instructed to *faire un blanc* (play an inch above the strings)! There was a vacancy in the band backing him, who were collectively known as Les Problèmes. Ralph got the job as guitarist, earning £4 per night.

"It was cash in hand, no questions asked. I was worried because I wanted it all above board – I didn't want to get busted working without a permit and they were on the trail of illegal immigrants." Les Problèmes had an excellent lead singer and were given a brief slot on the show, where they gave it their best shot. However, when they came on with Antoine, it was a different story. "The stage director decided the band should be arranged on a system of ladders and planks which did not allow for the bass player's vertigo. I will forever remember his expression of total fear, as he perched in the middle of a plank between two trestle ladders, moving involuntarily with his own weight."

They also had another problem with the keyboard player, as McTell recalled: "He was actually one of the better musicians but was a bit overweight, so they made him stand behind a curtain. I can still see the hurt in his eyes and, as far as I remember, none of his friends ever protested. I had to tune Antoine's guitar for him but, as French concert pitch is different to everyone else's, the guitar, harmonica and orchestra were all a quarter-tone apart. The audience never seemed to notice and Antoine constantly received rave reviews."

> Me and my buddy we're doing all right
> The girl who takes the money stays with me some nights
> My buddy thinks he stands a chance with the landlady's daughter
> On the Rue De La Montagne St Genevieve.
> **('Rue De La Montagne St Genevieve')**

The show came to the end of its three-week run in Paris, but not before further drama. Over the past weeks, Ralph had been living with the twin pressures of constantly running from the police while busking, and the manic Bill looking to kill him. Now having got this job at the Olympia, the pressure finally came to a head and one afternoon, after the matinee performance, Ralph collapsed backstage. He lay there for hours until he was found, when a doctor was summoned and, after a large shot of unknown medication was administered, he recovered sufficiently to complete the remaining shows.

He and Nanna were inseparable and, although very much in love, were undecided about the future. Ralph had vague plans to go to America: during his time in Paris, he had started to write songs. He was aware of how much he had changed over the past months, and needed to digest everything that had taken place. Besides, everybody else was moving on. Robin Best had departed with his three chords to Geneva in an MG sports car, and would not return to England for another eight years. Bunny Doyle too had left Paris, and was not seen for some time.

Tubs' penchant for drugs had reached the point where he had hatched a plan to become registered as a heroin addict; the idea was that he would only use part of his methadone prescription himself, and sell the rest to provide some income. Although he had been invited to tour with the Antoine show, Ralph decided to return to England, although he had enjoyed his four months in Paris. Soon after arriving home, he received a call from Wizz Jones, who invited Ralph to accompany him to Cornwall. The summer promised great times ahead.

Meanwhile, Nanna had also left Paris to return to Oslo, where she had found a job. She had promised Ralph that she would visit him in England later that summer. However, these plans were thrown into disarray when she discovered she was pregnant! "I told Ralph, but I knew that he wanted to go to America, so I made the decision that I would not stand in his way and also decided that I was happy to have the baby and would bring it up on my own in Norway. I put no pressure on Ralph. When he learnt that I was pregnant, he talked to me about marriage, but we made no definite plans. I also needed to think about what I wanted to do, so I moved in with my sister to relax for a while."

Tubs, when he heard the news, wrote to Nanna and insisted that she and Ralph marry. He was most concerned and was very supportive, belying his reputation as a womaniser, and even went as far as offering to marry Nanna himself if Ralph didn't! Ralph hadn't told his mother that Nanna was expecting his child, but chaos ensued when Nanna's mother decided to write to Mrs May and tell her the news. Eventually, they both agreed to do the 'decent thing'. The somewhat petrified father-to-be travelled to Norway by himself and, on 30 November 1966, he and Nanna became Mr and Mrs May.

"My parents arranged our honeymoon for us in a hotel in the mountains," Nanna recalls. "The only snag was that they came along too, with my sister and her daughter! My mother was aghast at Ralph – all he possessed were his brown desert boots, so she made him buy a formal black pair of shoes. Prior to the wedding, she had never met Ralph, and all she really wanted was for me to be married for the baby's sake. She told me I could always divorce him once the baby was born!"

Shortly after the wedding, Ralph and Nanna moved to Croydon, where they would live with his mother in her council flat. Although she came from Norway, Nanna wasn't prepared for the English winter. "I was in a state of shock when I came to England, though I never realised it. At least our home in Oslo was heated to help us get through the winters, but here I was in a strange country in a run-down area in Croydon. I remember the damp sheets on the bed. But Ralph's mother was so supportive and did everything to help me settle. It must have been very hard for her too. And when the baby was born she was so wonderful. She has always been great with children. She helped me get through."

While Ralph had been in Paris, Mick Bartlett had formed a group called the Levee Breakers, and had taken to playing a jug (a stone container into which one blew), and was now widely known as Henry VIII (due to a certain similarity in stature and the fact that he sported a beard). On Ralph's return, a trio was formed, with Mick North on mandolin, known as the Strimmed Implements. As Bartlett explains, the name came from "one of the characters from the Whitgift who used to get all his words mixed up and would come up to us and say 'Are you lads still playing them strimmed implements?'

"We did general club gigs playing jug band and 'good-time' music. Ralph had written a couple of songs for us, one being 'Sleepytime Blues' which we later recorded on his first album. We managed to get a gig supporting Chris Farlowe and the Thunderbirds at the Fairfield Hall in Croydon. Mick North turned up with a stinking cold and hardly able to speak. But Ralph said 'Don't worry, I'll sort him out' and went off to our local curry house. There he had a quick word with the manager and out came one extremely hot vindaloo. 'Get your chops round that!' says Ralph – and, sure enough, Mick played and sang beautifully."

Chapter
6 Cornwall

The first folk club in Cornwall was opened in 1964 at Botallack near St Just by a local businessman named Ian Todd. His idea had been to provide much-needed entertainment for the ever increasing numbers of holiday-makers visiting the area, in the form of a cabaret-style club. "I had moved from St Ives in the spring," said Todd, "and bought a place called the Count House which had a barn attached to the side of the house. The idea was to provide a place where holiday-makers could entertain themselves and each other by playing the guitar, singing a song, play harmonica, even the spoons…anything. Very soon, I realised that what was being performed was edging more towards folk music, about which I knew very little."

The set-up was very simple, with a stage made out of packing cases and bare boards and no amplification at all. Not being a licensed premises, it was initially a place where the whole family could congregate. Among the first performers to appear was a local character – a fisherman called, oddly enough, John the Fish. "Whole families would arrive and sometimes we'd just sing to one family alone. A real mix turned out." Todd persevered with the club and it gained increasing popularity. The original idea was to close at the end of the summer season, but many locals had started attending and let it be known they wished the club to continue, so it became a regular Saturday-night attraction.

By 1965, John the Fish had been joined by two other resident singers, Des Hannigan and Brenda Wootton. Hannigan was a journalist from Scotland who sang folk songs in the traditional unaccompanied style. "John the Fish had a personality which just lifted the place. There was a real innocence about the club in the early days which was sadly lost later on, when other performers brought a far higher degree of professionalism."

Brenda Wootton had originally visited the club to see what it was all about. "I'd done singing and drama for years, but never in the club until one night I was persuaded to sing. The audience would be in there, sitting on barrels listening to John the Fish doing 'So Long, It's Been Good To Know You'. It was such a tranquil setting in the summer, although it was so cold in winter we used to bring cardboard boxes along to rest our feet on to keep warm. Fishing nets hung down from the ceiling, not for effect but to stop bits of the roof falling down on

Ralph outside their first home at the Sun Valley Caravan Park, 1967.

people's heads. We'd have all-night sessions. There was no question of violence or trouble. It was innocent and lovely."

Among the audience at the Count House was a teacher named John Sleep, who travelled from Newquay. Like Ian Todd, he also wanted to find similar entertainment nearer to home. He had a friend named Willoughby Gulachson, who owned a farm in a village called Mitchell just off the A30. Gulachson's farm had a disused cottage on it which Sleep, and his friend John Hayday, set about renovating, also with the intention of setting up a club.

Electricity and a new staircase were among the improvements the two Johns undertook in order to make the place suitable for people to visit. By the summer, it was ready, and with Sleep and Hayday as residents, as well as relying heavily on both John the Fish and Brenda Wootton, the Folk Cottage was ready to open its doors.

Henry Bartlett remembers the Folk Cottage scene well. "It was shambolic. It would never get off the ground today, but, my goodness, it was the scene of some incredible sessions, packed to the rafters, and heaving. The police turned a blind eye on its lack of 'facilities' so long as the Police Inspector's son was welcomed to play, and it cleared Newquay of 'the rabble'. The top floor served as a club room, with a stage at one end in front of painted silhouette figures on the wall, there was a fire escape leading across the yard to 'Ye Olde Bog' (a chemical toilet that regularly overflowed on good nights). Downstairs was a coffee bar with old settees, where passing musicians would sit strumming, waiting their turn to go on." Now with two clubs, Cornwall's reputation spread, and by the summer of 1965 it seemed the place to be.

Ralph, Bob Strawbridge and 'Henry' Bartlett at the Folk Cottage. At Ralph's right elbow is Whispering Mick.

Meanwhile, Wizz Jones had been offered work in various pubs and hotels and by 1965 was well established on the British folk scene, working with an excellent banjo player, Pete Stanley. Jones now had a family, and his days of earning a living travelling around Europe were over. However, Pete Stanley was away in Italy and Wizz needed both the gigs and a partner, so he asked Ralph to deputise until Stanley returned.

"When Ralph got back from Paris," Wizz recalls, "he'd been playing with a little band he'd put together called the Hickory Nuts, but he was also playing some brilliant ragtime guitar in the style of Blind Blake – better than anything I'd heard before. I was quite amazed at how much he'd developed because the last time I'd seen him, I'd only heard him doing Guthrie-type stuff. He didn't have many gigs on at the time, and I remember he used to come around to the house always looking a bit forlorn and lost, and most of it was a bit of a put-on. He said, 'Oh, there's nothing on at the moment. I don't know what to do. I hear there's a job going on the dust (refuse collection).' So I said 'Well, come down to Cornwall with us."

Ralph: "I was hoping to be asked to go along. We worked out a few things – up to that point, I had barely started to write songs, and certainly would never have dreamt of playing them in public, so we worked off a few flat-pickin' numbers and off we went."

Wizz Jones: "He probably wondered what he'd got himself into on that tortuous journey, sitting on an old basket full of nappies in the back of our old Thames van with the kids jumping all over him."

They all spent that summer on a camp-site surviving on the proceeds of the odd washing-up job and a little busking. One of their gigs was at the Mermaid Inn at Porth Beach near Newquay, a regular venue down the years for Wizz and Pete Stanley. In fact, a couple of years earlier, Ken and Joan Woollard had wondered into the Mermaid while on holiday, and Ken later recalled that seeing how popular Wizz and Pete had become was one of the things that inspired them to launch the Cambridge Folk Festival.

"We used to get paid £3 per night between the two of us," Ralph recalls, "and, as Wizz had a family, I decided he should take £2. The place developed a sort of cult following – every night it was packed out. We'd share one mic between us, and whack it out all night long. Here I was playing with one of my guitar heroes, learning all sorts of songs and learning to sing harmonies. It was funny playing in hotels with Wizz where, a few years earlier, he would have been refused admission. Times really *were* changing."

While that summer was most beneficial to Ralph's developing confidence as a performer, it was a two-way street, as Jones remembers. "I learnt a lot from Ralph that summer, like how to get the thumb on my right hand alternating on the bass strings, instead of being rooted to the incessant Bill Broonzy thump. He also taught me how to take my music seriously, to be professional and finish a song properly!"

The chemistry Ralph and Wizz produced attracted larger audiences than anyone else in Cornwall at the time. Yet, despite their popularity at the Mermaid, the landlord sacked them – simply because he was unable to cope with the crowds of people who turned up to see them! But fate played a part, as one of the regulars at the Mermaid was John Sleep: Ralph and Wizz could see the potential of the Folk Cottage.

FOLK COTTAGE
MITCHELL
Thursday, September 8th
Last Late Night Session
WIZZ JONES and PETE STANLEY
Friday, September 9th
1st Session
JOHN THE FISH
2nd Session
RALPH McTELL
plus supporting artistes
Saturday, September 10th
RALPH McTELL
and
THE MITCHELL JUG BAND

On the fire escape, 1967

Shortly afterwards, Pete Stanley returned from Italy, and he and Wizz teamed up again to play regularly at the Folk Cottage. But Jones felt something wasn't quite right, as Ralph recalled: "When he put my name on the posters with theirs, Wizz reckoned that Ralph May just didn't quite look the part. He suggested I find myself a 'stage name', but I didn't have a clue what to choose. It was Wizz who suggested McTell, after Blind Willie McTell, whose 'Statesboro Blues' we both loved. So that was it."

Despite Jones and Stanley being the main attraction, McTell got his chance to play solo. "He didn't figure very much at the beginning," John Sleep recalls, "but he'd do one or two songs a week. In those days we used to give Ralph all we could afford, which might have been £1 or perhaps £2, so he wasn't exactly well paid, but he was glad of what he could get. He was nervous, but the audiences liked him very much, and he began to build up a reputation for himself."

The Folk Cottage went from strength to strength, even though John Sleep was amazed anybody could ever find it. "It wasn't very well signposted, but word of mouth gradually got around. We had a very small field across the road as a car park, but this would quickly fill up, and there'd be cars all the way back up the lane for a mile or so. We started having late-night sessions beginning around midnight, and these were very well attended – there wasn't very much else happening at that hour.

"One of the main attractions was the jug band that performed there, which everyone was very keen on. They used to centre themselves in a caravan across the road from the Folk Cottage (in which Ralph and Nanna would eventually live). There was Whispering Mick Bennett, Mick 'Henry the Jug' Bartlett, Pete Berryman, and anyone who could play was welcome. Clive Palmer would join in. They would practice in the caravan, and then put on their show during the late-night sessions. We extended the late nights to Wednesday, Friday and Saturday, and it was a great feature in the club. Ralph was always a major part of that – he really seemed to enjoy it. They'd do all sorts of stuff like Gus Cannon's version of 'Walk Right In'."

Tapes still exist of some of those nights in the Cornish clubs which provide a good indication of McTell's early promise as a performer, both as a soloist and with the Famous Jug Band. Despite an understandable hesitancy in his vocals, the distinctive guitar style is there to hear in its infancy, especially on ragtime features like 'Dry Bone Rag' and Blind Boy Fuller's 'Brown Skinned Woman'. On various nights, McTell would run through Alan Tunbridge's 'Earls Court Breakdown', 'Anji', 'Hit The Road Jack', 'Baby Let Me Lay It On You' and Joseph Spence's 'There'll Be A Happy Meeting', along with original material such as 'I'm Sorry I Must Leave' and 'Nanna's Song'.

One of his earliest songs, 'March Of The Emmetts', was always popular – Emmett is an old Cornish word for ant, and as Cornwall was starting to be invaded by tourists, the latter were referred to as families of Emmetts, and the song always gained a laugh at the visitors' expense. On one night, Stefan Grossman joined in with Ralph and the jug band – and, far from being unnerved, it stimulated McTell to demonstrate what a potentially great picker he would eventually become. The whole night came to an end with good-time versions of 'That'll Never Happen No More', 'Old Time Religion' and similar foot-stomping stuff. Those nights in the clubs were memorable evenings.

In turn, the jug band would play at the Count House in Botallack, another venue where McTell improved his reputation. "Ralph was developing all the time, no question," says Des Hannigan. "Every night you'd have this amazing situation where he'd come off stage and say, to me of all people, 'Was I all right?' He was singing the classic type of contemporary folk songs then." Wizz Jones: "What I remember about him especially in those early days in Cornwall was that boy-next-door personality. Everybody loved him."

The countless numbers who beat a path across to the west of England attracted by the Cornwall scene included Jacqui McShee. "I'd go across to Newquay for a couple of weeks at a time. It was an absolute haven for folk singers and guitar players, as there seemed to be so many opportunities and places to play…on beaches, in the town, and at various clubs that seemed to open up each week. Nobody seemed to mind you wandering around the place. These were pre-hippie days, I guess…

"I knew people who were going down there, like 'Jug Henry' Bartlett, as well as Ralph. But seeing Ralph play there made you realise just how good he was, even then. He really stood out as a guitar player. He just 'had it' – and everybody knew it." However the summer season passed and life began to get cold in the caravan McTell had bought for £50 as winter approached. Eventually, the caravan collapsed, and, by October, he moved back in London, continuing to play wherever he could.

At the Piper's Folk Club in the Village Hall in St Buryan. From left: Wizz Jones, Bob Strawbridge, Brenda Wooton, Ralph, John the Fish and Pete Stanley.

Chapter

7 Going Solo

Despite a growing reputation as a performer, Ralph was now a father, as well as a husband, after the birth of a son, Sam Bjorn, in early January 1967. Feeling a massive responsibility, McTell now felt that the time had come for him to attempt a conventional career, and college seemed the best option. Enrolling at teacher's training college in Tooting, he attempted to combine his studies with bringing money in from gigging, which wasn't easy: the steady demand for shows led to late nights and early-morning returns home, where young Sam keeping him awake was not conducive to concentration at college. On one occasion, following a drive back overnight from a club booking in Sheffield, he fell asleep at his desk.

While enjoying his time at college, he still felt out of place there. He had been accepted largely because a radical member of the board specifically recruited people with left-wing views, like McTell, in order to inject a radical stimulus into the college. However, the memories of the previous year in Cornwall were too great; as a result of his spell there with Wizz Jones and company, Essex Music had shown interest in his new-found ability as a songwriter.

At the end of his first year at college, he decided he could no longer combine both teaching and music. The time had come to take a chance at becoming Ralph McTell on a full time basis, and Nanna had no hesitation in encouraging him to take the plunge.

By then, he had started to play at the famous Les Cousins club in Soho, the seminal venue for acoustic performers at the time where the likes of Donovan, Cat Stevens and even Jimi Hendrix had played. There, in Soho, McTell began to gather even greater experience among the other emerging talents of the day.

"I remember being in there the night Roy Harper played his first date at Cousins. I used to run the all-nighter session and play on alternate weekends. The big thing about playing there was that I got to use a microphone! I would stick in plenty of ragtime pieces as I wasn't that confident about the strength of my songs then. But it was a great place in terms of building up my confidence."

Around this time, Ralph secured his first record contract with Transatlantic Records, then the leading folk music label. The route by which he obtained his record contract is worth explaining. He'd been asked to submit some demos and, aided by Ron Geesin, recorded four songs, 'I'm Sorry I Must Leave', 'Sleepytime Blues', 'Hesitation Blues' and 'Nanna's Song'. Though Graham Churchill at Essex Music wasn't much impressed, a live recording of 'March Of The Emmetts' with its usual audience appreciation interested Essex enough for them to offer him a contract

that gave them the option on his work for the next nine months. However, before the time was up they converted this into a record deal with Transatlantic.

McTell was building up his repertoire and gaining experience all the time. During the year he was asked to perform at a folk and blues festival in Bexhill on Sea in Sussex where sharing the bill with him were the Panama Jug Band and another up-and-coming singer-songwriter…Paul Simon. "At the end of the evening," Ralph recalls, "the promoter came up to me very apologetically. Though the event had gone well, he had not made enough money to pay the performers. Paul Simon was on £20 and he had just made enough to cover that, but not enough to pay me my £7. Instead, he insisted I take his most treasured possession, a copy of 'King Of The Delta Blues' by Robert Johnson.

"He was most insistent and I took it very reluctantly. Though I didn't get paid I came away from that gig far from empty-handed and was able to hear some of the most haunting, powerful and poetic music I'd ever heard in my life. I still have that record, and if I was ever allowed to only keep one of my records that would be the one."

Around this time Mick McDonagh, a college friend of his brother Bruce, caught one of his gigs. "Bruce was involved in running a club up in World's End Lane and Ralph was on there

one night. I had grown up with a love of blues and ragtime music and there was this young white English guy up there playing all that stuff: I thought he was just amazing. He wasn't doing that many of his own songs then. I became social secretary and started organising gigs regularly. Whenever the opportunity arose we'd try and put Ralph on in order to get him a bigger gig.

"He did one of our arts festival gigs and I remember a fantastic encore to it all where Ralph did 'Walk Right In' with his jug-band mates along with Brett Marvin and the Thunderbolts and Jo-Ann Kelly. Marvellous stuff."

Work began on his first album at Decca studios which was to be produced by a certain Gus Dudgeon. "It was Gus's very first album too," Ralph reveals. "He'd been an engineer for Decca for some years and his wife Sheila was Nat Joseph's secretary. When they were looking for a producer for me, Sheila suggested Gus, who'd never heard of me before. It was Tony Visconti's first arranging job, too, so it was a new experience for us all. In fact I had a bit of a fight to convince Gus that I was capable of playing guitar on it too! He wanted me to use someone else.

"I'd brought up the jug band from Cornwall along with Mac McGann who used to be with the Levee Breakers, which used to feature a then 17-year-old Beverly Martyn. We were all lined up to record 'Louise' and Gus suggested a run-through. I responded with 'Oh I think we'll be okay – we'll just do it' and there I was yelling out the cues to everybody. It's still there on that take. Gus wanted us to do it again but I felt we'd caught the right energy.

"I was fairly happy with the record, though there were couple of things I didn't think turned out as well as they should have. I wanted a feel to it similar to Bert Jansch's first record with just voice and guitar. I think Transatlantic had some odd idea of making me a pop star or something. We recorded Leonard Cohen's 'Suzanne', but Tony Visconti arranged it higher than I could sing it so it was left off. 'Morning Dew', which Essex had the publishing on, was a beautiful song but we should have never attempted to do it anything like the original. But I did get to do a few rags and some of my own songs on it so I was fairly pleased." There was also one other title that McTell decided he didn't want to record. It was a song written the previous year called 'Streets Of London'.

Titled 'Eight Frames A Second', the album was released in 1968 and was a passable if unspectacular debut. Some of the material did hint at his potential as a guitar player, though the tracks arranged by Tony Visconti didn't fit at all comfortably with the rest of the record. This was shown up particularly on 'Granny Takes A Trip' which ended up sounding similar to the early David Bowie track 'The Laughing Gnome' with its Cockney vocal and 'cor blimeys'. Since this awful 'song' was a minor hit for a Manchester group called the Purple Gang, it's a blessing – given Ralph's feeling of being typecast by his 1970s hit – that he never made it with this song!

Thirteen tracks, all but five originals, made the record. The instrumental pieces, in particular 'Blind Blake's Rag' (the guitar part of a song titled 'Buddy Bolden' which Gus Dudgeon mistitled) showed his potential as a guitar player. There was little on the record to hint at McTell's potential as a writer, but enough to suggest hope for the future. Ralph: "The title track is about the dawn and how light shades and colours change and that it happens every day. The thing about the reawakening that took place in the 1960s was a feeling that you were looking at things through new eyes. I was pleased with that song both musically and lyrically."

McTell had been given the princely sum of £12 to smarten himself up for the

First recording session at Decca Studios.

TRANSATLANTIC RECORDS LTD

120/122 Marylebone Lane London W1 *Telephone* Hunter 4363/6 *Cables* Xtra London W1

/ad

11th October, 1967.

Labels
Transatlantic
Xtra
Folkways
MK
Conversaphone
Storyville
Audio Fidelity

Associate Companies
Heathside Music Ltd
Cobral Recordings Ltd

Directors
Nathan Joseph
D Bassoon

Ralph McTell, Esq.,
29 Bracken Avenue,
Shirley,
Croydon,
Surrey.

Dear Ralph:

I am writing to confirm the sessions booked in connection with your forthcoming LP as follows:
Monday, October 16th, No. 2 studio, 8pm-11pm,
Monday, October 23rd, No. 1 studio, 8pm-11pm,
Friday, October 27th, No. 1 studio, 7pm-10pm.

The address of Pye Studios is A.T.V. House, Great Cumberland Place, London, W.1.

Yours sincerely,
TRANSATLANTIC RECORDS LIMITED

Sheila Dudgeon (Mrs)
Secretary to Nathan Joseph

cc.: Graham Churchill.

PRESENTING
RALPH McTELL
Transatlantic Recording Star
Guitarist / Songwriter and Britain's Representative
in Austrian Song Festival

IN CONCERT
THURSDAY, 21st NOVEMBER
At 8 p.m.

St. John's Hall, Penzance

SUPPORTING ARTISTES:
John The Fish - Pete Berryman
Clive Palmer
The Famous Jug-Band!!

TICKETS 6/-
Available at the Door or at your Local Music Shop
or The Folk Cottage, Mitchell

LICENSED BAR APPLIED FOR
A Splendid Time is Guaranteed for All!

Wardens of Cornwall Limited, Penzance

cover photo, which resulted in him buying a Marks and Spencer's pullover and cutting his own hair with a razorblade and comb. Not quite Transatlantic's vision of a pop star…more, as he described it, like a boxer!

'Eight Frames A Second' sold nearly two and a half thousand copies in its first year and its impact on his live work had him performing five nights a week throughout the country by the end of the year. In late 1967, McTell did a floorspot at the Horseshoe on Tottenham Court Road which reaped the impressive sum of ten shillings. There that night was someone with whom he was to form a long-standing working and personal relationship – Danny Thompson.

"I had never heard of Ralph before but liked what I heard very much. I can see him now dressed, as he seemed to for years after, in his denim jacket and jeans –what I called his 'Professional Busker's Outfit'. We spoke outside and he struck me as a really decent and down-to-earth bloke. I rated him from that moment as both a player and a person." Local press soon started to take an interest in him and in one interview he stated that "If I could make twenty pounds a week singing, I'd give up this teaching business."

Graham Churchill from Essex Music started helping Nanna deal with the ever-increasing demand for club performances but it was soon obvious that someone was needed on a full-time basis. While he could be quite critical at times, brother Bruce was an excellent business manager and it was decided he would take over from this point on.

McTell's second album 'Spiral Staircase' was released in 1968. Again produced by Gus Gudgeon, the finished album was closer to how McTell had hoped its predecessor would sound. He wrote 11 of the 13 songs himself, a clear indication of how his stature and self-confidence as a songwriter had grown over the last year. With the summer in Cornwall in mind, the jug-band sound was back on a couple of the tracks, 'Spiral Staircase' and 'Last Train And Ride', which includes the lines "There's fifty seven ways of being mean to me, fifty seven varieties like Heinz." Ralph: "The title song of the LP was a riff which went round and suggested a spiral staircase to me, and that in turn suggested a dilemma – like a nightmare where you're running up some stairs which are going down, and are only able to stay in the same place. An uptempo dilemma!"

Reaching back to his childhood, which would provide a rich source of inspiration throughout his career, resulted in songs like 'Mrs Adlam's Angels', recalling his days at the Mint Walk mission hall when religion was such a guiding influence in his younger life, while 'Daddy's Here' touched on the occasional visits to his home by his departed father to see his mother when he and his brother were tucked up in bed, leaving the adults to sort out their business.

One of his strongest and most under-rated songs was 'England 1914', which looked at a time when the world changed so much and so permanently. The song indicated McTell's potential as a songwriter of great ability in the way he could observe the feelings of people and convey them in a way that almost made you believe he had observed them at first hand. Having been surrounded during his childhood by a number of relatives involved in the Great War (his grandfather and great uncles Bill and Charlie all survived the 1914-18 conflict), he drew on their tales. The line describing the columns of marching soldiers as a "brown canal splashed with red" was quite striking.

The accompaniment of strings added to the overall picture and fitted in perfectly, in contrast to the first album. "Many people," says Ralph, "find the First World War more fascinating than the Second, which was just as brutal, but somehow the First signalled an absolute change in the world. The song is a sort of premonition of disaster and despair and destruction and the way it would be from then on. Never before had men had the power to destroy themselves quite so comprehensively. The song's about that and the sadness at England's loss of naivety – its rural phase. I'm not talking about Victorian values but the loss of peacefulness."

The final song, the haunting 'Terminus', was memorable for the mood McTell created of the parting of a couple with "bodies sweetly aching from the night before" playing out their final moments on a station platform. It's a theme he has revisited down the years: the scenario of a railway station being the location of a goodbye to a relationship, as also demonstrated in 'Last Train And Ride' (another track on this album), and, in later years, 'Slow Burning Companion'.

'Spiral Staircase' has to be regarded as one of McTell's most important albums, not least because it included 'Streets Of London' on record for the very first time. Having not felt happy about including the song on 'Eight Frames A Second', McTell was not even going to record it for his second release – clearly a sign that he was falling out of love with the song, even at that early stage. "After I'd finished all the tracks for the second album, Gus Dudgeon said 'Please have one go at "Streets Of London", even though I know you don't want to.' So I did just one take and Gus prevailed upon me to put it on the album."

Meanwhile, Mick McDonagh was on his usual summer trip around America, "bumming around doing whatever work I could. I ended up driving Sonny Terry and Brownie McGhee." It coincided with the release of 'Eight Frames A Second' in the US, and Ralph's agent, Julia Creasey at Blackhill Enterprises, asked if he could try get some reaction to the record while there. "I really believed in Ralph, and was happy to spread the word. While I was in New York, I saw a few agents and people who ran some of the coffee house clubs. I went to see Capitol Records who had licensed the LP, and, while they knew they had Ralph, didn't know what they were going to do with him. I went to see (Dylan manager) Albert Grossman and he said he'd listen to the album, though nothing ever came of that."

STREETS OF LONDON

The release of 'Spiral Staircase' had further enhanced McTell's reputation to the point where he was invited to make his first radio recording for the BBC as part of their *Country Meets Folk*, aired on 24 August 1968. Appearing on national radio helped to spread his name far more than gigging could and enabled him to get bookings throughout the UK. It was on one of the *Country Meets Folk* programmes that 'Streets Of London' received its first national exposure, after which the BBC's switchboard was jammed with callers wanting to know who was singing it!

The touring continued, as Bartlett recalls. "Ralph and I would often travel back from gigs together when the Famous Jug Band had supported him. I vividly remember one trip on a sleeper from Leeds. He was in a great mood, telling jokes, when the train stopped at a station around 3.00am. He decided to go and look for something to drink and had been gone for ages when the train suddenly moved off, leaving me worrying that he was stranded on some 'foreign' station. About half an hour later, he strolls back into the compartment, cool as you like, with two cups of coffee saying 'I bet *that* had you going.' He'd been chatting to the steward!"

McTell was starting to work almost nightly, zigzagging his way across the UK. One example of his ever-increasingly popularity is recalled by Stephen Clarke, a Hull University student at the time who in later years became a Crown Court circuit judge. "A guy called Ed Bicknell was booking the acts then, and put Ralph on at the Needler Hall. His fee was £25, and out of that he had to pay his own rail fare from London to Hull. I remember him arriving with his guitar slung over his shoulder, looking very much the travelling performer.

"Ed had done a really good job advertising the gig, which paid dividends as there must have been between 250-300 people there that night. Many didn't really know who Ralph McTell was, but they certainly did after that night. He was absolutely fabulous. His guitar-playing was so superior measured against the average performers we were getting on the circuit at the time. Also, part of the deal was that we had to put him up for the night, so Ralph ended up sleeping on the floor of one of our rooms! It didn't surprise me that Ralph went on to bigger things in the years afterwards. So did Ed, for that matter, who became the manager of Dire Straits!"

Chapter
8 Changing Times

As the year progressed, McTell started to get regular national radio exposure by playing many sessions on BBC's *Night Ride* and *Country Meets Folk*, as well as the influential John Peel's *Top Gear*. In July, he made his first appearance at the Cambridge Folk Festival, and the continual growth of his reputation as a writer and performer brought him constant bookings, although the number of dates he was getting were starting to take a toll. "There are far too many gigs at the moment," he told *Melody Maker*'s Jerry Gilbert. "They are never strategically placed and I seldom get any time for writing. On top of that, I just want to be sufficiently fit to put on a good show, as I can't stand the thought that I could have done a gig a lot better." But there were sufficient new songs around for McTell to start work on his third album later that summer.

He decided he would produce it himself this time, resulting in greater control and a record more sympathetic to his status as a songwriter. His suspicions about how others thought he had changed personally over the last two years surfaced in a new song, 'Clown', and there was another look back to his childhood in 'Factory Girl'. Then there was 'Michael In The Garden', one of McTell's most thoughtful pieces of writing, which would endure throughout his career.

'Michael In The Garden' was personal, in the sense that it was inspired by Nanna's brother, Olebjorn, who was born severely impaired, yet it has reached and touched very many people who have heard it over the years. It is unusual in being one of the few songs McTell has strummed rather than picked, but this adds to the anger and power of its lyrics. It is a song that seems to express something that exists behind the eyes of its subject. In the 1972 songbook *Ralph McTell*, published by Essex Music, it is preceded by the following introduction: "This song is not autobiographical, though there have been times when I wished it were."

Melody Maker *gig lists from 1968.*

And they in their wisdom say
'Michael's got something wrong wrong with his mind'
They must be blind
For they can't see what Michael sees.
('Michael In the Garden', 1969)

A LEGACY BEGINS

his instrumentation was first recognized in Paris. But it was at the Innsbruck Song Festival that the young man from London brought people to their feet cheering a non-uniform folk-blues voice. At first he is warm gentle song. The next moment he is wild ragtime guitar and suddenly there breaks out the old jug band sound. Always easy and sure. Always the fluid voice and limber rhythm. This is Ralph McTell newly lined up with the legacies who moved him: Jesse Fuller, Blind Black, Woody Guthrie. His album is now in America and so let the words end and the music begin.

Eight Frames A Second: Ralph McTell

Available on Records and on Tape Capitol

Ralph: "I wanted to write that song a long time before I actually did. I listened to descriptions of people suffering from what I now know as autism, a lack of communication with other people, and yet having a lot of intelligence and ability which are internalised and aren't expressed very well. I became intrigued with the idea of someone imprisoned inside their mind, and society in turn imprisons them in an institution, but actually they feel quite free and just choose not to communicate. Perhaps there are lessons for us in that, although it's a song that could only be written by a young person, which it was when I wrote it. Over the years, that song has produced as much correspondence as 'Streets Of London', and I've had books dedicated to it and letters from people who have children like that."

McTell was continuing to make a name for himself throughout the country. Rod Clements, a founder member of Lindisfarne, recalls their first meeting. "I had been aware of him from those Peel sessions around the time of 'Eight Frames A Second', where he was being presented mainly as a blues and ragtime player, which was exactly what I was into as well. I was then playing in an early version of Lindisfarne called the Downtown Faction.

"At the same time, Alan Hull was running the Rex Folk Club, which was held in a big hotel on the sea front in Whitley Bay. The club had a reputation of breaking away from traditional folk music and featured contemporary singer-songwriters, and it was there I first saw Ralph play. I had an impression that he would be very Guthrie-esque, living the life on the road and all that stuff. I remember Alan meeting him at the station and there he was, leather jacket, guitar and bag. Certainly not the scruffy individual I'd expected, but a bit downtrodden all the same! When he played, it was absolutely great, he just charmed everybody, and we all chatted with him afterwards over a pint or two.

"The band were having a bit of a low period at the time. We had a recording test coming up in London the following week, and we were wondering if we were really good enough to get a deal. That night we probably bored Ralph for hours with all our worries, but he was so encouraging, telling us 'Oh, you're fine. Really you are. Just hang in there and keep going.' And he really cheered us up. It was just the encouragement we needed."

Another up and coming performer who encountered McTell in the clubs was Christy Moore, a young Irishman looking to escape his bank job: "About 1968, I'd heard his name on the circuit quite a bit. I'd set up my base of work in the north of England, and I was playing at a blues and ragtime club in Manchester which was ran by an interesting guy called Rael Burns, a wigmaker whose proud claim to fame was that he'd made Edward Woodward's wig! Ralph played there that night and afterwards we went back to Rael's house, and it was there that he taught me 'Streets Of London'.

"I actually recorded it a short time later as a demo for Transatlantic, although they didn't offer me a deal, but Ralph was very supportive towards me which I'll never forget. When I came down to London, he helped me go about getting my first serious guitar, and took me to Ivor Mairants' shop where I got one for £40, which I still have. A short time later, I ended up putting an Irish band together for a six-show run on the BBC for the Sam Costa radio programme and Ralph was in our band. He was always willing to help out."

The folk clubs were providing regular work, but it was clear that if he was to develop beyond that area, McTell would need to start headlining shows of his own in order to break out of the 'folk singer' syndrome. Mick McDonagh: "Graham Churchill had been basically keeping a diary of dates for Ralph, but without any real creative input. He was only getting about £8 to £12 a gig then. Bruce and I were

Near the pond on Mitcham Common.

about to graduate and leave college; he was going to study at the LSE and I planned to go off to America and stay there. However, I decided to stay in England and continue in the music industry.

"I'd enjoyed the social secretary thing, so I set up a little company called Nexus with the idea that it would take English artists like Ralph and similar people and get them on the American coffee-house circuit where the singer-songwriter thing was very big. Both Bruce and Ralph wanted me to become involved, so I helped out as best as I could."

The autumn was spent trying to upgrade McTell's profile: McDonagh started to write press releases and get publicity pictures, with Bruce overseeing the operation. During all this time, McDonagh never signed a contract with McTell: "In hindsight, some warning lights should have come on then. Bruce and I were very good friends, but at the same time, there was a difference in our approach and opinions relating to what we both felt was best for Ralph. Being brothers, there was that sibling thing between them, but he was still very protective towards Ralph."

Nevertheless, Bruce May and Mick McDonagh continued together to elevate McTell to a wider audience. In December, they decided it was time he headlined a show for the first time, at Hornsey Town Hall. "I remember taking Ralph down the King's Road to try get him some better gear for the gig," says Bruce. "That must have been the first time I made a conscious effort to get him out of wearing jeans, which would always be a problem. We stood outside various railway stations passing flyers out, got some nice posters printed, and promoted it ourselves. Mick got Bonnie Dobson over to do the support, along with Roy Bailey, and about 200 people showed up: it was a great success."

Melody Maker reviewer Peter Gibson was enthusiastic enough to call him "a songwriter of very considerable stature and talent who is about to make a major contribution to music in general. He may well have come this far through the folk-club scene, but, like Dylan, he is destined for far more." Times certainly were a-changin' – and fast!

McTell's third album was released at the start of 1970. 'My Side Of Your Window' was well received and was given the honour of being *Melody Maker*'s Folk Album of the Month for January. In his review, Jerry Gilbert wrote: "Occasionally an album comes on to the market which stands beyond all verbal description or judgement. Such a case is Ralph McTell's third volume. His songs are ugly beautiful, a series of paradoxes with the emphasis shifting from the lyrical to the musical."

Initially, the songs on 'My Side Of Your Window' don't appear to have the same immediacy of those on 'Spiral Staircase', but McTell's writing had gained a more serious edge over the past year. 'Father Forgive Them' was written for the film *Staircase* by Stanley Donen which starred Rex Harrison and Richard Burton. The

My Side of Your Window
including:- Clown   Michael in the Garden
Factory Girl   I've Thought About It
Transatlantic TRA 209

film offered a sympathetic view of homosexuality, prompting McTell to ask that prejudice be laid aside: hence both the title and the line "Jesus was a man who kept the company of men, and He too was able to forgive those who betrayed him." The song was to have been recorded for the film soundtrack by Joe Cocker, but this arrangement fell through – and though the film bombed this remains one of McTell's most powerful but overlooked songs.

'I've Thought About It' has McTell complaining about social injustice and recognising his privileged position as a performer which enables him to speak out. The line "this guitar protects me" may echo the famous slogan written on Woody Guthrie's guitar, "This machine kills fascists", but McTell regards his guitar as his means of communication to comment on the world, and realises that without it he is just an everyday person.

Another of the key songs relating to his childhood is 'Factory Girl'. As a young boy he would hear the chatter of girls passing by his home *en route* to a nearby factory. The chattering of the girls would naturally be louder on their way home; with their working day over, their anticipation of the evening ahead grew and they could become individuals once more.

'All Things Change' is a song McTell rates as one of his most poetic, while 'Kew Gardens' found him accompanied by the Folk Weavers, with whom he had shared a club date in Peterborough the year before. 'Girl On A Bicycle', co-written with Ralph by Gary Petersen (who plays on the album with other members of his band Formerly Fat Harry), unfortunately suffers from Tony Visconti's string arrangement, which seems inappropriate. The album cover by Peter Thaine was originally a three-dimensional model made of cardboard, but the photograph taken for use in the artwork did not convey that fact.

'My Side Of Your Window' helped transform Ralph McTell from a jug-band singer into a singer-songwriter whose serious subject matter and thoughtful compositions made an impact. Following its release, he made one of many appearances over the years on John Peel's *Top Gear* on BBC Radio 1. Always a champion of new and underappreciated talents, Peel has helped launch many careers too numerous to mention. Exposure on Peel's programme often helped artists to break into the college circuit, which Jo Lustig (who would play a major role in the next phase of Ralph's career) hoped would provide an appropriate audience. McTell's performance on air on 28 February 1970 included a reasonably accurate cross-section of his songwriting so far in 'Clown', 'Michael In The Garden', 'Daddy's Here' and 'Eight Frames A Second'.

His reputation as a songwriter was beginning to grow, as was soon proved when Lustig found himself without a headliner for a date in May at London's Royal Festival Hall after Van Morrison was unable to appear. Lustig contacted Nat Joseph at Transatlantic, telling him that he needed somebody to fill the date – not the hall, just the date – and Joseph suggested McTell. "He took a chance on me and we did amazing business. Jo made me an offer there and then, before I went onstage, to manage me."

Jo Lustig originated from Brooklyn, New York. He had grown up there with, among others, movie star Charles Bronson, and had been involved in the early years of Elektra Records, a folk label until founder Jac Holzman discovered Paul Butterfield, Love and the Doors in the mid-1960s. Lustig had also been involved in the spiralling New York folk scene, even collecting money from the audiences during Bob Dylan's coffee-house gigs. He had arrived in England in the early 1960s, working as Nat King Cole's press agent.

Though McTell recalls Jo's reaction to his name as "Ralph who?", Lustig remembers their introduction a little differently: "My wife Dee first heard him on the radio, and liked him very much. At the time, I was managing Julie Felix and Pentangle, and had built up a mailing list of about one thousand names through which people would let me know which artists on the folk scene interested them. Ralph's name came up quite a bit, so I checked him out. I thought he was very good in the club environment, he had a good rapport with his audiences, and that his songs were very well formed. It was a gamble to elevate him to a bigger venue, but I felt that if he could realise that his appeal lay in a middle-class folk audience rather than the hippie types, he could transfer over."

Bruce May felt that for his brother to work with Jo Lustig was a more than positive move at that stage of Ralph's career. Bruce had basically gone as far as he could with his limited experience, and knew that being with a manager of some considerable reputation could only do Ralph good. "I was pleased when Lustig moved into the picture. He has at some time managed nearly every major British folk/rock performer, and he looked after Ralph's business very well. He was a guy who really wanted success for his artists."

When interviewed the day before his big show, McTell was already showing signs of being uncomfortable in the limelight, as he told Michael Cable: "I'm terrified. The mere thought of playing in front of up to 3,000 people makes me tremble. I don't want to be a big star, because I'd end up a nervous wreck; I'm much happier playing in the more intimate and friendly atmosphere of a small club." Nevertheless, Lustig's first decision was to move McTell onto the city hall and college circuit.

The 23 May show, advertised under the banner 'Where Trends Begin', was a great success. From there, McTell was able to develop rapidly. No longer was he in front of a row of people four feet away from him, and that extra room enabled his confidence to grow while still allowing him to retain the intimate style he had perfected in the folk clubs.

Reviews of the concert were positive, with even the quality press starting to become interested in Ralph McTell. In his review for *The Times*, Karl Dallas rather glowingly reported "when an audience breaks into applause during the introductory chords of a song, it's a sign that the solo singer is becoming a concert artist of international status. Not only can Ralph McTell almost fill the Festival Hall with paying customers for his first solo concert, he can fill it with his warm, sensitively human personality, peopling the stage with cameos that are almost Dickensian in their realism." Even the *Daily Telegraph* agreed, Maurice Rosenbaum noting "his voice has hints of power and the presentation of his material is free from affectation or gimmickry."

McTell had also caught the attention of someone else in the media – Arthur Taylor, a current affairs producer for Granada TV involved in the ground-breaking *World In Action* series. "I got involved in making a series called *Folk From The Two Brewers*, named after a pub round the corner from the Granada studios," he recalled. "I wasn't that up on 'folk music', but the more radical things in the folk world appealed to me, as well as the fact that folk clubs were somewhat like the old music halls in that there would be people singing, telling stories and humorous tales, all on the same night.

"I wanted to do a series of programmes reflecting that scene, and remember talking to a chap who ran a club at a place called the Sportsman's Guild in Manchester. I asked him who were the biggest draws on the circuit. He rattled off all sorts of names like Martin Carthy, Jeremy Taylor, etc, and added: 'But there's one other bloke, who, when he comes, the place is like a bloody church. They all file in and listen in silence to all these songs unlike they do for anyone else and his name's Ralph McTell.' So I got him up to Manchester to record some songs and was very impressed…he was such a talent that the idea of doing a programme on him started to formulate."

The mini-documentary, simply titled *Ralph McTell* and unfortunately screened only in the Granada region, was filmed in various locations including McTell's council flat with Nanna and young Sam, pubs and folk clubs as well as at the Royal Festival Hall, where the concert sequences are reminiscent of DA Pennebaker's filming of Bob Dylan in the famous *Don't Look Back* documentary. The sequence Taylor assembled for 'I've Thought About It', where McTell's performance in the studio is interjected with powerful images of protest marches, famine in the Third World, the Arms race, various world leaders and the recurring image of Christ, could be described as Ralph's first promotional video.

In the film, backstage at the Festival Hall, Jo Lustig was already outlining the new direction he saw for McTell. "Most singers today are mainly writing about their own hang-ups, but Ralph writes about things that concern everyone. He communicates so beautifully with people. He is not a protest singer but a commentator. He is going to be doing mainly concerts from now on. We are going to have to stop doing folk clubs – it's very unfair to turn fans away, as has happened recently. The clubs are just too small. Tonight we'll have over 3,000 people here, and it would be ridiculous to put him into Les Cousins which only holds 120."

McTell himself also spoke of an inevitable parting of the ways "I'll be sorry to leave the folk clubs completely, because I owe them so much, and I've had some great nights in them up and down the country. On the right night, there's a magic you won't get anywhere else." However, in Taylor's film McTell again appears to show concern at the speed of change: "I've not really thought about the future. I'm trying to live for the day as much as possible, because I know the life of a performer, professionally speaking, is very short. You can't go on forever. If I ever got to feel like a star, or that sort of pressure was being brought to bear on me, I think I would get out very quickly. I've seen too many people go crazy."

At the end of August 1970, McTell played the Isle Of Wight Festival to the biggest audience of his entire career, an estimated 500,000 people attending the three-day event. McTell appeared on the final day, 30 August, alongside Joan Baez, Leonard Cohen, Richie Havens and Jimi Hendrix (in his last major appearance).

"The Isle Of Wight is a natural setting for that kind of thing," Ralph reminisces, "a piece of Victorian England that still remains. The idea of an island is that it makes it exclusive, which is very special. I stayed in a great big Victorian hotel with a huge dining room, along with Sly and the Family Stone. Sly came down to breakfast in his stage gear – unless you normally wear a purple hat to breakfast. Jo Lustig thought I was ready for this event, but I felt daunted by it. These were the days before you plugged an acoustic guitar directly into the PA, and I had no idea if the crowd would hear me beyond the first two rows.

"I went on after Kris Kristofferson, wearing a red polo shirt I'd swapped for a second-hand set of guitar strings back in Milan in 1964, and got a really good ovation which amazed me. Jo Lustig said 'Ralph, get back on there' and started pushing me back on stage. I didn't believe him when he said that the crowd wanted me to do an encore, and hesitated. Meanwhile, DJ Jeff Dexter, sat high above the stage, had put a record on: Jo went mad and climbed up, grabbed him by his beard and yelled 'What are you trying to do to my artist?'

"I hung around backstage throughout the day and talked to one of Jimi Hendrix's roadies who said that Hendrix was very out of it, was lying in some debutante's

garden elsewhere on the island and that they were worried that he wouldn't be able to play. Halfway through Pentangle's set, a woman walked onstage and started talking to the crowd in German, and Jo went mad again. He was really wound up and only Hendrix's roadies prevented him from tearing that woman's limbs apart! I couldn't persuade him to stay, so we left after Jethro Tull had finished their set."

In October, a return concert took place at the Festival Hall, and a month later, a fourth album, 'Ralph McTell Revisited', was released. Lustig had thought that, with his charge now well-established in Britain, it was time to try to break him into the American market. The album, a compilation, was assembled to impress American labels and obtain a recording contract there. Lustig had made made a deal with Paramount Records, but they turned down 'Revisited', preferring to wait for a new set of songs on an album including 'Streets Of London'. Finally, Lustig bought McTell's contract from Transatlantic, who as part of the deal were also given 'Revisited'.

Opposite: Isle Of Wight Festival, 30 August 1970.

The whole business didn't impress McTell at all: "I've got very strong attitudes about that over-priced album. People have already heard the tracks, and I thought Transatlantic were a bit naughty. Originally, it was mixed for an American release, then it was decided to put it out here as well because they wanted another album and they didn't have one in the can."

Remixes were undertaken by producer Gus Dudgeon. Certain songs remained in their original state, but 'Factory Girl' featured additional pedal steel played by Gordon Huntley from Matthews Southern Comfort, while Hookfoot (a noted group at the time) added various bits to other tracks, and Ralph partly re-recorded some of the vocals. A completely new version of 'Spiral Staircase' with Hookfoot and Rick Wakeman of the Strawbs was released as a single; Danny Thompson was also involved.

Following the remixing sessions, McTell returned to his roots with a brief club tour of Cornwall, no doubt reflecting on how far things had progressed in the past twelve months. In an interview with Jerry Gilbert in *Melody Maker*, Ralph expanded on his worries: "I don't know when I'll be in the studio again. There are a lot of things under negotiation. I'm a very slow writer, and I'm getting back to how I started, with (Woody) Guthrie-type songs. I can do live gigs okay, but I never seem to release albums which sound like me. I've written a song called 'You Well Meaning Brought Me Here', which is a personal song about how I feel as regards my present situation."

As this highly eventful year drew to its conclusion, McTell played a nostalgic November concert at Croydon's Fairfield Halls, his first major 'hometown' gig. It was a time for looking back personally and musically: "Croydon is so sterile now. Do you know that before the war we had music halls, beautiful pubs, live music, everything? Then after the war, when Croydon had been bombed, they shot up office blocks and completely sterilised it."

On the stage that night, old friends joined him, among them Wizz Jones, who duetted with McTell on Woody Guthrie's 'Plane Wreck At Los Gatos (Deportee)' and the Famous Jug Band, who joined Ralph and Wizz on 'Will The Circle Be Unbroken'. A few weeks later, in February 1971, another child arrived for Ralph and Nanna, a daughter they named Leah Hanna.

The Banbury Guardian

"The Poachers," resident group at the Folk Cellar, Mount Hotel, Banbury, chat with Ralph McTell, centre, during the interval at the Folk Concert on Friday. Left to right are: Bob and Sylvia Mehta, Ralph McTell, Bernard Tompkins and Mick Mo...

Chapter 9

Alive in America

Though a man of principle, politics had yet to impinge on Ralph's career to any extent. But all that was to change in 1971. During an interview with *Melody Maker*'s Andrew Means the previous August, he'd been asked if there was anywhere he'd choose not to play on political grounds, and replied: "I wouldn't put money into a fascist system now. Once I went to Spain on holiday but I wouldn't go again. For that matter, I wouldn't go to Greece, although I love the country."

Looking back, he remembered his feelings: "We were supposedly very politically aware in those days, and I did feel it was wrong to play in Greece and Spain with the fascist set-ups there. Within days of that interview being published, I got a call from Jo Lustig telling me that he'd had some Spanish journalists on to him saying they wanted to talk to me. And I said to him 'You must be joking. I've just gone in print saying that I don't want to play in Spain.' Jo said 'Well, apparently that's what they want to talk to you about.' I thought that, as I'd gone into print, I'd have to face the music, and agreed to talk to them.

"I had to go and collect them from East Croydon station and take them back to my flat in Shirley. Among them was this guy, Ramon Trecet, who was one of the most intense people I have ever met in this business. Music had such a crucial importance to him. I said I was surprised they wanted to speak to me after what I'd said, and Ramon said 'Yes. That is what we want to talk to you about – because we are not Spanish, but Basques.'"

Ramon explained how the authorities had recently arrested some young Basques who had been tried and were to be executed by garotting. Morale in the region was understandably low. He wanted McTell to come out there and perform at a festival in San Sebastian, feeling that if a British musician were to play there for the people it would show support for them and their cause.

"His English was absolutely appalling and it was a bit difficult to get the full gist of his ideas out of him, but he was such a passionate bloke that he moved me. The idea was for me to go spend four days in Spain, for which I would only receive expenses. I just didn't know morally how it left me. In the end, because they were such nice people who obviously believed in what they were doing, I said I'd do it."

Arthur Taylor had become a good friend since making the TV documentary the previous year, and the pair had kept in touch. "I was on the fringes of Granada's *World In Action* programme, which in those days was very left-wing," Taylor explains, "and personally was very sympathetic to most left-wing causes. Someone at Granada told me that they were trying to establish contact with (the separatist movement)

ETA. The only contact they had was a priest and the word was that, if he approved, he would put us in touch with other people. But we needed to adopt an undercover approach.

"I had one of those old ten-year passports which showed my profession as teacher, and not as journalist – convenient when you didn't want to attract attention to yourself in such situations. So when Ralph told me he had decided to accept the offer to go to San Sebastian, I asked him if I could go over there with him. However, I didn't tell him about the ETA business. I was going as a friend!"

The festival was spread over a number of days with McTell, just one of many attractions, sharing the bill with local music, sports and poetry readings. Taylor's contact had instructed him to go to a village near the festival site and find the priest at the little church. The surrounding area was cut across by national boundaries, so that the Basque territory stretched slightly into France.

"During my set," Ralph remembers, "Ramon was standing at the side of the stage, and before each song, would go into long translations of what I was going to sing about. I'd have to stand there and wait until he'd finished, and the crowd would then erupt in wild applause." After his performance, McTell, along with Arthur Taylor, was well feted by their hosts, and there was a carnival atmosphere about the whole event.

"Arthur started to go off to make various telephone calls, and he then told me that he was going to have to go and see some people that would entail going over the border. I started to feel that there was something afoot, but when I asked him what it was, he replied only that he'd tell me later."

Taylor takes up the story: "I'd hired a car on the Spanish side, and we set off driving towards the border with my only instruction to find the priest, and then hopefully he would give us other contacts. It was obvious we were going to have to be very careful and watch our step. Eventually, we found the village and the church. The whole place was deserted. I remember Ralph was wearing this weird sheepskin coat and, with his long hair, looked like a guerilla or something.

"We knocked on the door of the church, but there was no answer, just a lot of shuffling noises from inside. Then the door opened a few inches, and a girl appeared who told me in French to go around the side of the church to another house, which we did. We knocked on the door, it was flung open and we were faced by a double-barrelled shotgun. I could make out two big lads inside, another with a small machine-gun aimed at us. I started spluttering things in French and the odd word in Spanish like saying 'It's all right.' We were made to hand over our passports, and after a while were allowed to see the priest, who was really annoyed that I didn't speak fluent Spanish, so we had to conduct the conversation in French."

All this time, McTell stood as still as he was able: "I would try and translate the odd thing, just to help keep the conversation going, but it was slightly difficult with a machine-gun in my back." Matters calmed down when the priest was convinced his visitors were genuine. Taylor told him that Granada TV in England wanted to make a programme that would express the Basque point of view, and he started to co-operate by giving Arthur several names and addresses. There were various conversations with others in the room, and then it was a quick exit and back across the border.

The programme was eventually made by Granada thanks to the contacts established by Arthur Taylor, although he was never involved with the actual production. However, something else subsequently emerged about the foray across the border, as Taylor recalled: "Later on, by chance, in a casual conversation with the guy who made the TV programme, he said to me 'You must have been quite

frightened that night in the priest's house.' He said the reason they'd been so jumpy was they had just kidnapped a German industrialist and had him tied up in the back of the house. They had sent out notice that, unless their demands were met, they were going to kill him.

"When we turned up in the middle of the night in a car with Madrid number plates, they thought we were Spanish secret police who had come to get him out. While we were in there, they had been checking our passports and sending people out to find where our back-up was, thinking the house was surrounded. Of course, we hadn't known about all of this!"

Eventually, McTell was let in on the story. "It was ages later when one evening Arthur and I were strolling down the Embankment in London, off for a pint, when he told me what had *really* been going on that night. I just trembled at the thought of it, thinking how near we were to getting our heads blown off. Thankfully, the German survived. But to think we were locked in to this sort of historical incident made me shiver."

Paramount Records didn't go overboard in a major hyping effort for McTell's first visit to America that October, but ran a press campaign using media like New York's *Village Voice* to spread the word about the arrival of their new signing, as well as pressing up a 12" single with just 'Streets Of London' on it. Not that they needed to, as the New York press responded in a number of positive pieces.

"There is something very real and timeless about Ralph McTell," the *Village Voice* noted. "It comes from rubbing shoulders with humanity." Certainly, if McTell had wanted to be regarded as a serious songwriter by the Americans, he was on the right track. The *Daily News* gave him coverage on successive days, speaking of McTell's "unique talent for reaching any audience without shouting about his personal hang-ups."

Faces in the curtains whilst the sirens were screaming
Disturbing the dreaming that I had without sleep
Hustler's on the block taking every cent I've got
So it's dollars for the barman to give my mind some ease.
('Standing Down In New York Town', 1972)

The following day's review found *Daily News* reporter Stanley Fields reiterating his initial view, having seen the live performance: "Ralph McTell, a 26-year-old folk singer from London, opened at the Bitter End on Wednesday night to the delight of everybody. Supporting LaBelle, he did not afflict his audience with esoteric soul-searching passed off as entertainment. His music and lyrics never ask 'Who am I?' He takes an honest, sensitive look at what he sees in his world and shares it with his listeners. His unique gift is that it touches us all."

Cash Box agreed: "It was just like old times. The spotlight gently shining on one stool and one performer – quiet with one guitar. The shadow on the wall was as softly formed as the songs of the artist – Ralph McTell."

There was no doubt the Americans were impressed with his debut performances, and among the crowd in New York that night was legendary performer Carolyn Hester: "The name Ralph McTell had began to circulate around the scene quite a bit. That night confirmed for me that what everyone was saying about him was true. The songs were little cameos of life, and the way he held the audience was as good as I'd seen anybody do for a long time. I was most impressed."

Ralph himself recalls that first show rather differently: "I was not on top of my form that opening night in New York. I was very anxious about what reception I would get." Karl Dallas from *Melody Maker* witnessed that first show: "During 'The Ferryman' and 'Birdman', you could have heard a pin drop. The pretty no-bra waitresses stopped bustling around to sell their quotas of non-alcoholic cider, near beer and ice cream sundaes, and hung on to his every word."

During his stay in New York, McTell appeared on a couple of radio programmes, including the famous underground *Alex Bennett Show* where his host spent a full 15 minutes enthusing about 'Pick Up A Gun'. Fairport Convention were also in town, playing support to Traffic at the Brooklyn Academy, and a most enduring friendship began with bassist Dave Pegg.

"That night was Simon Nicol's 21st birthday," Pegg recalls, "and there was much merriment in flow. Ralph showed up with Caleb Quaye from Hookfoot, and they were delighted to be in some English company all those miles from home. After the gig, we all went off to Greenwich Village to a bar called Nobody's, and got Ralph on to these lethal tequila slammers they served. That night was the start of a great friendship and many more drinking sessions than I care to remember!"

Following his stint in New York, McTell toured around various American cities. In Los Angeles, he played at the Troubadour Club along with Fairport Convention, and again received a positive verdict from both the west coast audiences and press. *Variety* wrote that McTell was "one of the better British imports. His tunes are universal commentaries based on zeroed-in observation of particulars others notice and easily forget. McTell will be a big hit on his campus tour." In Philadelphia, he shared the bill with Randy Newman at the Main Point and, at a reception after the gig, admitted to journalist Jonathan Takiff: "I don't know a soul here. Did they really all come out to see *me*?"

The *New Musical Express*'s US correspondent reported: "If his opening week is any indication, there are big things in store for Ralph McTell in America." As a result of all this enthusiastic press, 'You Well Meaning Brought Me Here' promptly sold out in the cities he played.

On his return to England, McTell found American enthusiasm for his new album matched by his own country's media, who rated 'You Well Meaning Brought Me Here' his strongest so far. McTell also felt that way, to the extent that he agreed to have the lyrics on the sleeve for the first time.

"Bruce said that I shouldn't have done that, as he felt it would leave me open to poetic criticism. But I had looked at other sleeves, and saw so much dross on them that I felt confident that mine would stand up. It would also let people see the way I set out to write things, and that I had actual rhyme schemes, and I set it out like a piece of poetry. It took a long time to get it word-perfect, you wouldn't believe how long. You sing a song and get a wrong word or change a phrase, so we had to correct it all."

The quality of McTell's lyrics warranted his decision, some very intricate songs showing how his songwriting had developed. 'Old Brown Dog', a song about dignity, was inspired by a short story in an issue of America's *Saturday Evening Post* which cover illustrator Norman Rockwell could have had a hand in writing. There was a look back to his period in the army, the previously mentioned 'Pick Up A Gun', although McTell felt on reflection that while it was not one of the most coherent songs he had written it was something he had to get out of his system. And, when subsequently introducing the song in live performances, he said that although conscription was no longer in place in Britain, it had been replaced by unemployment.

Also on the album was probably the most complex song he'd written, 'The Ferryman': "Following the release of my previous album, I had become very

depressed about a lot of things. The changes in my life had happened very quickly, and I was very confused. I knew this guy called Bruce Barthol, an American who used to play with Country Joe (McDonald) and the Fish. He was younger than me, and was one of the most laid-back people I'd ever met. He used to talk in this strange way almost as if he was trying to hold his breath at the same time.

"He knew how stressed-out I was feeling and he recommended this book called *Siddartha* by Herman Hesse. I'd read a couple of pages of it each night before I went to sleep and it really helped bring me out of the situation I was in. It was very inspiring. It was very rare for me to write about a book, yet I wanted to communicate a lot of ideas from it into the song. I worked on that for about six months altogether. I interpreted the story in my own way, and therefore changed the ending to it in my song."

The lyrics printed on the sleeve showed the beauty of some of his words, which fully stood up to being read in their own right.

> *Oh the traveller closed his eyes and he listened and he heard*
> *Only the river murmuring and the beating of his heart*
> *Then he heard the river laughing and he heard the river crying*
> *And in it was the beauty and the sadness of the world.*
> **('The Ferryman', 1971)**

McTell also became involved in a film of *Siddartha*, made in India using English-speaking Indian actors, working briefly with an Indian musician named Hemanta Khumah on songs that McTell translated. Sad to say, none of Ralph's music was used in the film, which was screened at the Berlin Film Festival, but sank without trace shortly afterwards.

Another song, 'Claudia', was somewhat political with its view of racism, and was based on two separate incidents which he had observed some time previously: "I married the two incidents for the song, and intentionally made it a bit obscure. The first one was when I was in the north of England with some blokes and a guy did actually get beaten up for being white. At the same time, I also got to know a bunch of people who were so called revolutionaries, and through them, I got to meet this woman from Harlem called Claudia.

"She was involved over there with the Black Panther party in a very non-violent role working on their arts programme for young blacks. We'd had several long and deep conversations, and even though we'd virtually agreed on everything we'd talked about, she ended it all by saying 'But you're white and I'm black', and that really made me feel let down after all we'd agreed about. I wrote the song to make a point that it's no good just talking about equality – you've got to get up and *do* something about it."

'First And Last Man' was inspired by a poster of an American Indian warrior that McTell had on his wall and by the perfect isolation from the modern world enjoyed by the remaining tribes in the jungles of South America. The song was a very artistic way of conveying what he was trying to say.

'Genesis 1 Verse 20' had a long history to it. "When I'd had the accident with the lorry and the glass window years back, I used to read lots of illustrated picture books that people passed to me. There was this wonderful one called *The Children's Wonder Book Of How, Why And What* that had all sorts of wonderful things in it. And in the centre of it was this picture of a thing called The Giant Lizard Of Tendagaroo, and I had no knowledge of dinosaurs and the like until I saw this picture. They had put a crocodile next to it so you could see the scale of it. It was pictured among trees and ferns, and I used to have dreams about this thing and imagined it to be a giant friendly creature. The biblical reference in the title – that actual verse has a reference to something about life in the water coming out onto the land."

> *Mother of Adam, how can I conceive*
> *The garden of light, oh father of Eve*
> *Lo something stirs, your still waters move from the land*
> *I see him turn 'twixt sea and earth, see him stand.*
> **('Genesis 1 Verse 20', 1971)**

Altogether, 'You Well Meaning…' was a strong enough record, yet some of Robert Kirby's arrangements resulted in songs being swamped by the string section. In many cases, they were best performed solo in concert where McTell was in command.

Shortly afterwards, Famous released promotional copies of a single by McTell titled 'Teacher Teacher', with a view to breaking him into the singles charts. "That song was written as a result of my spell at teacher's training college. Jo Lustig had wanted a single, and of the tracks we had recorded, Tony Visconti felt that 'Teacher Teacher' had the best chance – I was pleased with it and so was everyone else, but then the BBC decided they weren't going to play it."

> *Teacher teacher, when will it reach ya*
> *The writing on the outside wall?*
> *If you gained all your knowledge*
> *From the books you read at college*
> *Then you don't know nothin'*
> *Nothin' at all.*
> **('Teacher Teacher', 1971)**

By then, McTell had strongly established himself well away from the folk clubs and on the college and city-hall circuit. Jo Lustig still had high hopes that things would get even bigger, but there were further problems. Compared with Britain, Paramount in America. were more involved in the cinematic side of their business. The success of two blockbuster movies, *Love Story* and *The Godfather,* meant their record label was being neglected.

A new recording contract was obtained with Warner Brothers Records, and though the idea of a British 'folk' artist recording for a major American label was rare, it seemed to confirm Lustig's belief in his artist. However, once again McTell was forced to start from scratch with a new company, who would obviously need a new record as soon as possible – so new songs had to be written.

Chapter
10 Tomorrow Today

Ralph's fifth long-player, 'Not Till Tomorrow', was released in May 1972 and was the album McTell had been searching most of his career for. Gone were the arrangements that smothered the best of 'You Well Meaning…'s songs: here were simple arrangements with sparse backing from just three other musicians which left McTell and his guitar at the front of the mix. Another batch of confident songs made this his most accessible record to date, while the material contained a reflective look back over his life and included a number of songs that would remain among the most requested throughout his career.

The album opened with 'Zimmerman Blues', which in itself was a topical song. Bob Dylan had been a massive influence on McTell, but the past couple of years had been confusing. Dylan had all but disappeared from sight and the equally confusing 'Self Portrait' LP in 1970 had left many wondering what was going on with the "spokesman for his generation." McTell explained his feelings when interviewed by Fraser Massey in *ZigZag* magazine:

"Dylan was the beginning and the end of an era for a lot of people. 'Zimmerman Blues' is a kind of attempt to understand what happened, and to sympathise and to point the finger and ask a few questions…lines like 'Do a concert for Angela/Build a building or two.' Now I don't suppose Dylan ever did that, but he did do the Bangla Desh benefit concert, which is very commendable, whereas, at the same time, I read a rumour somewhere – and rumours have some sort of validity in this game – that he was going into a building project with Hugh Hefner, and I find the two hard to equate.

"That confusion is the Zimmerman Blues… 'It gets harder for me, and easier for you' – I would imagine him saying that. The more things go on, the more the media can capitalise on radicalism, left-wingism and so on. Give me a million dollars – what am I supposed to do with it? Give it away? Invest it?' I think if people saw me, the guy who wrote 'Streets Of London', driving around in a white Rolls Royce, then the same would be said."

Two reflective pieces – 'First Song' and 'Barges' – looked back to the past. 'First Song' looked at his and Nanna's relationship, how they'd progressed from the streets of Paris and the caravan in Cornwall to husband and wife with two children. 'Nanna's Song' was the third song he had ever written, although 'Third Song' would not have had quite the same impact as a title! 'Barges' was written with brother Bruce in mind, and recalled the days they both went to stay in Banbury with their Aunt Olive – of walking down the towpath of the Oxfordshire canal and fishing with the smell of wood burning from the fires in the gypsy camp behind the railway track.

With an introduction similar to Greig's 'Morning', its subject matter of canals is perfect when one considers children's fascination with water, and how they can wander by its edges for hours without achieving very much – 'Whilst summer rolled o'er us with no complications' – although reality returns with thoughts of mother back home in London. It is a song about innocence disappearing, using the canal, a man-made river, as a road into manhood.

'When I Was A Cowboy', inspired by a John Steinbeck short story *The Red Pony*, also recalls childhood days when visits to Saturday-morning picture shows fuelled games for the following week; in this case, Hopalong Cassidy was transported from the prairies of North America to the back alleys of Croydon. Elsewhere was found the traditional sounding 'Another Rain', intended for inclusion on 'You Well Meaning…' (and written for the Folk Weavers, who added vocals to 'Kew Gardens' on 'My Side Of Your Window') and 'Sylvia', a tribute to the poet Sylvia Plath.

Another tribute, 'Birdman', was dedicated to Soledad brother George Jackson (and written before Jackson's death) based loosely around the traditional song 'John Henry'. It compares two black Americans, John Henry, who was worked to death, and George Jackson, who, in his quest for freedom from prejudice, chose to take an intellectual route, only to meet the same fate.

Recent visits were also covered, holidaying in Wales in 'Nettle Wine' and touring in America in 'Standing Down In New York Town.' 'Gypsy' is about freedom and being vigilant in maintaining a watchful eye in order to preserve it before it is removed forever (a theme McTell would later revisit in 'Peppers and Tomatoes').

But the pastures close as the cowboy knows
And the world's cut up by fences
To catch the gypsy.
('Gypsy', 1972)

The broad range of influences McTell's writing encompassed for the first time on record, made the album his most complete recording to date, and it was well received by the press. Long-time champion Jerry Gilbert advised *Sounds* readers: "If you have been disillusioned by Ralph's records in the past, then this latest one is definitely for you." Tony Stewart in *NME* rounded his review off by stating "McTell has managed to offer us something outstanding again." Only *Melody Maker* had reservations, suspecting that, because it was McTell's first album for Warner Brothers, it was rushed to the point where it contained "sentimental meanderings that are disappointingly frequent", and that "the lyrics are trivial, the tunes undistinguished and the metre is ungainly."

This is hardly fair comment on the songwriter: in describing memories, a certain amount of sentimentality is only to be expected. Also, songs like 'Barges', 'When I Was A Cowboy', 'Another Rain', 'Gypsy' and 'Birdman' were all deliberately written out of 4/4 (straightforward rock) time.

The record's title is worth explanation. "The album was finished, mixed, final track listings, cover photos, the lot. I was in Jo Lustig's office one day, and a call came through from the printers saying that they were all ready to go and just needed a title. I didn't have a clue what to call it, and was trying to come up with something very arty. Paul Brown, one of Jo's assistants, was on the phone to the printers and, as we needed more time, his response to the question 'Have you got a title yet?' was 'Not Till Tomorrow'…"

STREETS OF LONDON

In the back garden of Barney Potter's cottage in Polmassick, 1973. Barney would later be the inspiration for Tickle On The Tum's Barney Bodger the builder.

A successful tour in the early summer of 1972, on which the support act was Hunter Muskett and another in the autumn with the Natural Acoustic Band continued to increase McTell's ever-growing following. Acoustic music was still very much the music of students, and he was doing great business on the college circuit. He was able to handle an audience, while the humour which remains an integral part of his live performances to this day was already evident.

Despite his deep thinking on life in general, humour is something which comes naturally to him, but is a side of his work for which he has received little credit. Many artists who emerged from the folk circuit at the time – Mike Harding, Jasper Carrott and Richard Digance – went on to become comedians when they realised that they were getting more attention for their patter than their songs, and McTell could arguably have gone on to be as successful.

One early moment when humour rescued a situation occurred in 1972 in Leeds where McTell had delivered his build-up to 'First And Last Man', with an introduction about the vanishing tribes of the rain forests, with the audience so silent that you could hear a pin drop. All of a sudden, out of the speakers came the crackly voice of a lost AA patrol: "Sorry, base, can you give me that location again? I can't locate a Morris Minor…over."

Naturally, this destroyed the audience, not to mention the song. It happened again on one other occasion later in his career, during the 1990s, McTell handling it with the same humour. Again, it was during 'First And Last Man'!

During 1972, McTell met one of his great influences in person, the Rev Gary Davis, when he was given the honour of introducing the legendary guitar player onstage at London's Shaw Theatre. "I couldn't believe I was face to face with him in the dressing room before the show. I eventually mustered the confidence to ask him if I could borrow his guitar for a moment. I said that I had recorded a tune of his on one of my albums, and proceeded to play him my version of 'Hesitation Blues'. When I'd finished playing it, the Rev looked at me obviously somewhat puzzled, and said 'And what was that one called, son?' He didn't recognise it at all!"

As the year progressed, relations between Ralph and Jo Lustig began to show signs of strain. Lustig, who had transformed McTell into an artist of considerable status, had hoped to set up another tour of America, but felt he never got much enthusiasm from the singer on the subject.

Throughout this time, Bruce May had continued to be a sounding board on a whole range of matters. Ralph had always talked over ideas for songs with Bruce and played them to him when they were completed, greatly respecting his brother's views, and when relations with Lustig broke down it was a logical move for him to take over the managerial reins.

No. 2519

THIS ASSIGNMENT is made the **30th** day of **June** 19**72**

BETWEEN **Ralph McTell**

of

(hereinafter called "the Assignor(s)") of the one part and **Essex Music International Limited**

of **Dumbarton House, 68 Oxford Street, London W1N 9LA**

in the County of London (hereinafter called "the Publishers") of the other part WITNESSETH that in consideration of the payment by the Publishers to the Assignor(s) of the sum of **5 n p (five new pence)** (the receipt of which is hereby acknowledged) on account of the Royalties and Fees mentioned in the Schedule hereto to the Assignor(s) hereby assign to the Publishers ALL the Copyright as defined by the Copyright Act 1956, throughout the territory to which that Act may now or may at any time hereafter extend together with all other rights of a like nature as are now conferred by the laws in force in all other territories throughout the world, including the renewal copyright as conferred by the law of the United States of America and such other rights as may hereafter be conferred or created by law or international arrangement or convention in any part of the world whether by way of new or additional rights not now comprised in Copyright or by way of extension of the period of then or now existing rights of and in the words and music of the composition(s) entitled

"BARGES"   "FIRST SONG"

"MAGINOT WALTZ"   "MY FATHER'S HOUSE"

"ZIMMERMAN BLUES"

(hereinafter referred to as "the said work(s)") TO HOLD the same unto the Publishers their successors and assigns absolutely AND the Assignor(s) hereby agree(s) on demand to execute and sign any other documents and to do all other acts and things which may hereafter be required of the Assignor(s) for vesting in the Publishers the premises expressed to be hereby assigned AND the Assignor(s) hereby warrant(s) and declare(s) that the said work is a new and original unpublished work and does not infringe the copyright in any other work and that he (they) the Assignor(s) has (have) good right and full power to assign to the Publishers free from all encumbrances the premises expressed to be hereby assigned and every of them in the manner aforesaid. AND IT IS HEREBY CERTIFIED that the transaction hereby effected does not form part of a larger transaction or of a series of transactions in respect of which the amount or value or the aggregate amount or value of the consideration exceeds £5,500 (five thousand five hundred pounds).

AS WITNESS the hands of the parties hereto the day and year first above written.

THE SCHEDULE ABOVE REFERRED TO:

SHEET MUSIC ROYALTIES
*10%(**ten** per cent) of the marked retail selling price of all copies of the said work(s) sold (except as hereafter provided) but so that no Royalty shall be payable on the first month's issue of sample copies of the said work(s).
50%: **fifty** per cent) of all sums received by the Publishers on the sale of Foreign and Colonial Editions of the said work(s).
The Publishers shall have the right to include the said work(s) in any Album, Folio or Newspaper and to licence others to make similar use upon payment of £5 (five pounds) in lieu of Royalties in respect of the inclusion thereof in such Album, Folio or Newspaper.

MECHANICAL ROYALTIES
50%(**fifty** per cent) of all Royalties received by the Publishers for reproductions of the said work(s) in connection with the manufacture of records (other than for use in or in connection with cinematograph films and television films) for sale to the Public.

SYNCHRONISATION FEES
50%(**fifty** per cent) of all Royalties and Fees received by the Publishers for the right to use the said work(s) in or in connection with any cinematograph film or television film.

PERFORMING BROADCASTING AND REDIFFUSION FEES
These are collected by the Performing Right Society Limited (and its affiliated Societies throughout the world) and are paid direct to its members in accordance with the Rules laid down by the Society and it is agreed that the Assignor(s) share shall be 50% (fifty percent) and the Publishers share shall be 50% (fifty percent).
If the Assignor(s) is (are) a Member(s) of the Performing Right Society Ltd., the rights hereby assigned are assigned subject to the rights of the said Society arising by virtue of the Assignor(s) membership of the said Society or otherwise but include the reversionary interest of the Assignor(s) in such rights expectant upon the determination by any means of the rights of the Society as aforesaid, subject to the payment to the Assignor(s) by the Publishers of the Assignor's(s) share of all performing right fees received by the Publishers, such share to be not less than the share previously payable to the Assignor(s) by the Society.
This Assignment may be regarded as the Assignor(s) certificate for the purpose of Paragraph (a) of the Performing Right Society's Rule 1 (e) authorising the Performing Right Society to treat the Publishers as exploiting the said work(s).

GENERALLY
All Royalties and Fees payable by the Publishers to the Assignor(s) by virtue of this Assignment shall be divided between the Assignor(s) in the following manner and shall be paid within 60 (sixty) days after June 30th and December 31st in each year:—

SIGNED by the Assignor(s) _____   Ralph McTell

in the presence of _____

Chapter 11
The Easy Blues

By the autumn of 1973, McTell was completing work on what would be his sixth album, 'Easy'. However, his decision to part company with Jo Lustig still rankles with the American manager who had helped elevate the singer's status.

"He was a very naughty boy to me about that. For some time he had not been, in my opinion, straight with me. Always to my face, but away from me, he would do things against my advice and was uncooperative.

"I remember when, for some reason, he wanted to play the Rainbow Theatre in London. I said to him 'Don't go there. It's just not your type of audience.' but he wouldn't listen. It was a total disaster: all sorts of problems with the sound system which packed in part-way through the night. Terrible. I was sorry to say I was proved right."

McTell remembers this sequence of events somewhat differently. "I never wanted to do that gig, and I say it was Jo's idea to put me on there. The Rainbow was a rock venue and not at all right for me. It was one of the worst nights of my career. The PA packed in and the soundman was nowhere to be seen. Tony Visconti was there, and could see there were problems before the sound went. He jumped out of his seat, ran down to the desk and eventually fixed it himself. While it was off, I sort of busked my way through 'San Fransisco Bay Blues', 'Creole Belle' and a flat-picked version of 'Standing Down In New York Town'. The whole night was a disaster."

Lustig recalls learning of the parting of the ways at a Steeleye Span gig in London when he bumped into Chris Coates, who went on to be Ralph's road manager. "That was how I heard he no longer wanted to be with me. I was very disappointed with him over that. I feel that Ralph never had any great aspirations to be any bigger than he was at the time I managed him. It was quite destructive, really. But I am happy with what I achieved for him.

"I'll always remember, years later, I was at an art exhibition and, as I was signing the visitor's book, a lady asked me 'Are you Jo Lustig?' When I confirmed I was, she said 'I was on your mailing list when I was a young girl. I went to a wonderful concert by Ralph McTell many years ago and it opened up my eyes to a world of great music…I'll always remember that night.' But, to this day, I still don't know why he decided to leave my management."

In fact, Ralph had reached the end of his contract and decided not to renew their association. Lustig was into many other things and McTell felt neglected, but looking back at their parting, today still regrets the terms on which they parted. "The whole way Jo received the news I'd decided to part company is something I bitterly regret.

He was a quirky kind of guy to deal with, but I still have the utmost respect for him."

As previously mentioned, McTell had asked his brother Bruce to take over his management. Nanna May: "Jo was very upset when Ralph left him, but he never appreciated the thought Ralph put into his decision to leave. I felt Bruce was able to talk and deal with Ralph in a personal manner in a way Jo couldn't."

Mick McDonagh assesses Lustig's influence on McTell's rise differently: "My view on Jo Lustig was that all he had done was spotted this artist that was blossoming of his own accord, and that 90 per cent of Ralph's rise was down to no-one but Ralph himself. He was exactly right for that time. He was doing excellent shows and was cutting through to a cross-section of audience. It was down to him." However, there were problems with Warner Brothers to be dealt with, as McTell was dropped from the label after 'Not Till Tomorrow', and one of Bruce May's first tasks was to find a new record deal.

"Warners' Des Brown, who believed in Ralph's ability, and was genuinely sorry that he had been dropped, advised me to go out to Los Angeles and see if I could rescue the deal. I didn't go, since I was setting up a very big tour for Ralph, so I felt that I would concentrate on that part of the business and see what happened when the upcoming record was finished. Derek Block was promoting the tour, and had

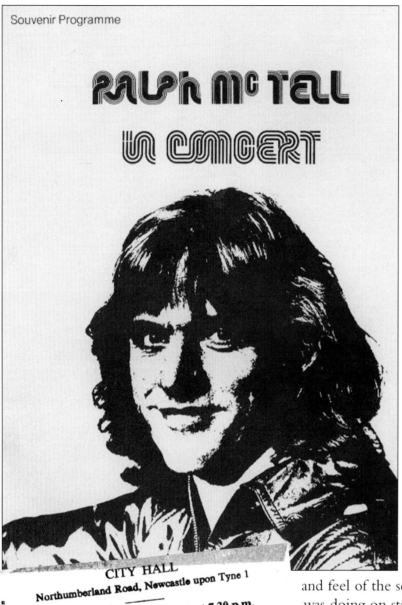

Souvenir Programme

RALPH McTELL
IN CONCERT

CITY HALL
Northumberland Road, Newcastle upon Tyne 1

Thursday, 7th February, 1974, at 7.30 p.m.

DEREK BLOCK
presents

RALPH McTELL
IN CONCERT

AREA £1·25   SEAT   E 18

Booking Agents: City Hall Box Office
Northumberland Road, Newcastle upon Tyne (Tel. 20007)
This Portion to be retained

booked Ralph in for a date at the Royal Albert Hall. When Des, who'd been trying to get Alice Cooper a date at the same venue, caught wind of this, he realised Warners' had made a mistake and quickly offered us a new deal."

Up to this point, McTell had been performing considerably better on stage than he had on record, but the tracks he was laying down at John Kongos's studio would resolve that problem. He also felt that his writing had become rather serious, and wanted to change that image. "That was why we used a picture of me clowning about for the tour publicity. I hated the picture at first, but then I thought 'It's me, I'm like that, so why not?'

"It was the first time that I ever had more material than I needed for an album, but we still had a few problems completing it. Tony Visconti was in the midst of setting up a new record label, which meant that he was unable to finish the album, so Danny Thompson and myself took over production. We were under pressure to deliver it by a certain date, so we had to keep the recording very sparse. As a result of that, there's a greater degree of consistency about it, and the finished work reflected the mood and feel of the sessions. I think it was fairly close to what I was doing on stage, and things were going from strength to strength."

Visconti recalls his brief period working with McTell with fondness. "Ralph was one of several legacies I got from Gus Dudgeon. Ralph had been a bit disenchanted, because Gus had been going through that over-production, throwing-in-the-kitchen-sink syndrome. Ralph wanted to be recorded simply, and that was what I provided for him on 'Not Till Tomorrow', which was a lovely album. We only did part of 'Easy' together, but I thoroughly enjoyed working with him, and I'd enjoy working with him again."

Danny Thompson looks back at the recording sessions as somewhat pressured: "There was a deadline to complete the record which Visconti, among other pressures he had, just couldn't achieve. So Ralph asked me to help him out. I'd produced before with Bert Jansch, so I roughly followed the same way of working. It's a difficult situation when you work for a mate, and it can put a strain on things, but he's so good to work with that I just did the best I could, and thankfully it seemed to please everybody."

Indeed, McTell's confidence in the period since the release of 'Not Till Tomorrow' had made an enormous difference to his songwriting, bringing to the sessions the strongest batch of songs he'd ever had at his disposal. Another major factor in producing the sense of togetherness on the album was that he'd known most of the musicians for a long time: "I could do what I wanted, I was able to relax with my mates, and I think that came over on the record: that's why we called it 'Easy'. I think when you have friends playing with you, you don't feel the need to impress them or win them over."

Wizz Jones appeared on 'Take It Easy', playing rhythm guitar, which helped drive things along. Danny Thompson added his usual solid bass playing, and Bert Jansch put in three weeks' effort to learn his guitar parts on 'Run Johnny Run'. McTell tried to pick specific people for specific songs, and Tony Visconti suggested Paul McCartney to play on 'Sweet Mystery'. Ralph demoed the song with Danny Thompson, and sent a tape to McCartney, who told Visconti he felt it was too difficult for him to play!

Jazzman Stan Tracey played piano on 'Summer Lightning', but the finished version had such a different feel from the rest of the recordings that it was decided to remove his contribution from the final mix. 'Easy' shows a whole range of influences within its songs. Initially, he had wanted a pianist on 'Would I Lie To You', as he felt that the song contained echoes of Fats Waller. 'ZigZag Line' is very Derroll Adams, 'Stuff No More' is Blind Willie McTell, and 'Maddy Dances' is obviously a tribute to Steeleye Span vocalist Miss Prior.

'Take It Easy' is back to the old days busking around Europe, but also looks at the innocence of those times when McTell, Tubs and the rest of the crew were all so innocent and naive. 'Maginot Waltz' was inspired by seeing an old photograph of a group of people setting off for a day trip, recalling that the first time McTell ever saw the sea was on a trip to Brighton as a young boy. "I pictured them all going off there. The photograph was dated around 1913-14, so I wondered just how near to the outbreak of war it had been taken, and whatever became of those people, especially the men, on that photo. So I just set the whole thing around summer, 1914.

Danny Thompson, Pat (a fan)'s mum and Ralph, 1972.

"Unfortunately, I got it wrong with the title as it was some time later that I realised the Maginot Line was built just prior to the outbreak of the Second World War, but it was too late by then. It was essentially an obscure anti-war song, so my cop-out for getting the title wrong was that it was a premonition for all wars!"

Elsewhere, 'Sweet Mystery' is all about courtship, doing it right in the old Fred Astaire manner with flowers. 'Run Johnny Run' is a complicated song, in which McTell uses the idea of a prisoner on the run, but beneath the surface, it's much more: its subject is a dream-like sequence of events spread over a night, a day and a second night, when someone is running away from something they can't quite identify.

Well its briars and brambles tore his skin
And there's time he fell down but got up again
And his steaming breath in the starry dark
He was straining his ears for the guard dog's noise
And that's why he ran through that icy stream
For to throw them dogs from off his scent
And though he knew it would slow him down well
They would not know which way he's gone.
('Run Johnny Run', 1974)

'ZigZag Line' was inspired by a holiday some years earlier when the family were driving around in a car and his son saw what he thought was a mountain. Ralph, who saw it as a hill, agreed to climb it, although halfway up he reached the conclusion that it was in fact a mountain. Remembering school lessons, he adopted the technique used by mountain climbers who would take a zigzag line to reach the summit. The song's message is that, to achieve one's desires, one sometimes needs to adopt a roundabout route.

McTell explained that 'Let Me Down Easy' was written about a friendship that was drawing to an unavoidable sad conclusion: "It was a way of saying 'If it's all over, try not to hurt me too much.' 'Would I Lie To You' is again influenced by the sort of music I grew up with. 'Summer Lighting' is about that situation which everybody has been in at one time or another where there is an uncomfortable silence between two people, and no-one is saying just what's wrong, but you just know that there is and you're waiting for the big bang.

"It's trying to put the situation right before the day is through and not letting it drag on to the next day. Using lightning, where there are blinding flashes but sometimes a long delay in the following crashing noise, is a marvellous way of capturing that uncomfortable silence between people."

Don't let the day go down
The two of us still fighting
It's not a storm at all
No it's only summer
Only summer lightning
And we've still got the night
So there's time to put it right
Let's go to bed.
('Summer Lightning', 1974)

Reputedly due to a world-wide oil crisis, a vinyl shortage prevented release schedules being met, and 'Easy', a late 19th century painting by Enrique Serra on its striking sleeve, was eventually released in March. McTell went on a winter tour in 1974 to promote the album which had received the best reviews yet: most critics rejoiced that at last he had produced an album to match his live performances.

'Easy' was McTell's first album to reach the charts, hitting the dizzy heights of Number 30 to equal the Beatles and Diana Ross! "That was a terrific tour," recalled the chart debutant, "one of the most enjoyable I ever did. I had decided to take Danny Thompson and Mike Pigott with me to facsimile the sound we'd got in the studio. It was great fun. That was the last tour I ever did with Danny. He'd been going through a bad period at the time so it was good to get him away and working for a while.

"We were playing a gig in Holland with Randy Newman. Randy doesn't like playing much, and each night as we'd come off he'd be waiting in the wings asking 'What was the crowd like?' I'd say it was fine and he'd go down great. The tour over in Europe was rather gruelling, and before a rather big gig in Amsterdam, Danny had gone on a bit of a bender and was completely stoned by the time we got back to the theatre where Randy was doing his soundcheck.

"He was looking pensive as usual and Danny got up on stage with his bass and shouted to him 'Wahay Rand! Fancy a blow?' and started banging away on the bass. Then it came to Danny that he'd actually backed Randy in London on an *In Concert* for the BBC and he said all the wrong things from there on in like 'I remember when we played that time and everyone was saying "Just who *is* this bloke? He can't sing, can't play the piano."' Randy's face dropped. 'What do you mean, can't play the piano?' I'd never seen him so animated: 'How about *this* then?', and he launched into a long classical piece. Danny yelled 'Wahoo' and started jamming along.

"Shortly afterwards, Danny passed out and didn't wake up again until two minutes before we were due on. We got on stage and all I could see were these two bleary eyes peering out at me from behind his bass. Anyway we got through the gig all right and, since Holland were playing in an important football match the next night, we had to wave these little flags at the end of our set. All the audience cheered and Danny called out 'utter rubbish'."

Despite McTell's portrayal, that gig is still vivid in the mind of the bass player. "Ralph has such reverence towards some musicians – it's as if he feels in awe of them when he's as good as most of them himself. We were backstage and Ralph is talking to Randy and he turns towards me and says 'And this is my bass player, Danny Thompson.' I say 'Hello Rand' and Ralph looks on aghast as if I've insulted the guy.

"It was really funny, especially as I'd worked with Randy before. To me, he's just another bloke, a musician who likes playing with other musicians. But for Ralph…I'd overstepped the mark. To see his face that night was so funny."

On the road, McTell was met with great enthusiasm by an ever-growing public. Bruce May was happy with his progress, as Danny

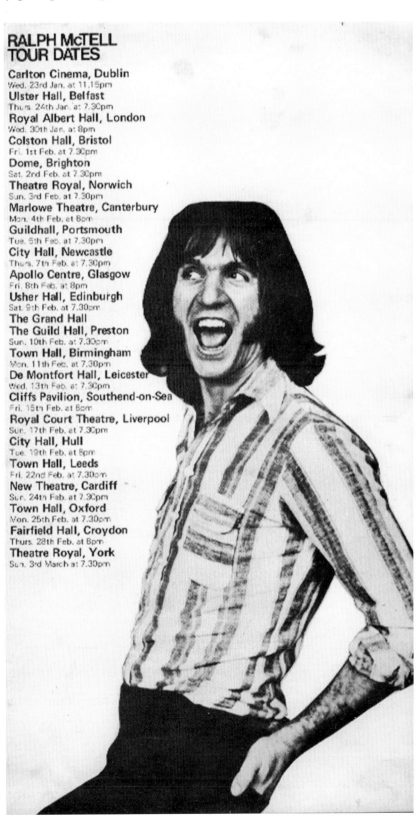

RALPH McTELL TOUR DATES

Carlton Cinema, Dublin
Wed. 23rd Jan. at 11.15pm
Ulster Hall, Belfast
Thurs. 24th Jan. at 7.30pm
Royal Albert Hall, London
Wed. 30th Jan. at 8pm
Colston Hall, Bristol
Fri. 1st Feb. at 7.30pm
Dome, Brighton
Sat. 2nd Feb. at 7.30pm
Theatre Royal, Norwich
Sun. 3rd Feb. at 7.30pm
Marlowe Theatre, Canterbury
Mon. 4th Feb. at 8pm
Guildhall, Portsmouth
Tue. 5th Feb. at 7.30pm
City Hall, Newcastle
Thurs. 7th Feb. at 7.30pm
Apollo Centre, Glasgow
Fri. 8th Feb. at 8pm
Usher Hall, Edinburgh
Sat. 9th Feb. at 7.30pm
The Grand Hall
The Guild Hall, Preston
Sun. 10th Feb. at 7.30pm
Town Hall, Birmingham
Mon. 11th Feb. at 7.30pm
De Montfort Hall, Leicester
Wed. 13th Feb. at 7.30pm
Cliffs Pavilion, Southend-on-Sea
Fri. 15th Feb. at 8pm
Royal Court Theatre, Liverpool
Sun. 17th Feb. at 7.30pm
City Hall, Hull
Tue. 19th Feb. at 8pm
Town Hall, Leeds
Fri. 22nd Feb. at 7.30pm
New Theatre, Cardiff
Sun. 24th Feb. at 7.30pm
Town Hall, Oxford
Mon. 25th Feb. at 7.30pm
Fairfield Hall, Croydon
Thurs. 28th Feb. at 8pm
Theatre Royal, York
Sun. 3rd March at 7.30pm

Thompson recalls: "We get up to Glasgow and find we've been booked into the Albany Hotel, which was really posh. When we got in, there was a message from Bruce saying 'Dear All… Tour going great. Exceeding all expectations… Well done all… Have booked you into the Buchanan Suite. Fill your boots… Bruce.' And sure enough, we're in this fabulous suite. So we all pile in and I make straight for the mini-bar. 'Great, lads, Campari' I yell…we're really pleased.

"Our driver, a bloke called Stan, who was an ex-stuntman, is doing these rolls and stunts which were absolutely pathetic. We couldn't stop laughing at him. He was awful. So I say 'Let's get room service…yeah! Steak…yeah! Oh look, Ralph…Scottish Salmon – let's get that,' and Ralph is all cautious…it's this lovely working-class streak which has never, ever left him. He asks 'How much is it?' I look down the price list…'30 bob, Ralph, great', and he goes all iffy. 'Oh, I don't know…I'll have half of yours.' I can't believe him.

"I'm a London lad, and if anyone puts me in a top hotel suite and leaves me a message to 'fill your boots', I'd do exactly that… Not Ralph. Can you imagine someone like Dylan saying that – 'Oh, I'll have half of yours'?"

McTell's first appearance at the Royal Albert Hall reminded him of two of the best shows he had ever seen, by Bob Dylan in 1965, and the Band in 1970. Now it was his turn to stand on that same stage. The show was a 6,500-capacity sellout, and the *Melody Maker* review noted: "The whole aura of the Albert Hall and its vastness seemed to weigh heavy on him."

Ralph: "I couldn't believe it. I was so nervous before I went on, in case they didn't like me, that I had to down a couple of stiff brandies to give myself a bit of Dutch courage. Listening from backstage to the stamping and whistling after I'd come off was an amazing experience."

However, one review of McTell's Albert Hall show annoyed Danny Thompson so much that he went as far as hitting back personally. Thompson had stayed with McTell after the show, and the following morning had perused the morning papers before Ralph to see if there were any reviews. When he saw one by Robin Denselow in *The Guardian*, he was annoyed and tried to prevent Ralph from seeing it.

"The only problem," wrote Denselow, "was his lyrics. They varied unevenly between the intelligently emotional and the appallingly twee, and the overall effect ranged from pleasant to pleasantly boring. Too many songs were about children, girlfriends and country cottages, and suffered from sentimental overkill. Some things come just too easy."

Thompson begged to differ. "That Albert Hall gig was wonderful. Ralph was absolutely stunning. There's just Ralph in his Levi's, guitar and a bass player. At the end of two and a half hours, the place erupts. Six encores. You come off walking on air. Doing that gig was no small achievement. And then you see this review where Robin Denselow goes on at Ralph for writing 'twee songs'.

"Ralph never saw himself as a pop star or anything like that. He is just a guy who wrote honest, decent and truthful songs about life and how he sees it. Why Denselow couldn't celebrate the fact that here was a Croydon lad who'd lived in poverty as a child and had lived the dream in selling out the Albert Hall really got to me.

"A couple of weeks later, I was doing a gig with John Martyn at Drury Lane when I took the mic onstage and said 'Something has just occurred to me – while you audience are in here having a wonderful night, these journalists are here as well, who haven't paid at all, who will eat our food and drink backstage and then creep off again into the night and write all about what you have listened to. In their homes, they have their guitars on the wall, because they don't know how to play themselves…' It just all got to me, these critics who don't have a clue what it's all about: going onstage nervous and handling a show the way he did that night."

Another show, at Oxford, had to be rescheduled because a General Election campaign was in full swing at that time in England and various parliamentarians were using the theatre. At one venue, McTell drew as big an audience as Prime Minister Harold Wilson had the week before!

Later in the year, McTell took a break of sorts, playing a session for singer-songwriter Lynsey De Paul. "The connection there was Robert Kirby, who had done the string arrangements on 'You Well Meaning…'. He'd liked the way I played guitar and was producing the debut album for a young lady who was called Lynsey Rubin at the time. I was really pleased to be asked to play, as I had only done one other session before that. I thought they'd want a bit of fingerpicking, so it wouldn't be too complicated.

"When I arrived at the studio, there was the lovely Lynsey with her shirt unbuttoned to the waist and six leering sessionmen in tow. Then I saw a music stand with the arrangements and dots and notes and everything – and I panicked, as I can't read music at all. I asked Robert to leave me till last, which was an excuse to let the other musicians run through the tracks so I could watch their hands. And I just blagged my way through the entire session.

The next time I saw her was at Pentangle's last gig at the Festival Hall. I went up to say hello, and she said "Oh, by the way, we *loved* your playing so much we put it right at the top of the mix. You've *got* to hear it." I said I had to make a confession, that I left that session without a clue of what I had put down or what I sounded like! I had a similar experience with Fairport Convention doing 'Me With You' on their 'Rosie' album. The studio resembled a London fog, with Swarbrick puffing away, and again I left the session without a clue about what I'd done."

McTell's career was clearly going from strength to strength, and a major factor in Danny Thompson's opinion was Bruce May's management: "When Bruce arrived on the scene, he very quickly saw things that needed to be done in terms of making Ralph more professional in his personal life. Like whenever any of us were in London, it was always taken for granted that everybody would be able to stay at his place. And there would be that inevitable scene going on at his house – God knows how Nanna put up with it all. Bruce got rid of all the dead wood in Ralph's personal scene and made him more aware in a professional sense. He was very good at doing that, and in turn it gave Ralph a greater edge as an artist."

Chapter *12* Singled Out

fter McTell had completed his third LP for Warner Brothers, the label requested a single for release before the year's end in advance of the album. There was no obvious track among the new recordings, but Bruce May suggested re-recording 'Streets Of London'.

"He pointed out that Transatlantic were free to release it in March of '75," Ralph recalls, "and since I was on such a lousy royalties deal with them, why not? Plus I knew I could do it so much better now and felt that it could actually be successful. When you look at it, the song had had one of the longest promotions in record history. There was a belief that it had at one time been a single because it was always getting radio airplay, and when Capital Radio ran their 'All-Time Top 100 Singles' chart, 'Streets' was on it. The fact was that Transatlantic had never released it because they thought it wasn't commercial enough."

Warners had been very pleased with the sales of 'Easy' and, since McTell's concert tours were selling out, they were hoping for great things from his next album. There had been staff changes within the company, and it had been Ron Kass who had listened through the tapes McTell had recorded to see if there was anything that could make a single.

Some years earlier, Kass had been involved with the Beatles, and, at a time when they had no new album scheduled, he had asked them for a single to bridge the gap. 'Hey Jude', their biggest-selling single ever, was the result. With this in mind, and with the album some way from its final mix, he'd suggested a similar ploy to Bruce.

"I chased around checking any legal tie-ups there might have been on the song once Warners had said they'd go for it. I recall Noel Edmunds, who was then a DJ with enormous influence, playing it on his programme regularly as soon as it was released. We then got Ralph on the *Russell Harty* programme, but while Ralph was in the studio recording his slot the producer told the head of promotion at Warners that, according to the figures he had, the single wasn't happening and they weren't going to put Ralph's slot in the show. Just then, a phone call came in to tell us that they have shifted 22,000 copies of 'Streets Of London' that very day! So in the space of 60 seconds, we didn't care if he went on the programme or not!"

No-one could have expected what happened next, as 'Streets Of London' was playlisted by radio stations nationwide. Indeed, at a time when glam-rock dominated the UK charts a song like 'Streets' almost assumed the mantle of a novelty hit. "I'd had no wish to create a commercial single," Ralph insists, "and yet that's what it is. There are no drums on it, just an acoustic guitar. It was done absolutely straight, as I always sing it anyway. It was just one take. It ought to be after eight years!"

STREETS OF LONDON

The success of 'Streets Of London' caught everybody by surprise – not least a member of the production crew of BBC-TV's *Top Of The Pops* who asked a camera-ready Ralph when he was going to put his 'proper stage clothes' on, and a BBC executive who asked Ralph how it felt to be making a comeback. Jimmy Savile, introducing Ralph, said: "Once in a while in the entertainment business, a fairy tale comes true."

"I was rather bemused by *Top Of The Pops*," the singer admits. "They all said nice things about the record, they were all pleased to see it up there, but I felt a little uncomfortable. I did quite a bit of TV – I was on *The Lulu Show*, and I mean no offence to her when I say the show was awful. Part of the deal we made for her programme was that I got to do another song, so I did 'Maginot Waltz' as I felt it would show I didn't know just the one song. But they didn't use it, they just showed the other thing.

Ralph at Essex Music.

"That had a disastrous effect because, when I went out on the road after all this massive exposure, attendances were slightly down on the previous tour. Perhaps the reason was that I had only toured a few months before, but I felt that a lot of the old stalwarts had felt a bit let-down by me going on those sort of variety shows."

Though it topped at least one of the music-paper charts, 'Streets Of London' peaked at Number 2 in the official UK singles listings, which it entered on 7 December 1974. It was headed by Mud's 'Lonely This Christmas' in the 11 January 1975 chart, or Status Quo's 'Down Down' the following week.

The single's runaway success made the upcoming tour take on a different look. The forthcoming album had been recorded at Air Studios in London and, with a line-up of musicians including ex-Lindisfarne bass player Rod Clements, Fairport Convention members Dave Pegg and Jerry Donahue, and Steeleye Span's Maddy Prior, a far fuller sound was produced than ever before. Apart from 'Streets Of London', 'Grande Affaire' and 'El Progresso', which he had performed on the autumn dates, all the songs were new to McTell's followers.

There was also a change from previous records with a distinct variation of musical styles: the country-ish 'Interest On The Loan', the traditional 'Red Apple Juice' (aka 'Honey Babe Blues') providing a blues feel, and the Latin-American influences on 'El Progresso'.

With the musicians gelling well together in the studio, and with Ralph as producer, his vocals possessed a greater range and depth than at any other stage of his recording career. While there'd previously been a definite division between his vocal performances on stage and in the studio, 'Streets' almost sounded like an album by the Ralph McTell Band.

And that was clearly the singer's aim. "I had been planning to put a band on the road for ages, and we were already rehearsing when the single started going up the charts. Prior to that, I'd told Bruce I couldn't face touring on my own again. I had been starting to get stale doing the same things over and over again. I needed to give a bit more on stage, and I felt the best way was to put a team of friends and musicians around me."

First in was Rod Clements on bass, followed shortly by American drummer Danny Lane, a member of Michael Nesmith's house band at the ex-Monkee's Countryside Records who'd also played on Ike and Tina Turner's hit single 'Nutbush City Limits'. Mike Piggott was on fiddle and mandolin, and had previously toured with Ralph as a member of Paul Brett's Sage. Finally, backing vocalists Sian Daniels and Joy Askew had been with local London bands.

Rod Clements had left Jack the Lad before they supported Ralph's previous tour, but had gone to see them play at their warm-up gig at the Howff in Hampstead, which was where he met Ralph for "the first time in years. Ralph got me into Air Studios the following week, as he had a co-production job on Bert Jansch's version of 'In The Bleak Midwinter', which we finished fairly quickly, and he recorded 'Streets Of London' the same day, complete with him playing tubular bells too!

"Shortly afterwards, we started rehearsing for the tour, but problems arose almost straight away, which I must say were not helped by Danny Lane, who didn't arrive in the country until three days before the tour started. We'd rehearsed as much as we could without a drummer, but could go no further, and I had Pick Withers (later of Dire Straits) almost waiting in the wings to come in and take over. I felt that Danny brought a lot of angst and pressure to the band, which got things off to a bad start. He seemed to be wanting the 'star treatment' bit, which didn't help morale.

"We had guitarist Sammy Mitchell in the band too. He got the push on the eve of the tour which Danny had a hand in, as he didn't rate him – though to be fair, what Sammy was doing wasn't gelling with what the rest of the band were doing. I went out on that tour hardly fired with confidence, and I think we all felt that way. There were some good players in that band, and when we did get going, there were some very good performances; no-one was trying to upstage Ralph but just trying to do their jobs as best they could."

Ralph: "After three rehearsals, Danny Lane turned to me and said 'It's all wrong. These guys aren't good enough.' We should have called it off right there and then, as soon as there was any dissent. He didn't pick on anyone in particular and say they weren't good enough, but he did say it wasn't as good as it could have been, it was taking too long to get it together, and that we weren't rehearsed properly. There was only Mike he rated, and Mike should have been allowed to play more guitar in the band which was originally the idea. I'd never worked with bands before and was inexperienced, looking back."

Prior to the start of the tour, McTell made one of his customary visits to Northern Ireland. The Troubles were at a height, yet he was one the few performers who would play there, and Belfast always gave him one of his best receptions. Before the show started at the city's Grosvenor Hall, he received a ten-minute ovation from the 3,000 crowd, and the audience applauded for 15 minutes at the end. After the show, a large crowd of enthusiastic fans followed him back to the hotel. Not even a bomb alert during the evening could spoil the show, and everything looked good for the upcoming tour.

Meanwhile, the single continued to rise up the British charts. "We were trying every conceivable angle to maximise its success," recalls Mick McDonagh. "During that dead period between Christmas and New Year where little news is generated, I put a call into the BBC press office, reminding them about 'Streets Of London' and the fact that there were so many people spending Christmas on the streets. As a result, they sent a crew out around London for a feature on their *Nationwide* programme, which helped sustain the single in the charts. We were hitting everything at the time, and the amount of press we generated was amazing." However, when McTell learned about this, he was appalled at what he considered tasteless exploitation of a serious situation.

The 'Streets' tour opened at Queens Hall in Barnstaple, Devon, on 21 February 1975. Supported by ex-Steeleye Span founder members Gay and Terry Woods, it was McTell's biggest ever tour, comprising 28 concerts in just over a month. The format of the show was for him to play two or three numbers solo, and then bring on the band. Yet while the addition of musicians gave him the opportunity to perform different material, the sound seemed distorted on many nights, the vocals lost among the rhythm section and the backing singers. PA problems seemed to dog the crew, and audiences at many shows seemed perturbed at Ralph's new style of performance.

His new-found status had brought him a new audience who were only there to hear 'Streets Of London', yet his on/off feelings towards the song had arisen again and he decided not to perform it on most nights. There was almost a sense of mischief in omitting the song on that particular tour, the excuse being that people were sick and tired of hearing it, and its creator convincing himself that people had not just come for that particular song. The fact that had escaped him was that many had, and audience reaction was mixed.

"Oxford was probably the worst, because there were people shouting out. Other nights there were calls of 'On your own, Ralph!'" The initial enthusiasm of being freed (in a sense) to perform with the band was tempered by both the audience reaction and continuing problems of faulty monitors and guitars and speakers humming and buzzing. McTell's usual 'happy to be up there performing' mood was clearly wearing thin. What was to have been the crowning moment of his career became a sad experience indeed. Although not quite as bad in terms of crowd behaviour, there were certain parallels with Bob Dylan and the Hawks in 1965-66.

"With the rehearsals not as good as they should have been," Rod Clements feels, "we got off to a bad start and never really recovered. Being a nervous performer anyway, Ralph was under an awful lot of media scrutiny, and possibly jumped off into the deep end by using such a big band instead of maybe just two or three other musicians. It seemed that Bruce also had a downer on the band from the start, and felt that there was an awful lot of money going down the plughole for very little reward. All this must have been rubbing off on Ralph, and didn't help in building his confidence for such a big tour."

Everything came to a head at the New Theatre, Southport, on 22 March.

Derek Block in association with Bruce May Present   Autumn Tour 1974

RALPH McTELL

Opening solo with 'Nettle Wine', basic mistakes in the intro were made and the usual fluid guitar runs were not in evidence. McTell made several barbed comments to the soundman before eventually stopping one song shortly after it had begun. "I cannot work under conditions like this," he shouted to the mixing desk, and stormed off. As he later explained, "That was a disastrous night for a number of reasons – the sound was so bad, I just walked offstage. I had never done that before."

The crowd were cleared out of the main hall into the bar area – and, with the Southport complex housing two halls, they were greeted by the strains of chart stars Mud playing their hit 'Tiger Feet'! There was a sad irony to it all, as Rod Clements recalls: "The band were all in the dressing room listening to Ralph's opening numbers over the relay tannoys. We heard him stop, the clunk of the guitar and wondered what was going on. The first we knew was when he came into the dressing room very upset, followed by radio people who were there recording the show. Eventually we got him calmed down."

The concert resumed later, but the tension was still tangible and, at the end of the show, Ralph walked into his dressing room and sunk a half-bottle of brandy alone. Rod Clements: "Ralph took me and Mike Piggott out for a curry, and really poured his heart out to us about how he felt and where it was all going wrong. It was a friendly little gathering and we were being as sympathetic as we could, and tried to give him as much positive encouragement as possible. At the end of the meal, we felt that he was feeling a lot better, had got a lot of problems off his chest and that things could only improve from there on in."

Back at the hotel, however, the tension soon returned. After asking for a drink several times at the hotel bar, he was refused, and proceeded to smash the bar up and even uncharacteristically offered to take outside a top-ranking policeman who chanced to be drinking there. The rest of the band looked on stunned. The galling aspect of it was that here he was, with this new-found enthusiasm to play live with a band, while audiences were wanting him to play solo.

Amid all the confusion, Bruce May decided he would find out what was happening for himself. "I went along early to one of the venues and they were running through their soundcheck. There was Danny Lane sitting in the stalls with his feet over the seats. Ralph is on the stage and Danny calls out 'Well come on, Ralphie…let's see you show us just what you can do' in his laid-back American drawl. That got my back up straight away. I thought 'They've got no respect for Ralph at all. No wonder he's going under.' There and then, I knew it wasn't going to work. Something quick needed to be done to save the day."

Ralph: "We pushed on for another three nights. It was after the Theatre Royal, Drury Lane, gig that I told the band it was all over, although there were just a few gigs left. Unfortunately, after the Southport concert, I'd done an interview with a guy from BBC Radio Blackburn, and I was so wound up, having drunk a half-bottle of brandy as well, I just effed and blinded into his tape recorder. He sent the tape up to Radio One's *Newsbeat*, so by the time I'd got to Drury Lane all the press were there waiting for me."

That night, after announcing on stage that he wouldn't be doing any more live shows after the remaining dates, he finished his concert with a poignant performance of Bob Dylan's 'One Too Many Mornings' – a song McTell had referred to as being "a goodnight song to a whole generation." Rod Clements: "We had a day off on the tour and were back in London and were all invited out for a meal by Bruce, but due to the way things were going I didn't fancy it at all. It was there that Danny was given his plane ticket back to the States.

"The following day I got a frantic telephone call from Danny saying 'We've all been fired!' so I got into my car and tore off down to Putney to have it out with Bruce – and, indeed, had already started having it out with Bruce when he told me to hold on... Ralph, Mike and myself were going to continue on for the remaining gigs. From there on in, there was a total change in Ralph's temperament and it was a joy to do those shows."

Ralph: "I did most of the show on my own and they'd come on for the last five or six songs at the end. It was beautiful, the tension was gone and it was so easy. But I'd already made my mind up that it was over, no more live appearances. That was it – I was retiring from gigs, and was just going to concentrate on recording."

The announcement even made the national news. In an interview with the *Daily Mail*, he said: "I know I'm turning my back on a lot of money, but I only ever wanted to sing, to express myself, to be happy. Since I've had a hit record, life has become a misery. I keep getting hustled into doing things I don't want to do and I'm losing the respect that I had for myself. I have to get out of Britain for a while. As it is, I haven't written a song for six months, and there's a real danger of my drying up completely."

For Bruce May, too, it was a frustrating time. Here he was placed in a situation where he had an artist who had achieved a big hit single, but had then decided he didn't want the trappings of stardom. Yet perhaps the key was that, as an artist who had always tried to make each song an improvement on its predecessor, he had achieved so much recognition on the back of an old song. What he saw as a natural progression over the years had been interrupted by four minutes 24 seconds of one of the earliest songs he'd ever written – one which, by his own admission, was not one of his best.

Danny Lane, Sian Daniels, Joy Askew, Ralph, Rod Clements and Mike Piggott.

Danny Thompson views McTell's on/off love affair with 'Streets Of London'

with typical bluntness: "I've heard this moan many times over the years. I keep reminding him just how many people know that song the whole world over and wished they could have written it. It's an international song; even if some people don't even know who wrote it, they know the song. That's no small achievement. I can't count how many times I've said to him 'Don't put yourself down about that song, you shouldn't have written the bloody song if you're going to be that way about it.' I have to give him a slap about it every now and then!"

Bruce May felt his brother deserved to take a break. "He'd worked very hard for some years to get where he was, and I knew that keeping his family life together was more important than his career. If, by taking time off, that helped preserve it, then so be it. If he'd had someone else with more experience than I managing him after the success of 'Streets Of London', they may have guided him better. But I respected his wishes totally."

Meanwhile, the new LP, completed before the re-recording of 'Streets Of London', had been released with the single included – despite protests from both Ralph and Bruce May. Both felt that it didn't belong on the album, but label pressure won. Warners then wanted the album to be titled 'Streets Of London' – and, and after yet more debate, a compromise was reached with 'Streets' the eventual choice.

"Originally," Ralph reveals, "it was going to be called 'In The Blue Corner' or 'Off The Ropes': something to do with the boxing cover. That picture was done on my birthday. I'd taken Danny Thompson and a few other friends to see Joe Bugner fight at the Albert Hall. Everybody on that picture has had a go at boxing at some time or another. Eventually, after much discussion, we went for 'Streets' in very small letters.

"It infuriated me to have 'Streets Of London' on the album, but business-wise it's suicide to have a hit single and then leave it off the album. I thought it was ripping people off to have it on yet another album. Then they said they wanted to put a sticker on the sleeve saying 'Containing the hit single', but I must admit they did it quite tastefully, in the form of a boxing ticket. I was upset that 'Streets Of London' went on instead of 'Country Boys'. The album took a long time to record and cost a lot of money too. I thought I'd be able to overdub everything but found I couldn't, so we did things a few times and got Dave Pegg and Danny Thompson in to do the bass work."

Ralph's plan was to record the tracks with bass and drums and everything would be built on top of it. "I'd wanted to do it that way after all the bad experiences I'd had of working with drummers who weren't turned on to acoustic music: I didn't want to run that risk again. Although (Danny Lane) played beautifully, it just wasn't happening, so we scrapped everything we'd done except 'Pity The Boy' and 'El Progresso', and started working again with bass, drums and rhythm guitar. And it worked. I was delighted. Those sessions gave me the extra confidence to work live with a band."

Some songs included on the finished album had been a long time coming. The tune of 'Grande Affaire' he'd written circa 1971, but had only completed the lyrics (about being young, broke, in love and politically aware) in the summer of 1974 while in Norway. 'Pity The Boy' was written in 1970, around the time of 'Heron Song'. 'Lunar Lullaby' was originally intended for 'Easy', but missed the cut. 'El Progresso' went back even further: he had actually started working out the tune back in 1968.

'Henry' Bartlett has reason to remember this particular song in some detail: "One time I went around to Ralph's place after he had arrived back from a holiday in the

Canaries. He nonchalantly offered me a cigarette, from which I took one drag and rasped as an unbelievable pain hit my chest… Everybody fell about laughing! The cigarette was called 'El Broncesso' (*sic*), and Ralph wrote a song about it all."

Despite the age of some of the material, 'Streets' was a very carefully assembled album, and one McTell felt included some of the strongest songs he'd put on record. 'Red Apple Juice' was retitled from the original 'Honey Babe Blues', which McTell had tried to credit to Dock Boggs, but could find no trace of the latter having written it. Both Ralph and Wizz Jones used to play different songs called 'Honey Babe Blues', and during the sessions, started playing them together.

Ralph: "We had just been over to the pub, and when we got back everything was still set up and I started to play it. So I called out 'Get behind this, Danny', and it sounded great. Just at that moment, the engineer walked in and I told him to press the button. So it was recorded as it happened, live vocal, everything. It actually went on for five minutes and there's an edit in there which you can't hear. It sounded great when they played it back to us."

The album met with quite positive reviews. A variety of feelings were expressed throughout the songs, with two songs in particular, 'Grande Affaire' and 'Heron Song', recalling the travelling days in Europe on the road. But the maturity in his writing continued. 'Pity The Boy' tells of being at the crossroads in life when trading in 'rambling ways' for stability and safety within a relationship, but with a warning that it doesn't always work out that way. This could also be said to apply to the success he had now finally found – but at what price?

> *Better by far to marry for love and stay broke for the rest of your days*
> *Than to settle down for the sake of ending your rambling ways*
> *They won't end, and thinking about them, your time you will spend.*
> **('Pity The Boy', 1974)**

'Lunar Lullaby' is a reflective view of the world from afar, inspired by an evening walk by the Thames one clear dark night during one of the moonshots of the 1970s. 'Streets' entered the UK album charts on 15 February 1975, spending 12 weeks there and peaking at Number 13.

Having made the decision to stop touring, the plan was to go alone to Los Angeles, where no-one was to meet him on his arrival. It was important for McTell to get the space he craved to try and make sense of what was happening, and see why it had resulted in this sorry state of affairs. The decision to step back from his success and what it was doing to him should not really have come as a surprise: in Arthur Taylor's documentary five years earlier, McTell had hinted that he would 'Get out very quickly' if he was ever made to feel like a star. In America, without distractions, it was hoped the way forward would become clearer.

This was also a time when McTell needed strong managerial guidance. As Bruce May points out, it might well have all turned out differently if someone else had been managing him. It was a period in McTell's life when he wished his father had been around for support and advice. After all, it's hard to seek guidance from one's younger brother at the best of times!

Chapter 13
The Hit Hangover

On his arrival in America, McTell took refuge in his motel room on Sepulveda Boulevard, only venturing out at night to find solace in alcohol in the many bars along the nearby Sunset Strip. Los Angeles at the best of times can be an unfriendly city, but more so when one is in the state of mind in which he found himself during that spring of 1975.

"I hadn't told anybody I was in Los Angeles, as I needed time alone. I did try a few attempts at writing while I was there, but it was obvious that I wasn't up to it. All I was able to do was drink; I was very confused and didn't know what to do. Eventually I phoned Danny Lane, who was amazed to discover I'd already been in LA for three weeks."

Even though Lane had been fired towards the end of the 'Streets' tour, he was nevertheless pleased to see Ralph and provide the support he needed. However, Lane had returned from England to a domestic situation that had left him rather crazed, and the situation was probably not as relaxed as McTell really needed. Some efforts were made at recording with Lane and a bass player from Blood, Sweat and Tears, which produced little. Meanwhile there were plans to re-record 'Let Me Down Easy' for a single release, but this plan too was shelved, perhaps because the whole scenario of a possible hit with another older song terrified McTell.

He had suffered a near nervous breakdown after the events of early 1975, and came back to England hoping that the turmoil in his mind would evaporate, but soon discovered that things were not right. As a result, he returned to America hoping to do some recording there. Bruce May went out to try and lend a helping hand, offering his support not just as a manager but as a brother. McTell returned to Britain again and, a few weeks later, took Nanna and the children back to America for a family holiday.

He resurfaced as a performer that November, playing an unpublicised concert at Belfast's Queen's University, and another at London's Queen Elizabeth Hall. Nanna May: "I went along that night, which I don't do that often, and it was a joy to see him so relaxed. He talked to the audience in a way he hadn't done before. He seemed so confident introducing the songs and played wonderfully. It was such a positive performance. The pressure seemed totally off him."

Back in England, he recorded a demo of a new song, 'Dreams Of You': "I was just playing around on a 12-string one day at home, and started playing Bach's 'Jesu Joy Of Man's Desiring', and Bruce walked in and said that it sounded really good. So I just added some words and put a rough demo down before I returned to America. When I came back for Christmas, I got Rod Clements in to overdub some

bass and mandolin, and we put it out. It was quite an honour to see the credits as a joint Bach/McTell song!

"It was a simple little song about comparing the memory of someone from a long time ago with an old tune going around in your head. It sold 90,000 copies and got to about Number 30 in the charts. They asked me to do *Top Of The Pops* again, which surely would have put it into the Top 20, but I never really believed in the song, so I didn't do it."

In January 1976, McTell went into the studio with legendary producer Shel Talmy, who had previously worked with the Who and the Kinks in the 1960s. The pair had met via American lawyer Marty Machat, and Ralph had felt that using other people's songs as well as his own would enable him to sing in different styles and perhaps go on to other things. As it happened, Talmy was himself looking for a similar project.

McTell: "I was introduced to Shel because it was felt the reason my records weren't selling in America was that I needed an American producer. The (record company) felt that the album would be more geared to the American market, but I thought that philosophy was wrong. If you want to sell to the Germans, you don't need a brass band on every track, you don't need accordions to sell records in France…

"Shel worked very, very hard and put together a very commercial, middle of the road album. That's what it was, MOR, and when I heard it I was very upset. It put me in a difficult position, because I didn't want to hurt Shel's feelings."

The sessions lasted over a month and the album was completed and mixed, but the results were not to McTell's liking. "It was the correct move to ask for a second remix. After all, it's one of the things you work for in this business, the right to say no if things are not quite right. It was my fault. I take full blame. I should have been stronger and stopped it immediately I realised it wasn't going to work, but due to the events following 'Streets', I was still unsure of myself."

To describe the album as unrepresentative of what Ralph McTell was about is a massive understatement. The production was of the standard expected from someone with Talmy's pedigree, and the musicians, including legendary guitarist James Burton from Elvis Presley's band and pedal steel player Hank de Vito (who, like Burton, was a member of Emmylou Harris's Hot Band at the time) played impeccably. But the album was closer to Don Williams than anything one might expect from a Croydon Cowboy.

Among the original songs recorded were 'Tequila Sunset', 'Another Star Ascending (The Boxer)', 'Van Nuys (Cruise Night)', 'Country Boys', 'Big Tree' and 'Winnie's Rag'. Also laid down were 'I Recall A Gypsy Woman' (which Talmy had introduced to Ralph, but which became a hit for Don Williams), Randy Newman's 'Marie', the classic Jim Reeves weepie, 'He'll Have To Go', Patsy Cline's 'I Fall To Pieces', 'Ladies Love Outlaws' (written by Lee Clayton and included in the repertoire of Waylon Jennings), 'Don't Make Promises' by Tim Hardin, a new original song, 'Sweet Girl On My Mind', and the neo-traditional 'Abilene'.

"We tried an experiment doing some old country songs," Ralph concludes, "but it just didn't work out. I'd have liked to do some of them again, but in England we haven't the players to do those kind of things. I made the mistake of recording material for which I didn't really feel much enthusiasm just to make up an album, and neglected my own songs because my confidence was low. Looking back, putting things on like 'Winnie's Rag' and 'Big Tree' just didn't fit in with the rest of the material, so I just ditched the whole thing. But looking back at working with Shel, I knew him as a great producer and I still think he is. It just didn't work between us."

However, Wizz Jones heard it differently: "I remember Ralph playing me some of those tracks he'd done with Talmy, and I thought they were good. I felt that it could have opened doors for Ralph in the country music scene and in America, but he wasn't having any of that." Two of the tracks from the Talmy sessions did see the light of day, 'Sweet Girl On My Mind' as the B-side of 'Heroes And Villains' in 1979, and 'I Fall To Pieces' as a single in 1982.

In the middle of January 1976 McTell commenced a 15-date tour that fulfilled some of the commitments postponed the previous year. After the opening concert at Folkestone, he explained his feelings: "All I'm trying to do is feel my way back into a position where I'm really happy performing. I'm still not really sure of myself. The audiences were great, but I've got to do a few more before I start making decisions." 'Streets Of London' reappeared on the set list and, at his concert in Derby, was introduced thus: "If you haven't heard this song before, you must have been living in Outer Mongolia for the past ten years. It's one I've stopped running away from."

Following the tour, McTell topped the bill at the Montreux Folk and Jazz Festival, which also featured Leonard Cohen and Tom Paxton, making further appearances in Scandinavia as well as a sellout show at the Royal Albert Hall, before heading off to Australia and New Zealand for his first tours of those distant lands. Here was a chance to try out some of his new songs. like 'Weather The Storm', 'Tequila Sunset' (which was released as a single to coincide with the tour) and 'Naomi' (or 'Nail Me' as the reviewer from the *Christchurch Press* called it). For his concert in Sydney, a clause in the contract was included at McTell's instigation stating that complimentary tickets were to be issued to local buskers. The idea of a live album had been mooted and his performance at the Sydney Opera House was recorded. Reviews of the concerts were good, and the tour had proved the tonic he needed.

Following the unsuccessful Talmy sessions, McTell continued to prepare songs for the next album – a release which, after the trauma which had followed the success of 'Streets Of London', had to be of the highest standard.

Prior to an Australian tour, McTell had taken a batch of new songs into Air Studios to begin recording what would eventually become 'Right Side Up'. Co-producing again was Peter Swettenham, who had worked on the 'Streets' album sessions. McTell considered it imperative to work with a producer who was familiar with his work, especially after Shel Talmy's ideas of how he should sound. Also, having friends like Danny Thompson and Dave Pegg present helped give the recording sessions a relaxed atmosphere.

The result was that when 'Right Side Up' was released, it showed that no permanent damage had been caused following the depression of 1975, and was also one of McTell's best albums to date. There was a confidence in his singing, while the new songs showed a continuing maturity. "I needed to put my own identity on it. I'd been asking myself a lot of questions over the past two years. This is the first album I've made where I've stated my case." The title of the album was designed to emphasise the positive feelings, and was suggested by Bruce May: "You've come down heads, you're right side up."

'Right Side Up's songs echoed to how he had felt over the previous year. 'Chairman And The Little Man' may appear on the surface to be a rather lightweight, but it hints at the struggle between artist and big business which he had experienced following 'the hit'. The album also contained two songs that would become his most requested and popular songs for many years to come, 'From Clare To Here' and 'Naomi'.

"'From Clare To Here' came from a little incident many years back when I was working on the building sites in London. There were a lot of Irish lads there, and they would keep themselves to themselves and socialise within their own groups. It was an achievement if they accepted you. Anyway, one day I was working alongside one of them down in the trench and, while stopping for a blow, I just said to him 'It must be strange for you lads to be here all that way from home' and he stopped and sort of gazed past me and said 'Aye. It's a long way from Clare to here.' And that always stuck in my mind. I somehow knew it would result in a song that would say something about these lads who have left their homes to come over here for work, yet still dream of making enough to return to their homeland."

The song has become a standard, recorded by innumerable Irish artists. Yet 17 years later, it received its biggest airing to date when Nanci Griffith covered it on her highly acclaimed 'Other Voices, Other Rooms' album. It was also released in Europe as a single. "I've loved that song since I first heard it," Griffith reveals. "I've known Irish people the world over, and they've all had that same sad expression in their eyes when they talk about their homeland. Only later, when I got to really know Ireland myself, I could then see what that sadness was about, and the way they missed their beautiful country. 'From Clare To Here' perfectly sums up that feeling of homesickness and longing.

"Oddly enough, I'd always believed that Ralph was Irish. That sums up the excellence of the song in the way I felt only an Irishman could have written it. When it came to my recording, we had all these different versions of the song, and by the time I'd got through them they were all beginning to sound different and far removed from Ralph's original recording. So we contacted him and said 'Come on, send us your favourite version of the song', and he sent one of his own recordings. I agree that him doing it is the definitive way."

Christy Moore also has reason to recall the song: "One time, Ralph told me that he had nearly finished a song he thought would suit me down to the ground, and he'd let me know when he'd finished it. I waited, but never heard any more. Then the Fureys had a big hit in Ireland with a Ralph McTell song. It was 'From Clare To Here'. I wished I'd have got it!"

'From Clare To Here' was also the starting point for McTell's long association with John 'Jonah' Jones, a man who'd been involved in the music scene for years, mainly working with rock'n'roll acts. "I'd worked with people like Long John Baldry and Georgie Fame in the 1960s, but I was really impressed with Wizz Jones and began to get more and more interested in the acoustic folk and blues scene. Alan O'Leary, who became one of Ralph's road managers, later asked me to work on one of the Fleadhs, so I got interested in how the tradition still ran within the anglicised Irish in London. It gave me a tremendous insight to folk music.

"One night in the mid 1970s I was at the Nag's Head folk club in Battersea and remember Wizz Jones coming in one night with this tall guy, dressed all in black with an air of mystery about him. He was very quiet and shy. He got up and played, and I was really impressed. That was the first time I met Ralph. Shortly after that, I went to see him at the Royal Albert Hall and thought he was amazing. I was caught in particular by a song he did that night that would stay with me for ever, called 'From Clare To Here'. I wrote in my diary that night that if he was ever to have another hit record, then that would be the song that would do it.

"There were covers of it by the Fureys and Noel Murphy. And it wasn't until 1993 when Nanci Griffith played at the Royal Albert Hall and asked Ralph to play it with her that I remembered that diary."

'Naomi' also instantly stood out when the album was released. Dealing with a couple who had grown with each other in the confines of a lifelong relationship, it has remained one of McTell's most requested songs. Ralph: "We had decided one day to go visit some elderly relatives but wanted to surprise them, mainly so that they wouldn't go to too much effort on our behalf. Unknown to us, another side of the family decided to do exactly the same. So there was this situation where there were lots of children from both families all running around together making so much noise.

Below: Ralph and Jessie.

Bottom: Ralph's 1934 Rudge bicycle, purchased from the Royal Military Academy at Sandhurst, bearing the registration RA1!

"While I was driving home, I wondered what the couple must have been thinking now everybody had gone and all the noise too, and the quietness had returned to their lives once again. It is about other relationships too, where as the years go by and the inevitable changes happen, communication takes on different forms, where just a glance or a touch can say more than any words."

Surviving from the Shel Talmy sessions (though re-recorded) was 'Tequila Sunset', while 'Country Boys' (omitted from 'Streets', much to McTell's annoyance) finally made it onto record and was also re-recorded. John Martyn guested on 'River Rising', and McTell reciprocated with a version of Martyn's classic 'May You Never'. 'Weather The Storm', which was released as a single, could almost have been a wry look in the mirror at having survived the past year with a telling line 'when the break has mended, it can be stronger than before'.

The record sounded positive and confident, yet reviews were mixed. Colin Irwin in *Melody Maker* complained "It's frustrating because it could have been *the* Ralph McTell album. It doesn't make it because the man is in the middle, playing it too safe."

Following the release of the album, McTell played a few dates and recorded a BBC-TV *In Concert*. Reviews of the shows were varied. Summing up the performance at London's Imperial College on 20 November, *Sounds* writer Christopher Middleton stated that the set McTell was now presenting had become too cosy, unexciting and uninspiring, and there was a danger that if things didn't change, it could result in a slide back down from major concert halls to clubs. Yet *Melody Maker's* Karl Dallas considered the new songs to be strong and praised McTell's ability to hold an audience. He added "It was one of the most beautiful and inspiring concerts I have been to." If Ralph was unsure about the future, then so were the critics.

McTell, however, had every reason to be pleased with the reaction 'Right Side Up' had generally

received. It showed that the confidence was back and that the public had not forgotten him. Plans were made for major touring in the first six months of 1977, and January found McTell doing a week of shows in Germany with four appearances on local television before a return to England.

For many years now, the university circuit had provided McTell with the backbone of his audience, so the tour was split into two halves, with the first running from February to mid-March in front of the students, and then in May at major theatres. But 1977 was the year when the music industry experienced its biggest revolution for many years. as punk exploded onto the scene. Anarchy in the UK was spreading, and few performers of McTell's type were expected to survive the revolution. Not that those who continued to go to see McTell bothered too much.

Supported by Magna Carta, McTell contained to deliver what his audiences had come to expect. The *New Musical Express* review of the show at Bristol University mused: "It all could easily be a university gig ten years ago. The old and new songs tend to sound too indistinguishable. I was bored." Yet just a fortnight later, *Sounds'* Howard Fielding commented on the packed Bath University audience who "managed to maintain a breathless silence during the songs and their introductions which only a great performer can command."

After the tour, McTell and classical guitarist John Williams gave a charity concert at the New London Theatre in opposition to the Chilean Junta. The concert was organised in memory of Chilean folk singer Victor Jara who, after the military coup in 1973, was arrested and beaten to stop him singing for the other prisoners. After he was shot dead, his hands were chopped off as if to signify that his spirit would never be able to play guitar again.

Two days later, McTell found himself back in Australia at the start of his second tour there. Following the success of the previous year's performances, 15 shows had been set. But restlessness was starting to creep in. Speaking to the press in Sydney, McTell started to yet again express doubts: "I've done all I can in England. I've done this for ten years and made a lot of money out of it, had a lot of fun and a lot of downers as well. I want to try something new."

One week into the tour, in Perth, his voice failed. A doctor told him that the best cure was not to sing for at least four days, and then asked for tickets for that night's show! Aided by brandy and milk, McTell got through the next few nights in Adelaide and Melbourne before returning to Sydney where he ran into Douglas Fairbanks, Stanley Holloway and Stephane Grappelli over the course of the day. Next stop America.

After a 22-hour journey from Sydney via Auckland and Hawaii to Los Angeles, he was met by Bruce May. "I put a lot of pressure on Bruce to get me back to the States to work," Ralph recalls, "because I felt we were losing touch with people there. I wanted to get back, even if it was only club work, and even if I had nothing to sell. The tour was very low-key, but you have to start somewhere." Four shows were played at the famous Troubadour in Los Angeles, during which time a visit to pedal steel player 'Red' Rhodes's Guitar Shop led to the purchase of an old Fender Stratocaster. Ralph shared the bill at the University of California with fiddle player Byron Berline.

McTell then moved on to San Francisco, Chicago, Philadelphia, turning Americans on to Old Holborn rolling tobacco wherever he went, before the final stop at the Bottom Line Club in New York, where he was watched by an enthusiastic crowd including John Prine and Steve Goodman.

A week in Europe preceded the second part of the English tour of major halls. McTell had returned from the American jaunt on a high: "I have been enjoying going to new territories tremendously," he told the press as the tour began. "I have reached the point where I have more confidence and I feel I can work with other musicians, but I must break the mould. I hope to play electric guitar as well as acoustic. I believe using a band will lead to a change of style. I want a group as tight as an American band." But for these shows he was accompanied by just Dave Pegg on bass.

Shortly afterwards, McTell appeared at the 13th Cambridge Folk Festival. A lot had happened since his only previous appearance in 1969: "In a way, Cambridge is where it all started for me. I am always grateful for what Ken Woollard did for me." Following Woollard's death in 1994, McTell performed at a tribute concert at the Royal Albert Hall (with Christy Moore and Loudon Wainwright III) and closed the 30th Cambridge Festival in July that year.

August saw the release of 'Ralph, Albert And Sydney', the result of the previous year's live recordings from concerts at the Sydney Opera House (where 80 per cent of the album was recorded) and the Royal Albert Hall. It captured McTell perfectly with a mixture of songs, rags and anecdotes, and reviews hardly contained an adverse comment. In addition, two 'new' songs appeared – 'Winnie's Rag' and 'Big Tree', both originally recorded with Shel Talmy – and, despite being somewhat throwaway songs, they fitted in well.

Also unleashed upon the public was an example of McTell's Joplin-esque ragtime piano-playing on 'Five Knuckle Shuffle', a nod in the direction of one of Tubs' sayings which brought a wry smile to a few south Londoners, and a brief instrumental version of 'Waltzing Matilda'. *Sounds* called the album: "A must for the fans," while *Melody Maker* simply described it as "outstanding".

Releasing a live album is often a sign that an artist has run out of ideas, a device to keep the record-buying public happy or a contract-filler. However, Bruce did not see 'Ralph, Albert And Sydney' fitting any of those categories. "This is a guy who has sold out the Sydney Opera House and the Royal Albert Hall. Just listen to the applause on that record! Basically, what we were saying was that we may not be making commercial records for Warners, but this is a commercially viable act."

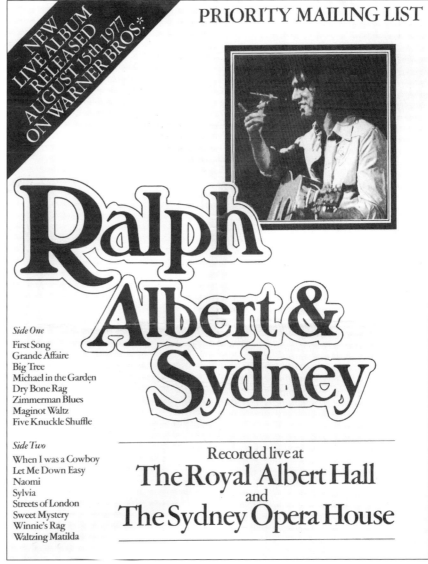

PRIORITY MAILING LIST

NEW LIVE ALBUM RELEASED AUGUST 15th 1977 ON WARNER BROS.*

Ralph Albert & Sydney

Side One
First Song
Grande Affaire
Big Tree
Michael in the Garden
Dry Bone Rag
Zimmerman Blues
Maginot Waltz
Five Knuckle Shuffle

Side Two
When I was a Cowboy
Let Me Down Easy
Naomi
Sylvia
Streets of London
Sweet Mystery
Winnie's Rag
Waltzing Matilda

Recorded live at
The Royal Albert Hall
and
The Sydney Opera House

Chapter

14 Screens and Scenes

Before paying another visit to America, McTell again tried working with a band when he performed at London's Royal Festival Hall in March 1979 with the Fairport Convention rhythm section of Dave Pegg and Dave Mattacks plus Nigel Smith on keyboards and Mike Piggott (a survivor from the short-lived 'Streets' tour) on guitar and fiddle.

The mixture of well-known songs with a few covers thrown in appeared to go down well, but *Melody Maker*'s Karl Dallas questioned the wisdom of such change. "It's puzzling that he persists in performing with a band, almost as if he is determined to prove it can be done. So far, Ralph hasn't discovered the secret of how to do it. I suppose we'll just have to be patient while he goes on looking."

McTell then returned to America with Bert Jansch for a brief east coast tour. He later mused: "It was strange coming from England where, at the height of punk, everyone was saying that there isn't anything in acoustic music anymore and the singer/songwriter was dead. And there's me and Bert, with no hit records and no record-company promotion, finding over 1,100 people coming to hear us in Boston. It was tremendously rewarding."

One particular night on that tour holds memories for Bert Jansch. "We were playing some gigs with David Bromberg and his fiddle player, and were at a place called the Belle Star Lodge in Buffalo, upstate New York, and the audience there were completely out of control. The stage was about two foot by two foot, with one chair in the middle and the audience standing around it. It has got to be one of the craziest gigs I've ever done, and I'm sure it's the same for Ralph. It was bizarre!"

Indeed, McTell remembers it very clearly: "It was complete mayhem. The place was heaving, obviously expecting a band or something. Both Bert and I always played sitting down, and when Bert sat down to play the set, he just disappeared. David Bromberg saw this and said that it would be better, when I went on, if I stood up. So I did, and there were people literally two feet away from my face.

"When I'd finished my opening song, one says to me 'I really liked that'. And another guy a bit further along said 'Yeah, I did too'. They were breathing right at me. The bar staff there were completely off their heads. They had so much cocaine up their noses it was falling out onto the bar! God, it was a crazy scene."

McTell had been writing new songs over the past year, and started work on a new album in the summer of 1979 at Chipping Norton Studios in Oxfordshire. There was a definite plan to record with a fresh approach, using musicians who could capture a band feeling in the studio. The sessions had a Fairport Convention feel to

them, with past and present members Dave Pegg, Simon Nicol, Dave Mattacks, Jerry Donahue and Richard Thompson among those contributing.

Produced by Bruce May and Dave Pegg, the results were released the following March under the title of 'Slide Away The Screen', and the finished article was unlike anything McTell had released before. Here was the sound he'd been searching for since he'd first toured with a backing band four years previously. There was a modern freshness about the overall sound and the production was bright. Oh, and there were some good songs too!

With uptempo tracks like 'Love Grows' (written for his two youngest children, Tom and Billy) and 'Heroes And Villains', the album featured a real variety of sounds. McTell turned in a delightful version of Dave Swarbrick's 'White Dress', respectfully dedicated to the late Sandy Denny. "When I asked Dave if I could change the words, he readily agreed and generously gave me a writing credit. The song alone is a tribute to the guy as it means a lot to people who have read more into it than perhaps Dave intended.

"I first met Sandy at 'Les Cousins' in the 1960s. She could be difficult. So many facets of her personality were in conflict with the inner one that emerged through her songs. She could be one of the boys on the surface, yet carry the ache of the artist's responsibility just underneath. At her best, she was heartbreakingly beautiful, her smoky, sexy voice cracking in just the right places to touch the emotional heart of the song. At her worst, she stretched the patience of those who loved her to

In the office at Charlewood Road, Putney.

despair. Those who are really honest would not have been surprised that she died so young, possibly before her best work, but the tragedy of losing her leaves a gap that will never be filled. I still cannot listen to a whole album of hers all the way through."

Probably one of the best songs he had written of late was 'Traces', a string of bitter-sweet memories sung alone at the piano, that produced a powerful performance. But there were a couple of older songs too: 'Van Nuys (Cruise Night)' had been originally recorded in 1976 with Shel Talmy, and `Harry (Don't Go)' had been performed on his 1977 tour.

"Harry was a member of my crew on the 'Streets' tour in 1975. He was from Guyana, and was a great guy to have on that tour as he could have a marvellously calming effect on us all. Anyway, after the tour we all went our separate ways, and later I ran into him and found he was currently working in an old people's home. His methods of dealing with people, many whom were very set in their ways, were somewhat off the wall, but he won a lot of them over with that way of his. Backed against a lot of racist feeling in Britain in the mid-1970s, I wrote him this song." Rounding the album off was a fun version of the Drifters classic, 'Save The Last Dance For Me', which its co-writer, Doc Pomus, told Ralph was one of the best versions he had ever heard. (However, legend has it that Doc Pomus is famous for saying this to everybody who covers his songs!)

Things continued to happen with 'Slide Away The Screen' after it first appeared in 1979, for the album was later released in two more versions. In 1982, McTell re-release it under the title of 'Love Grows' on the Mays Records label in a remixed and remastered form. "I just thought that the original sounded a little too cluttered, and thought that putting a bit more air between the vocals and the instrumentation would add a lot more, because I thought it was as good an album as I could come up with and those sessions were among the most enjoyable I had ever done.

"We gave the tapes to an engineer called Martin Levan, and he brightened the sounds generally, and gave a lot more space to the overall sound. With the track 'Love Grows', I felt I'd taken it a little too slow, so we speeded up the track, re-recorded my voice so it was a semitone higher, and then remixed it at that speed." The running order was changed, and two songs, 'Van Nuys (Cruise Night)' and 'Save The Last Dance For Me' replaced by 'Banjo Man' and 'If I Don't Get Home', which had been originally recorded with a band and was re-recorded for this release.

The 'new' songs were a welcome addition, but the remix took away much of the overall force of the original album's sound. 'If I Don't Get Home', a heartfelt cry from the road, of being away from home with a yearning to be back, fitted in with a sleeve now showing photos of Ralph with his four children. 'Banjo Man' was a spirited uptempo number in tribute to American banjo player Stephen Wade.

Finally, 1994 brought a second re-release on Road Goes On Forever Records, again titled 'Slide Away The Screen' and digitally re-mastered by Ralph and Martin Allcock from Fairport Convention. The original running order was restored, along with the additional two songs from 'Love Grows' and three further previously unreleased songs from the sessions, the most interesting of which was 'I Wish I Could Pray'.

"Religion has always flitted in and out of my life, and this linked in, I guess, with 'Mrs Adlam's Angels' as a feeling of lost faith. I did have plans to add a gospel choir originally, but we never got around to it. Bruce always felt I would have alienated a lot of people who held deep religious beliefs if I had gone ahead and released the song on the original album, but I don't know."

It echoed gospel hymns and was reminiscent of the sort of song to which the late

Richard Manuel (of the Band) would have done justice. The other two added songs were 'Trouble I'm In' and 'Looking Over My Shoulder For You' – and, while it's interesting to hear them, it's also clear why they were left off the first two versions of the album.

The spirit of the recording sessions were to remain as a focal point for where McTell next went. In 1981, he reunited with Messrs Pegg, Mattacks and Thompson under the guise of the GPs. Time to strike up the band once again? "It all started to become a real possibility at those sessions. But even before that, the other guys in Fairport had become rather reverential towards Richard, who had become a private person, whereas they had their bonds firmly formed with the drink, the *craic* and so forth. And when Dave Pegg was suggesting musicians for the sessions, he mentioned Richard and I said 'Sure'. I didn't know the man, and didn't know if he'd want to do it, but when I phoned to ask him he said he would. As the sessions went by, he started to join us in the pub, though he didn't drink. But I forget who actually suggested we form a band. It sort of just grew."

The GPs were very much a group, all four members making equal contributions. While they did perform some of McTell's and Thompson's songs, they were able to incorporate everything from Smokey Robinson to Hank Williams on stage. The name of the band originated from Dave Mattacks. These were the heady days of punk, where bands selected names for their shock value – and with the Dead Kennedys on the loose, the recent assassination attempt on Pope John Paul led to the Grazed Pontiffs (GPs for short).

"We rehearsed the GPs for over a month or so at Ralph's house," Dave Pegg recalls, "and they were great rehearsals. We'd start early afternoon in one of the upstairs bedrooms with the drum kit, and Nanna would be downstairs cooking dinner for everybody, which we'd eat about eight o'clock…by six, the smell drifting up from the kitchen was driving us crazy! It was such a fun thing to do, as we knew it was never going to be a permanent band."

Once again, McTell was in a position to work live on stage with other musicians, although this time the pressure was not as great: he no longer had to be 'Ralph McTell, Songwriter', but could be Woody Guthrie, Eddie Cochran and Hank Williams all on the same night. The mood was right, and having a real pal in the band in Dave Pegg was a contributory factor to the good spirit and occasional mayhem.

Dave Pegg: "After dinner each night, Ralph and I would go down to the Half Moon, where we'd drink a fair bit before returning, opening the odd bottle of wine and putting the world to rights until about five in the morning. At this time, Ralph had got the jogging bug and was going out each morning no matter what state he had got into the night before. One morning I was determined to join him, and despite a huge breakfast and Ralph's attempts to talk me out of it, off I went on Putney Common with him. I kept up with him for about 15 minutes, and then I started having palpitations, and when we got to this bridge over a little river, I said 'I can't go on. I've got to stop.' I was so hung over I leaned over the bridge and was sick right over the edge.

"Now I've got a plate in my mouth with my front tooth on, and I'm afraid it went over the edge with everything else into the river. Ralph's really worried, grabbing me and saying 'Dave, Dave, are you all right? ' And I'd say 'I'm sure I will be, but it's my tooth. It's gone down there and we've got a gig tonight!' He clambers down the bank and lo and behold, finds my plate, washes it in the river and brings it back up to me triumphantly! If *that* isn't a sign of real friendship, I don't know what is!"

That the legendary career of the GPs lasted just five shows may partly be to do with Jo Lustig's presence putting a stop to Richard Thompson's further involvement. Those shows were performed during the summer of 1981 at the Tramshed in Woolwich, the Half Moon in Putney, Horsham Town Hall, the Fairport Convention Reunion at Broughton Castle in Oxfordshire and a not so memorable visit to Ireland for the Ballysodare Festival.

John Jones was stage manager there as well as at Broughton Castle. "Karl Dallas said in his review of the Broughton Castle gig that if you missed the GPs, then you've missed one of the greatest musical events ever. I agree totally, but they didn't think so at Ballysodare. They sent a van to the airport that was so small the gear had to go on the roof with the lads inside. They got halfway there, the weather got worse and they needed some polythene sheeting to cover the gear. So they pulled over under a tree, and the driver said he'd go and try to find something to use. He left the lads in the van for hours, and it was freezing cold. Eventually the bloke comes back, and they ask if he's got the cover. The bloke says 'No, lads, couldn't find anything, but I got some chips as I'm starving. Anyone want one?'"

McTell: "That was a total disaster. We played to absolutely bewildered faces. It wasn't what they expected and they just didn't like it at all. It broke the lads' hearts. I thought it was great, myself. Maybe if we had played more of Richard's or my stuff, we might have got away with it."

Dave Pegg: "We got to the hotel pre-gig, threw our stuff into a room and went down to the bar. I said 'We'll have just one pint of Guinness', because we wanted to be on our best behaviour, and then went off to soundcheck. The reception we got wasn't great, and we all thought we were dying a death. Afterwards, we were in the festival bar and then went back to the hotel and the bar there was really jumping. Ralph and I then sat in this circle along with about 30 other people, drinking Guinness, telling stories and singing songs, generally all having a hoot. All of a sudden, I looked at my watch…it was five to nine the next morning and Ralph and I were still at it.

"There was this guy sitting next to me who I'd been talking to for a couple of hours, and he'd been keeping up with me as I'd had about 12 pints by then, and I said 'Oh shit. It's five to nine! Sorry, mate. Ralph! Quick, drink up, we're going to have to go. The van's leaving at nine!' and the guy next to me, who'd had as much as I had, says in a broad Irish accent 'Oh don't you go worrying about it, now. I'm the driver. We'll go when I'm ready!'"

Chapter *15* *Water of Dreams*

The early 1980s were difficult times for singer-songwriters like Ralph McTell. The punk-rock explosion of the late 1970s had left many of the old guard terminally 'unhip' and as the decade began, the sound of synthesisers and new romantics had left thoughtful lyrics and acoustic guitars very much yesterday's news. Many still regarded McTell as a 'folk' musician, which was light years away from what the youth of the 1980s wanted.

It was hardly surprising that at this time McTell was fairly disinterested in looking for new directions with his music. He continued touring, but the fact that his contract with Warner Brothers had expired, and major labels weren't exactly queuing up to sign him, can hardly have helped inspire him. He had continued writing songs but was unable to finish many of them and was surrounded by loose ends.

Unexpected light relief came in late 1981 when punk quartet the Anti-Nowhere League released their version of 'Streets Of London' as a single. Prior to McTell's annual concert in aid of children's charities, the group decided to visit the writer in person, an occasion road manager Alan O'Leary recalls: "I'm wandering around backstage at the Dominion on Tottenham Court Road when suddenly these guys in leather punk gear appeared with the most unbelievable spiked haircuts imaginable. 'What the hell is *that*?' I thought.

"'We've come to see Ralph,' one said. 'We want to have our photo taken with him.' I tried very tactfully to get rid of them, having no idea how they'd found their way back there. I looked at these guys and thought 'They'll frighten the life out of Ralph if he sees this lot.' They frightened me!"

By 1980, McTell had reached the end of his contract with Warner Brothers and no renewal offer was forthcoming. For some time, the label had wanted another hit from him and, while he had great credibility and was still selling out theatres, he only generated small sales compared to the vast units groups like Fleetwood Mac were shifting. McTell and Bruce May saw the best way forward as releasing future McTell product on their own label. Mays Records took a year to set up, after which it was time to see if there was anything to release. McTell had one song that he was particularly pleased with – so pleased that he decided to release it as a single.

"'England' was, in some ways, influenced by the Irish, oddly enough, in the way they somehow convey the beauty of their land in many of their songs. I felt songs about England never reflected that feeling of beauty, you know, in things like 'Land Of Hope And Glory' and 'Rule Britannia'. I wanted a song that could be appreciated and enjoyed by anyone, whatever their ethnic background, who was born here. So I used the images of green hills running through city streets, that

England is a multi-racial land and tried to convey that through the song."

A great boost came in a phone call from Billy Connolly, who had heard a demo of the song and was really enthusiastic about it. "That was great as the Scots, as well as the Irish and Welsh, have sung about their own homeland with great passion throughout the years, and yet we English are a little too reserved in doing the same. I was pleased with that song."

'England' was the first release on Mays Records in 1981, but, unfortunately, the true meaning of the song was lost on most people. This became apparent in the spring of the following year when Britain went to war in what many felt was a rather fruitless conflict thousands of miles away in the Falkland Isles. A wave of jingoism was sweeping the nation and, for many, a song like 'England' matched the euphoria abroad in the land. A major record label became interested in the song for that very reason, and after some discussion, McTell only allowed its re-release after the troops had returned home at the end of the conflict. "No-one wants to make money out of that sort of thing. 'England' nearly made it as a hit, and in fact some people think it *was* a hit, so that'll do for me."

'England' succeeds in what McTell was attempting to convey. Here, again, he touches on images from the Great War of 1914–18 which interest him; we find an echo of Rupert Brooke, Britain's celebrated war poet, who in 1914 wrote: "If I should die, think only this of me. That there's some corner of a foreign field that is forever England", while McTell states:

> *What is it about you, that took men into war*
> *Rows and rows of crosses — who remembers why or what for?*
> *The corners of these foreign fields, the dust in them concealed*
> *Out of sight but not out of mind — don't you know that England feels?"*
> **('England', 1981)**

Live in Berne,
Switzerland.

What was needed now was a new album, as McTell realised: "I had been in and out of the studio for quite some time putting things down. Eventually I said to Martin Levan, who was engineering the recording sessions, that I was fed up doing things that seemed to be getting us nowhere. It had to come to an end, and we had to see what we could use for a record." Those recordings eventually formed the 'Water Of Dreams' album, which was released in the autumn of 1982.

Once again there was an impressive array of musicians of the calibre of Albert Lee, Richard Thompson, Dave Pegg and even Phil Collins on the album. Yet despite this, many long-time fans felt it sounded like a curious collection of songs of variable standard lacking the expected sense of unity. Among those songs, however, were two of the most hard-hitting and political McTell had ever written in the title track and 'Bentley And Craig' – and, in retrospect, the presence of these alone made 'Water Of Dreams' a worthwhile release.

STREETS OF LONDON

"Those events of 1952 never left me, despite me only being young at the time. I kind of felt with that song that it was always one I was going to write at some time in my life, if only about the sheer injustice of it all. I was inspired as well by Alan Clarke's documentary in 1972 called *To Encourage The Others*, which laid out the facts of the case very clearly, and that there were all these doubts. I wrote the song very much in the way Woody Guthrie would have done it – whether or not Derek Bentley used the words 'Let him have it' is debatable, but I did it in the way that it was 'let him have the gun' not 'let him have the bullet' which Woody would have done – he would have left the debate open, I felt.

"The more I played the song, the more intense I felt about it, and then the better I played it, because it's quite a tricky guitar part as well. Everywhere I've played throughout the world, I've had people come up to me afterwards who can't believe that it was a true event, and it did actually happen." 'Bentley And Craig' was rightly singled out as a key song when the album was released. Eventually, it came to the attention of Derek Bentley's sister, Iris, who throughout her life led a devoted campaign to obtain a full pardon for her brother from the British government.

She recalls a neighbour who had been to see Ralph playing at the Fairfield Hall in Croydon coming to see her. "She then told me that he had sung a song that night about Derek and that the audience just went completely quiet. All you could hear from the crowd was tears, you know, people sniffing. She said 'Iris, it was *magnificent*.' So I went to try and make contact with his management and they then sent me a tape: that was the first time I ever heard it.

"I felt a sense of shock when I listened to it. I couldn't believe somebody could put it together so well. It was so meaningful. Everything in those few minutes he's singing is told so truthfully. It is a remarkable song. I felt it really came from the heart. It's let a younger generation know about Derek's case, which is very important, and many people have got in touch with me, to help with my campaign, who've only got to know about it through hearing Ralph's song. There was another song written about the case by Elvis Costello, but I can say unquestionably that it is Ralph's song that has brought the greater response."

The influence of Woody Guthrie carried over to the album's title track, 'Water Of Dreams', which closely echoed Guthrie's 'Ballad Of Joe Hill'. The song touches on the subject of suspected miscarriages of justice, in this case relating to three people who died in police custody in the UK in the late 1970s and early 1980s. "I was shocked rigid by the reaction to 'Water Of Dreams'. It seemed to me that people were saying 'Well, Jimmy Kelly was a drunk, Liddle Towers was throwing punches at policemen and Blair Peach was a "leftie", so they got what they deserved.' The basic fact is that these people were unlawfully killed, yet there was no outcry.

"I suppose, looking back to Germany in the 1930s, when things were shifting radically to the right, people were saying that they didn't know what was going on, and I saw all these things as symptoms of what is going on here, and that if you could put it so that it would be a song about the people's individual conscience – the word 'police' isn't mentioned anywhere in the song – that if things worry you and you put them to one side, they will come back to you in dreams, they will not be ignored.

"I know that many people in my audience were shocked about me taking a political stand on that album. Bruce said to me once, with the best advice in the world, 'Don't sing that and "Bentley And Craig" in the same set.' I thought long and hard about it, and I told myself I had to do it. If I lost a few people, fine, but I may have gained a few."

> *If you can learn to live with your doubt*
> *You will soon learn to live with a lie*
> *But the questions will rise on the water of dreams*
> *And be washed to the shore*
> *To be seen by your sleeping eyes.*
> **('Water Of Dreams', 1982)**

It is a timeless song that, like 'Gypsy' and the later 'Peppers And Tomatoes', is a reminder that freedom is in danger of being lost if one does not remain vigilant. Another song that should be singled out on 'Water Of Dreams' is 'Song For Martin', written about his old friend from Croydon and Paris days, Tubs.

"In the years after Paris," Ralph explains. "Tubs had really got deep into using heroin and had become a totally unreliable guy, but despite that was so well loved by people that they all used to cover up for him. He was injecting pretty badly, to the point where he was running out of veins to inject into. He'd tried various heroin substitutes but was still drifting all over the place.

"He was living in a caravan in Devon when one night he came home drunk, knocked over the stove and fell asleep, and was burnt to death. It was such a waste as he's been such a great chuckling, wonderful character who'd always see the funny side of life before the drugs got hold of him."

> *Don't leave Martin alone tonight*
> *Just because he looks alright*
> *He's only got to pick up the phone*
> *And one of them guys in the car'll be round*
> *Give him just enough on account*
> *They know that he'll be back for more.*
> **('Song For Martin', 1982)**

Despite a determination to give his work a harder edge, things had started to slide away from McTell commercially. Attendances at shows were smaller, and he was in danger of becoming another 'turn' on the concert circuit. With no sign of a further breakthrough, the feeling was that he had become a reliable but predictable artist. There were continued appearances on television shows, but the image had become safe and almost too folky in most people's eyes.

However, one of the BBC-TV appearances, *6.55 Special*, included a gem that has sadly remained unrecorded. Filmed on the Severn Valley Railway in Shropshire, McTell performed an excellent tribute to the pioneers of steam trains called 'Stephenson And Watt' as well as a Sonny Terry/Brownie McGee-influenced blues shuffle, 'Steam Train'. But these were rarities tucked away where many potentially

interested listeners would miss them. If ever a radical rethink in terms of future direction was needed, it was now.

One small but very significant practice pioneered on the concert tours in the early 1980s was that McTell would actually meet and greet his audiences after the show. Road manager at the time Alan O'Leary had done a tour with Tom Paxton and seen him do it. "It became almost an essential part of his gig, the little after-show appearance to say hello to people. Not everyone can do it –- you've got to have the ability to talk to people and Ralph definitely has that. I'd say 'Look, they're lovely people out there who have made a great effort to come out and see you. They're not going to bite you.' He's naturally very shy.

"He fought like crazy before he started to do it. I'd say 'What else would you be doing? Sitting in the dressing room having a fag?' It was such a positive thing to do. And as he did it more, the better at it he got. It amazes me to this day that wherever we went, no matter what town we were in, he remembered everybody's names who came up to him."

John Jones also saw the positive effect this had on his audience. "He'd be up there on his own playing for 90 minutes plus, and then he comes off exhausted and hot and he's got to come out and face the public. Not an easy thing to do after a show. But he'd do it. That contact with people is very important: the guy is one of the best guitar players in the land, and there would always be people out there who would want to know how he does this and that."

O'Leary had become friends with McTell via Ralph's favourite watering hole, the Half Moon in Putney. Known for many years as a musicians' pub, it was a place he could keep in touch with normality. "It was my brother who met him first," O'Leary recalls. "He was running the folk club there and he'd tell me that Ralph used to drop by and see various acts at the club quite regularly. Often, he'd tell me, Ralph would put his head around the door and if there weren't many people in, he'd put a tenner into the takings box which was a nice touch. He'd also drop by some of the Irish sessions I put on at Fulham Broadway, and he really got into the music and would sometimes sit in and play as well as getting off on the general *craic* of the place.

"I got involved in making a tribute record to a guy called Des Donnelly, an amazing fiddle player who was tragically killed. Ralph learned of this project and, through his connections and contacts, put the wheels in motion. He'd go off on tour and then come back and pick it up again. It was mixed at Olympic Studios for a bottle of Irish whiskey. He gave up an awful lot of time on that project, and that's really where our friendship began."

As a working musician, McTell continued to tour extensively across Europe and the road continued to throw up varying adventures, just as it had in the 1960s. It might have been only ten years since he'd trodden the boards of the Royal Albert Hall, but the misconception that touring is part of a glamorous life was emphasised on his May 1983 tour of Austria, when he played a gig in Amstelten he remembers only too well.

"It was in a big pub with a big room with tables all set out. My dressing room was at the side of the stage and smelt very strongly of what I can only describe as manure! I went in and changed my strings and worked out my programme for the show, all the time aware of this unbelievable smell. I was relieved to get out of there when it was showtime – a quick schnapps, and I was into 'Pretty Boy Floyd' and on my way.

"The gig went very well – but after two encores I was dying to go to the loo, and there didn't seem to be anywhere to go. I pushed open the door in my room and there was indeed a great big pile of manure. I had no option but to aim for that! However, as soon as I did, I heard breathing sounds in the darkness and panicked, as I certainly didn't want to be caught this way by any fans.

"I cautiously pushed the door open wider, and there looking straight at me are two enormous pigs. I just couldn't believe it but there they were! Meanwhile, the audience are still shouting for more, so I just got out quick and went back on stage and did a couple more songs. Oh, the glamour of it all!"

On the same tour, he was asked to play at one of the oddest events he'd ever experienced. "The Longinus are people who are over one metre 90 centimetres tall, and there was this press conference at a hotel about them. I was to be made an honorary member and, despite being 'only' 189 cm, I was told it didn't matter. We

Receiving a sales award for the 'Streets Of London' sheet music.

went to the wrong hotel and, by the time I found the correct one, the press conference was over – which I was relieved to hear, as by now I wanted to get out of the whole daft event. However, they still wanted me to appear, so I'm put into this land of the giants where everyone is at least six inches taller than me – even the women.

"There's a TV guy there and he wants me to do a couple of verses of 'Streets Of London' and chat with a Longinus, which I reluctantly agree to. I'm just ready to do it, when in walks the tallest human being I've ever seen who was the champion Longinus, a Dutchman, standing at two metres 20 cm! After a chat, I'm just about to do my song when in walk about 50 of these giants who all tower above me, leaving me feeling like a gnome. I do the song, then they all converge on me for autographs. But worse was to follow. One of these guys had composed a song called 'The Longinus Blues' and they all want to sing it with me. What could I say? It was terrible, one of the worst songs I've ever heard.

"I did a brief radio interview, did a runner to the van and got out as soon as I could. Soon afterwards on the Salzburg road we hear the radio slot announcing that yours truly is 1 metre 95 cm tall, that I've now joined the Longinus Club and that, if you tune in tomorrow, you can hear me singing 'The Longinus Blues'. Thankfully, I never heard it – and hope no-one else did either!"

Ralph and the late Trevor Lucas.

Chapter
16 Child's Play?

Soon after his encounter with the Longinus, McTell was to embark on a new career that, while a resounding success, was to prove an even greater risk to his credibility. Granada TV had planned a children's programme with a six-month season of 26 ten-minute slots. Someone had the idea of structuring this round the alphabet, each programme featuring an animal whose name began with that week's letter. McTell had recently done some music for a Granada educational programme and, when they were looking for someone to do the music, one of the production team put his name forward.

"I told them that I wasn't interested in doing that type of thing but they persisted and said they'd really like to come and talk to me about it. Bruce was quite in favour of the idea and pointed out that being the father of four children did give me some experience of what children like on TV. Besides, Woody Guthrie and Leadbelly had done children's songs and it didn't harm them. The show's producer, Stephen Leahy, came down to London personally and assured me they didn't want me to dress up and act silly or anything like that. I could do the songs in my own style."

Ralph, Duster and Nerys Hughes.

McTell was immediately inundated with scripts from which he had to try to construct songs: "Some of them were really difficult. I think I was scraping the barrel a bit with 'Daphne The Dolphin', but it wasn't my idea. But some, like 'Kenny The Kangaroo' in particular, became enormously popular." Co-presenter on the programme was actress (and erstwhile *Liver Bird*) Nerys Hughes, who became an enormous source of encouragement to Ralph as he struggled to learn the ropes of regular TV work.

When the *Alphabet Zoo* series was broadcast in 1983, Granada had a success on their hands. Suddenly, Ralph McTell was being recognised on the streets again, only this time by children as well as adults: "My brief wasn't just to entertain children, it was to entertain unemployed Dad at home and alleviate Mum's boredom, so the songs may have had other meanings. Like 'Holly The Hedgehog', where no-one wants to sleep with her because of her prickles. I got away with that one. The kids hear it one way, and maybe Mum got a little smile out of it in another way."

Due to the success of *Alphabet Zoo*, 14 of the songs were released as an album on Mays Records, featuring Mike Piggott and the Lindisfarne duo of Rod Clements and Ray Laidlaw. A special song on the album was 'Sally The Seal', a duet between McTell and his youngest child, Billy, who was then aged three. (In 1994, Road Goes On Forever Records released 'The Complete Alphabet Zoo', a 78-minute CD with detailed notes indicating the depth of thought and care Ralph had put into the whole project.)

After a second series of *Alphabet Zoo* came another show featuring McTell this time in a slightly different setting as a resident of a fictitious town called Tickle, which nestled beside the slow-rolling River Tum. The series, called *Tickle On The Tum*, included star names like John Wells, Billy Dainty, Kenny Lynch, Penelope Keith, Willie Rushton and even long-time friend Billy Connolly all playing odd characters who dropped into the post office where Ralph sang his songs, helping to add some credibility to this rather inane show.

McTell called time on his career as a children's TV presenter after two series, yet old friend Wizz Jones had his own views: "I thought he was mad to pack in the TV role he had created. Once you've got your face known to people, you're there. It could have led to all sorts of things for him. He was a natural, and I thought he was very good at it. I'd have jumped at the chance to get something like that."

Whatever one's opinion of McTell doing children's television, the care and craft that he put into the numerous editions of *Alphabet Zoo* and *Tickle On The Tum* has to be commended. While many would see the job as money for old rope, he went about the projects with the same levels of seriousness and effort that were a feature of his regular composing. However, seeing him as a 'children's entertainer' was, for many, an indication that he had embarked on the slippery slope to oblivion.

It was, indeed, rather odd to observe one of the world's best guitar players using his skill gleaned from Blind Blake to tell the tale of 'Gordon The Goat', but if you forget the title 'Albert Ross The Albatross' stands up as a 'normal' Ralph McTell song. Many of the songs contain very correct and moral messages, and certainly, viewed on its own merits, McTell's children's TV work was of the highest standard, even though it seemingly helped alienate many of his long-time fans.

In the summer of 1983 Ralph fronted his own BBC Radio 2 series, *Ralph McTell And Friends*, which gave him the opportunity to perform with a host of fellow musicians like Billy Connolly, Mike Harding, Simon Nicol & Dave Swarbrick, Earl Okin, Alan Hull, Georgie Fame and Jake Thackray. He sounded a natural broadcaster and presenter, no doubt helped by his experiences with *Alphabet Zoo*.

A notable performance on one of the shows was one of the very first songs he'd ever written, titled 'To The Kentucky Miner (Alexei)'. Penned after the Soviet invasion of Czechoslovakia in 1967, it was an open letter comparing the lives of a miner in America and his Czech counterpart, and showed the singer's early political leanings.

In June 1984, McTell embarked on a tour of the North America where, despite never achieving the success his first visit in 1971 had promised, he had built up a cult following playing the club circuit. Following two shows in Bermuda, he moved on to Toronto to play a club called Larry's Hideaway ("The roughest place I'd ever been in since the Hotel du Commerce!"). Before the gig, while in a bar, he was discovered by members of China Crisis, in the city supporting Simple Minds, and promptly requested tickets for his show. It was satisfying that the younger breed of writers were still full of respect for his work.

After Toronto came New York, returning to play the Bottom Line club. Keeping a diary while on the road, his entry for that night reads "My support act is an

Bobby Binns (Billy Connolly) and Ralph on the set of Tickle On The Tum.

Ralph in the Tickle On The Tum *store, first series.*

extraordinary singer called Suzanne Vega. My set goes well. Every song is greeted with thunderous applause and, after one and a half hours, I come off to a standing ovation. I feel terrific. I'm visited backstage by Tom Paxton, Doc Pomus and Loudon Wainwright III."

Further shows were played to fairly small, but unanimously positive audiences. McTell has never taken his position as a performer of international status for granted. All he ever really wanted to do was to tell the truth via his writing and show some compassion for people through his work. That is why he has never been able to brush off criticism easily. If they are dismissing his words, they are questioning his intent. This whole feeling of being misunderstood hangs heavy over him at times, even to the present day.

His diary on the road in America reveals the feelings he has to the point where he questions himself and his ability. "It seems that I will never amount to anything here in the US without a radical rethink about my music. Whenever I play, I always go down well or very well, but this audience is used to excellence and, without the sense of occasion, I am only a part of the constant musical tapestry that they take for granted. Has my modest talent been pushed too far, spread too thin? What of the future? Will I ever write anything that captures the public concern?

"When I think back to Al Stewart, Bert Jansch, Roy Harper, John Martyn, they all believed in their work. I never did. I enjoyed crafting a song like a child with a lump of clay who pulls and prods it until it resembled something which grown-ups could admire, and after I had milked that offering I might have another go, and so on. This probably explains why there is no pattern to my writing, why it is not guided by any overall philosophy except trying to please people."

But by the beginning of 1986, whether he liked it or not, he was saddled with the reputation, in the eyes of many members of the public, as a children's TV presenter – reinforced, fairly or otherwise, when he provided the vocal for the title song for a TV adaptation of Kenneth Grahame's *The Wind In The Willows*. Meanwhile, Mays Records had secured the rights to his last three Warner Brothers albums. 'Slide Away the Screen' was retitled 'Love Grows' (with an amended running order), 'Right Side Up' became 'Weather The Storm', while 'Ralph, Albert And Sydney' retained its original title. Also re-released was his 1971 album, 'You Well Meaning Brought Me Here' as 'The Ferryman'. Despite this body of work being available again, it failed to re-establish the image of Ralph McTell as a serious singer-songwriter.

Also during this period, TV viewers heard McTell proclaiming the wonders of Skol Lager in a commercial based around a new composition, 'The Winner's Song'. Skol had commissioned some 36 writers, and Ralph's contribution won. The commercial was a hit on both on TV and radio, prompting Bruce May to suggest that McTell release his own version as a single. Ironic, since the singer is a keen real ale drinker!

But from this rather barren and confusing period came one of McTell's most under-rated, and largely forgotten, songs which showed his compassionate and socialist beliefs had not been lost in the Thatcherite 1980s, when unemployment rocketed at a pace not seen since the Depression and minister Norman Tebbit issued his invitation for the unemployed to 'get on their bikes' and seek work. Released as a single (which never stood a chance of making any impact on British radio, let alone the charts) 'Stranger To The Season' was a song in classic McTell mould that displays a major songwriter tempering force with compassion.

> *When the factories close down*
> *The life bleeds from the town*
> *Some politicians tell us*
> *'Move and build another home'*
> *But weren't they voted into to lead us?*
> *No-one said they had to feed us*
> *If they give us back our jobs*
> *Then we will take care of our own.*
> **('Stranger To The Season', 1983)**

The title came from old friend Billy Connolly, who had seen an Asian trade union delegate quote from Kahlil Gibran's *The Prophet* in his address to the Liberal Party Conference with a speech that used the line 'a man without a job is a stranger to the season'.

"Billy told me about the speech and I was moved by the poetic line about unemployment and what it does to a person. Unemployment is a downright disgrace and, in my belief, was planned by the Thatcher government of the time to keep people down and prevent strikes. Before that, people had been able to strike without fear. In the 1980s, suddenly there was massive police presence at many industrial disputes, I'm thinking of the miner's strike in particular, where labour disputes turned into open warfare all because of people standing up for what is their right: to withdraw their labour in order to improve their life and conditions.

"My belief is that work is a pulse to life and, without it, life is a grey nothingness. There's such a thing as pride. I'm not talking about people who don't want to work – there's always going to be them – I'm talking about people who really want to work in order to have a bit of pride in themselves."

Though we get by on the dole
It feeds the body, starves the soul
And stirs the bitterness that's growing
In the ones who've been betrayed.

One of the most famous record reviews in history is appeared in *Rolling Stone* magazine in 1970 when Greil Marcus, reviewing Bob Dylan's 'Self Portrait', opened with the question "What *is* this shit?" The album was a disappointing collection of mainly non-original songs no-one would have imagined Dylan ever recording. It's been suggested that its release induced him to return to his original label, Columbia Records, for fear of a second volume, though it seems unlikely that such an icon could allow himself to be blackmailed in this manner. McTell released his own 'Self Portrait' in 1985 under the title of 'At The End Of A Perfect Day' – the album he would be least proud of recording throughout his career.

Ralph in Brooklyn, New York.

McTell still had a fan base out there, but post-*Alphabet Zoo* the problem seemed to be getting people to listen to him as a writer of serious, crafted songs. If they weren't going to do it by means of a hit record, then other avenues had to be investigated, one of which was a TV-advertised album.

Mick McDonagh had been working with Telstar on similar projects, so Bruce May struck a deal with the label for them to do such a record with May working with McTell on the recording and McDonagh handling the business side. The idea was that Ralph would record other songs as well as some of his own, so a list of songs was mutually agreed between Telstar, Ralph and Bruce.

McTell spent the whole of the summer in the studio trying to work up enthusiasm for a project he'd been reluctant to undertake. However, Telstar were offering major advertising support and he could see the advantages if the project were to take off. However, he was unhappy about being offered songs like 'Bless This House', and his lack of enthusiasm can be heard in the finished recordings. Clearly McTell could not be poured so easily into such a commercial mould. After getting nowhere with the sessions, he drafted in Graham Preskett to try and rescue something tangible from what had been recorded, and with his help was able to complete the sessions.

The title, 'At The End Of A Perfect Day', was combined with a bland cover, the nausea-inducing subtitle '16 Songs Of Love And Friendship' and an awful illustration of Ralph walking down a cobbled street complete with a sweet little old lady looking on. If that wasn't enough, hearing McTell trying to do justice to such songs as Roger Whittaker's 'The Last Farewell', Lennon and McCartney's 'Penny Lane' and the Mary Hopkin hit 'Those Were The Days' was a sad and painful experience.

Despite including five of his own songs, the only decent thing to emerge was an inspired performance of the traditional 'Scarborough Fair'. Ralph: "That song gave me the chance to acknowledge Martin Carthy as having come up with the version that Paul Simon launched his career on. Myself and (ex-Cat Stevens guitarist) Alun Davies worked out Martin's guitar part and we got my daughter Leah to do backing vocals on it. So the record is a little keepsake for her in that way."

As if recording the album hadn't thrown up its own share of problems, then so too did the plan to film a TV commercial for it. Mick McDonagh: "The TV shoot was the biggest one I'd ever been involved in. We shot it in Wilson Street, north London, which, oddly enough, Bruce and I had lived in at various times. It was a night shoot, so we had to light it up using big arc lights on top of some nearby council flats. We also had to clear the entire street of all cars but, as we were ready to shoot, found that there was one remaining. After searching around, we found it belonged to Jo Durie, the tennis player, who was in a tournament in Flushing Meadow! So we had to call America and track her down. We also tried to do some photos for the cover but they didn't turn out very well and, for whatever reason, the cover became that awful painting."

Looking back on the project, McTell is in no doubt how he feels about it: "A totally commercial venture and a miserable failure. I had big discussions with Bruce and, while I was reluctant to do it, the possibility of getting the kind of back-up that Telstar were offering was too good to miss. I'm kind of relieved about its failure, in a way, as I'm trying to forget about that record. I've had fans come up to me and tell me that they cannot bear to listen to it."

If the project had worked, it might well have achieved what Bruce had hoped and given McTell a new lease of life in commercial terms. If, however, the artist has no real enthusiasm for the project, it is almost inevitably doomed to failure. It didn't help that K-Tel, another TV marketing label, used the title 'At The End Of The Day' for an album by Irish folk group the Fureys & Davey Arthur, resulting in an unfortunate coincidence – two TV-advertised albums being released almost simultaneously with very similar titles.

Playing his Keith Johns hand-made guitar.

Also, the McTell TV commercial was only shown in certain parts of the UK, and as a result Telstar were left with thousands of copies of the album which are still available at knock-down prices. All in all, it was a project undertaken with the best of intentions, but one which ultimately failed in every respect.

Chapter 17

Throw Out A Line

Continued touring kept Ralph's name in the public eye as the 1980s progressed, reinforced by radio work which was still coming his way. Alan O'Leary recalls a BBC session at Maida Vale: "Producer Johnny Gregory came in with the string arrangements, which looked more like a large book. A big curtain ran down the room, behind which to my amazement was a full orchestra – about 40 musicians in all – waiting for him to arrive. I was shaking in my boots. Ralph just went in there with his guitar and did everything straight off…there may have been one retake.

"The musicians went ape. Having been booked for three hours and finished in 45 minutes, they all headed for the bar. Another time we were doing a session at the BBC, and as I was taking the guitars in who should be coming out but Paul McCartney? He sees me with the guitar cases and says 'Who you with, mate?' I say 'Ralph McTell'. 'McTell! What guitars have you got?' He recognised the name as a player of renown."

Finally, after a year of gathering material, McTell was once again in a position to go into the studio. The result was 'Bridge Of Sighs', released in 1986, an album which thankfully showed that McTell remained a songwriter of considerable ability. He later reflected: "The hardest part of creativity for me is decision, and I brought that to bear on quite a few unfinished songs I'd found to be too complicated or which were leading me in a direction where I was going to end up with eight verses instead of the three I'd planned.

"I brought that new discipline into mind when selecting the songs. It was clear I had to have an 'adult' album out after all the kids' stuff of the past few years. And I wouldn't have been able to put that decisive way of thinking into practice had it not been for what I learnt in terms of confronting the problem when I was doing all the *Alphabet Zoo* and *Tickle On The Tum* songs. If I didn't have a guitar part or basic tune ready, I disciplined myself to press on with the lyrics.

"My writing has always followed the pattern that I write the tune first, then the lyrics, and adapt the tune to fit. But here I changed a lot of that. I had done it a few times before. With 'First And Last Man', 'Barges', 'First Song' and 'From Clare To Here', I wrote all the words before I had a melody and they all became quite important songs in my repertoire, so I knew I could do it the other way round."

Among the songs on 'Bridge Of Sighs' that had been around for some time were 'Bad Girl' from 1977-78, 'Holiday Romance' and 'Words I Couldn't Say' (both from 1979-80), while the title track was started in 1982. The album's key song, 'The Setting', saw McTell return to his Irish influences and told of someone leaving their home to explore new lands. Although the song is based on a girl departing, it unfolds to suggest that the narrator, the girl's brother who has gone to wish her *bon voyage*, has done it all himself before and returned home. The implication is that it failed for him, and he fears that it will fail again for his sister.

Inspired by the writing of Sean O'Faolain, it leaves the listener wanting to know more about what happens, illustrating the disciplined writing technique McTell described. Ironically, it was a long time before 'The Setting' was generally accepted by McTell's audiences, and the song spent years as an occasional inclusion in his live set. From the opening four lines, the lyrics immediately paint the scene in a most visual way, almost akin to the directions of a stage play. 'The Setting' is one of McTell's finest pieces of writing, with beautifully crafted poetic images scattered throughout.

> *And outside the trees grew starlings like apples*
> *Their hustle and chatter not dampened by the rain*
> *That washed down the pavements and into the gutters*
> *That soaked through my clothes as I set out again.*
> **('The Setting', 1986)**

Another song on the album, 'The Girl From The Hiring Fair', would become one of his most requested. Alan O'Leary had loaned Ralph a book called *The Children Of The Dead End* by Patrick Magill, which featured a scene where men lined up in fields to try to 'sell their labour'. But the song which the story helped to inspire was not written initially for McTell himself but Fairport Convention. "I felt they needed a song in the 'folk tradition', but not one where the hero gets drowned at sea or dies in a far-off foreign land, leaving the woman he loves behind forever. I based it on the hiring fairs that were prevalent at the turn of the century where both men and women would go and offer themselves for work on the farms – especially at harvest time.

"I finished the song and gave it to them, but word came back that they weren't too keen. I liked the song so I started performing it and eventually recorded it for the album. Then they decided they were going to record it after all and it came out on their 'Gladys' Leap' album." In fact, the group abbreviated the title of the song to 'The Hiring Fair'.

The rest of 'Bridge Of Sighs' featured a variety of writing styles. The title track was another powerful song that deals with conflict, two sides taking their own futile positions when reconciliation is so far away – yet by meeting halfway the world could be a better place.

> *Don't be afraid*
> *There is no disgrace*
> *No one's betrayed*
> *There's no loss of face*
> *In meeting on the bridge.*
> **('Bridge Of Sighs', 1986)**

Set to a driving backing which featured Richard Thompson on lead guitar, this again suggested McTell should take this sound on the road and belie his 'comfy' image. 'Little Actress' is about melodrama, how people will sometimes draw as much sympathy as possible from a crisis and play on their misfortune, while 'Mr Connaughton' was another visit back to his childhood, to the father-like figure he and Bruce recalled in the days at the Waldrons. But if McTell had experienced a difficulty in obtaining inspiration in recent years, this was to be one of the quickest songs he'd ever written, as he explained.

"I did a gig at the Barbican in London in the early 1980s, and onstage recalled the days of my childhood. Afterwards I went out to see some friends, and I noticed a young woman waiting. Eventually, she came up to me and said 'Hello Ralph. You don't remember me', which I confessed I didn't. She said 'Oh that's all right. You won't have seen me for 30-odd years', and introduced herself as Josephine Connaughton, the daughter of the Irishman from upstairs when I was a kid. All the memories of those days came flooding back. The next day I was alone at home, picked up the guitar and everything just fell into place. We had released it three years previously on the B-side of 'Stranger To The Season', but I felt it should be on the album."

'Bridge Of Sighs' was a strong album with expert backing from the Fairport Convention connection of Dave Pegg, Simon Nicol, Dave Swarbrick, Richard Thompson and Gerry Conway, as well as a newcomer, the multi-talented Martin 'Maart' Allcock, with whom Ralph would subsequently form a long-standing working relationship. Allcock had been called in to replace Dave Pegg, busy playing with Jethro Tull, "so I guess it was a bass session for me. I was given more or less a free rein to do what I wanted with Ralph giving me a few pointers here and there. I remember finding 'The Girl From The Hiring Fair' quite difficult to play as I was used to playing it with Fairport, where it has a slightly different chord sequence, but I got there in the end."

Backstage at the Albert Hall with the Everlys, 1987.

Also making a valued contribution to the sessions was guitarist Alun Davies. Their playing helped along some fairly uptempo numbers like 'Throw Out A Line And Dream', 'Something The Matter With Mary' and in particular the title track. A new recording of 'Dreams Of You' finally made it onto record at long last, and overall the album showed him to be in fine voice – but by 1987, McTell's career seemed to be on a downward spiral.

"The damage to his credibility during the years as a 'children's entertainer' had begun to bite deep into his audience figures. But out of the blue, he was given the opportunity to regain some credibility on a large concert stage, albeit as a support act.

Promoter Derek Block contacted Bruce with an idea he had conceived for a package to tour the UK. He wanted Ralph to support the Everly Brothers, as McTell recalls: "Bruce said to Derek 'But Ralph doesn't open for *anybody*', to which Derek replied 'I know!' When it was put to me, I said to Bruce 'Of course I'll do it.' It was like being asked to open for Buddy Holly. For me, it was touching base, as the first record I'd ever bought was by the Everlys. Their songs had sustained me in times of real misery and I'd loved singing them.

"I was treated like a kid, but I got the respect of the band, mainly due to the fact that Albert Lee, who'd played on 'Water Of Dreams', liked my guitar playing. Phil used to come and stand at the side of the stage after the second night because he'd heard the applause after 'Streets Of London', and he used to say to me 'Ralph, you're going down too well!' He brought Don down, who said to me 'You sure paint a pretty picture.' They were very kind and complimentary and they proved to be the most sociable big stars I've ever met. Every fourth night, they'd come and hang out with the band and have a beer with us. They were great fun and told some great tales about being on the road with Eddie Cochran and Buddy Holly. It went so well I got another tour with them."

McTell toured quite extensively after 'Bridge Of Sighs', but the working relationship with his brother was slowly drifting to a conclusion, and by 1988 was history. "It had been coming for some time," Bruce now admits. "Managing him through those years was an awful long time to stand in someone else's shadow, especially your brother's. When we split, I said to Ralph that it was either six months too soon or seven years too late…I would still be hard-pushed to say which. I firmly believe that he should have done another series of *Tickle On The Tum*, and then moved into late-night TV. Ralph's back catalogue is so vast that who knows what he could have achieved if it had been reworked to a new audience? I don't think there's a hatchet to bury between us, but more a common ground to be discovered. Looking back on my time managing him, what I can say is that from me he had total loyalty and total honesty. What he didn't have was the best professional advice."

Alan O'Leary recalls the period as "very acrimonious…Bruce used to say 'Well, when Ralph gives me something to work with, I'll go for it.' He was very good at some areas – if you gave him a record, he would get it played on radio. He'd storm into the BBC, get the job done. For Ralph, I know the writer's block he was experiencing was very frustrating. I used to remind him of the mess Thatcher was making of the country and try to cajole him into trying to say something about it all: 'Come on Ralph. We need people like you to write songs about what's happening,' but he always seemed to have excuses for everything. He'd say 'I can't write about that. Young people write about those sorts of things. I'm not young anymore.' He got himself into that frame of mind."

Clearly, McTell needed a direction – and into the picture came a face from the past, Mick McDonagh. "Following his break with Bruce, Ralph asked me to take over: it was very much on a loose basis, with no contract. From my point of view, I just wanted a one-to-one relationship where we would get on well with each other."

The proposal that the one-nighters should end in favour of formal tours did not meet with total approval from those around McTell. Alan O'Leary: "Where McDonagh came from, goodness knows. Where he snatched him from is anyone's guess. I asked Ralph this and why him, and he'd say 'Well, he's had the Fureys', and I'd say 'What? You want to be another Fureys?' I think he was setting his sights too low again. For me, Ralph is up there on ability with the likes of James Taylor and Joni Mitchell, that sort of songwriter, not an act like the Fureys."

Chapter
18

Blue Skies Grey Future

In the wake of of 'Bridge Of Sighs' in 1986, new songs were very slow in coming. After more touring in Australia, the US and Europe, McTell began recording what was a long-overdue album exploring his blues and ragtime influences. "When I was 15 or 16 and heard this stuff, it changed my life. Up until then I was a mere strummer, but it opened up a whole way of playing the guitar for me. I have to accept the fact that, as a boy from South London, I'm never going to have the blues voice I'd wanted all those years ago, but I do have the voice of a grown-up male, and singing and playing these songs is fun. It has a freshness about it that I really like. Recording those tunes was a way of acknowledging my debt to those people. and my wish is that it will turn people on to that music and they too will go on and develop an interest in it, as happened with me."

The album was recorded live at Raezor Studios in London in February 1988. Danny Thompson returned to play bass on four songs, but the rest was pure McTell as he was live. Titled 'Blue Skies Black Heroes', his own detailed sleeve notes explained his love and passion for the songs he'd recorded, which ran from Robert Johnson's 'Kind Hearted Woman' and 'Love In Vain' (the latter previously recorded by the Rolling Stones, among others) to Mississippi John Hurt's 'Louis Collins', the Muddy Waters classic 'Can't Be Satisfied' and Jesse Fuller's 'Working On The Railroad'.

"Jesse Fuller came to England in the 1960s at the time when interest in the blues was huge, and people seemed to be combing the United States for men who could still play in that style, but of course most of them had either died or were very old. Jesse was still around, and was in his 60s when he came over to England to play. He played nearby in Worthing and I missed him! But when I heard his records he blew me away. He was a railroad worker, and he evidently used to entertain the guys laying the track by playing to them."

Also finally on record was Blind Boy Fuller's 'Truckin' Little Baby', which opened Ralph's live shows during the 1970s. Additionally, two new pieces appeared, one being an instrumental, 'Leah's Favourite', so titled after his daughter commented on how much she liked the tune, and 'Arthur Blake', the tribute to Blind Blake who had been a lasting influence on his guitar style. "There wasn't much to know other than that, for some strange reason, he changed his name from Phelps to Blake, was born in Florida, moved to Chicago and in the late 1920s made some recordings. Armed with this wealth of material, I attempted to try to tell a little about him in a style as near as I could to his."

Danny Thompson thoroughly enjoyed working on 'Blue Skies Black Heroes', but has a message for McTell regarding any future tributes he may undertake: "I've said to Ralph, whatever may happen to me in future, do me a favour – when I die, please *don't* write a song about me. Please let me be different. In a world full of people who will let you down, he has already proved his worth to me and he has been unshakeable as a mate. And that's fine, enough that I know it. But please, don't write a song about me."

McTell promoted 'Blue Skies…' on a summer 1988 tour of England, taking with him a large collection of guitars. With no support act, he was able to showcase as many of the songs as possible, showing how black music's range of styles had influenced him with anecdotes about his discovery of the music.

The album underlined McTell's reputation as one of the best English guitar players with a feel and respect for the blues, gaining the approval of another great acoustic guitarist, John Renbourn. "For those that got into Ralph's music a bit later and know him mainly as an outstanding contemporary songwriter, this was a real ray of light on the man's roots. To us old-stagers, it came as no surprise that Ralph should have come out with a collection of folk-blues classics, recorded pretty much straight down the line in the spirit of the originals. The only surprise, I suppose, is that it didn't happen sooner.

"In many ways, the recording sounds like the old Ralph but somehow amazingly fresh. The choice of material is really nicely varied and balanced and, in a way I suppose, revealing. A few of the songs are a little off the beaten track, the choice of 'Fables Ain't Nothing But Doggone Lies' from the repertoire of Jesse Fuller, for example, and even a tune from Peg Leg Howell, 'Coalman Blues'. But they are all just wonderful. I guess what it really comes down to is Ralph's feel for the music: it really flows and there's that almost indefinable yet infectious swing that runs through it all – something that so many imitators never quite got."

Away from the road, the struggle to find new songs continued to weigh heavy, with inspiration increasingly difficult to find. However, amid all this he came up with 'Red And Gold', one of the best songs he has ever written – and once again, the grateful recipients were Fairport Convention. "They will often ask if I've anything lying around that I think would suit them. Having been to their annual festival at Cropredy in Oxfordshire, I'd seen the place and one day Dave Pegg told me all about the battle there during the English Civil War on the same fields as the festival site. It occurred to me that a song about this event would suit Fairport well and it got me thinking.

"I aimed to tell the tale, which in essence is an anti-war song, through the eyes of a common field worker caught up in the conflict. I asked Simon Nicol for a suitable name for this central character and he said that Timms was a common name in the area. Originally he was called Daniel Timms but they changed it to William." (As it happens, in the churchyard in Barford St Michael, the village where Pegg lives, there is the grave of a William Timms, although he dates from the 1800s.)

The main priority was for McTell to secure a recording deal with a company who were willing to invest both time and financial backing to promote both himself and his records. This proved a major frustration for McDonagh: "The basic problem was that Ralph wasn't writing, and hadn't written a song of note for quite some time. I continued to try and get him TV work and the odd cover version here and there, but a new record deal was what was needed.

"He would always say to me 'Well, you get me a record deal and I'll write the songs.' But, sadly, record companies don't deal like that anymore. He was in a very uncreative mode at the time, so my first thoughts were to rationalise the back catalogue. There seemed to be a lot of mid-priced McTell compilations of past material, so we decided to put out a decent-priced compilation (that didn't include 'Streets Of London', as we didn't want any further trading on the back of that song) aiming to bury the whole *Alphabet Zoo* and *Tickle On The Tum* business once and for all and get Ralph's name back as a credible singer-songwriter."

Digging around in media circles, McDonagh had found what he feared – that the children's TV shows had greatly damaged McTell's credibility. In drawing up long term plans to raise McTell's profile again, he arranged a tour which would be based around the new compilation album. This would then hopefully fill in some time until McTell had emerged from the writer's block he was experiencing, and he would then be able to write new material.

A deal was done with Castle Communications to put out a set of love songs entitled 'Affairs Of The Heart'. McTell was contractually unable to use certain songs from his past records in their original versions, so he went into Dave Pegg's Woodworm Studios to re-record them. Martin Allcock retains vivid memories of the project: "Those sessions we did at Woodworm were before Peggy extended the control room, and I remember it was absolutely freezing in there. There was Ralph, (engineer) Tim Matyear and myself all huddled around the mixing desk for warmth. I was half-familiar with the songs Ralph wanted to record, so I had to follow him very closely to get what he was after. We did all the tracks in one day, and I even got to use my Casio MIDI horn to trigger an oboe sample on one song."

An extensive UK tour comprising 53 dates was scheduled to run from mid September to early December 1989, with the aim of going some way towards rejuvenating McTell's career. Colour tour brochures bearing the slogan "Staying in touch on tour" were produced, and the new album was released to coincide. On the road McTell performed with his usual polish and there appeared to be signs of a new spark about his performances compared with recent years.

At the old stomping ground, Fitzrovia Street, Soho.

One of the main reasons for the raised spirits was that accompanying him on the road was a dependable three-man crew, as tour manager John Jones explains. "We tried to improve the way he was touring. In recent years, he had been banged up in a car with a couple of guitars, but here we were all together in a van, a complete little unit. We tried to take the strain off him and get him from A to B without too much hassle and generally keep him happy in order for him to be fully focussed on performance.

"I think the 'Affairs Of The Heart' tour and record (inspired) the best publicity that he'd had for years – the mailing list and the whole idea of the 'Keeping in touch with the fans on tour' thing. There was some great marketing done for that. It all

Ralph McTell

OFFICIAL PROGRAMME

costs a lot of money to do, but that investment was what Ralph's career desperately needed at that time."

McTell returned to the studio to record another batch of his favourite songs to be released in 1990 under the title of 'Stealin' Back'. Whereas 'Blue Skies Black Heroes' was an album McTell was always likely to tackle (the other 'lost' McTell record still unrecorded is 'Ralph McTell Sings Woody Guthrie'), 'Stealin' Back' seemed to be going through the motions until the time he could eventually amass a batch of new original material.

One of Ralph's favourite films, Laurel and Hardy's Way Out West, *provided the inspiration for 'That'll Do Babe'.*

In what was an uncannily similar situation, Bob Dylan – one of McTell's greatest influences – was also going through writer's block and hoping to rediscover a way forward in terms of revisiting his influences.

The playing on the album was excellent, with McTell again providing some background to the songs in his sleeve notes. The album also gave him the chance to recreate the jug-band sound of his days in Cornwall in the late 1960s on 'Stealin'', which featured 'Whispering' Mick Bennett. Highlights were a gentle treatment of Gus Cannon's 'I'm Going To Germany', a revisited 'Hesitation Blues' from his debut album ("I can play it better now. I should after all those years!") and a beautifully passionate version of Big Bill Broonzy's 'When Did You Leave Heaven'.

The only original piece on the album was 'That'll Do Babe', an instrumental tribute to Oliver Hardy that was to become a great live favourite. "I've always been a great Laurel and Hardy fan since the Saturday-morning picture shows I used to go to when I was a kid. As I get older, their films just get better and better to me and can serve as a real tonic when I'm down. I'd had the tune for some years and eventually based the final version on the scene in *Way Out West* where Stan and Ollie do that famous little dance routine in front of a quartet.

"I'd learned that Ollie was, despite his size, a very nimble

dancer and at all the swish Hollywood balls at the time, the ladies would often stand in line waiting for the opportunity to dance with him. I called it 'That'll Do Babe' as 'Babe' was Ollie's nickname. If you watch closely, in some of their early silent films you can see Stan sometimes mouth 'Babe' to Ollie. It turned out to be one of the most difficult pieces to play I've ever written. It's a real challenge to do live as it's usually different every night."

Around this time, Mick McDonagh says, "We then set about doing new publicity shots and posters to try and present Ralph as a stronger personality, and the PR shots we did are among the best images that Ralph has ever had."

The team spirit being on the road engendered was reflected in the relaxed way McTell was starting to approach his live work, despite still suffering pre-gig nerves. As with a lot of working musicians, the banter and general leg-pulling alleviated the boredom, and John Jones would often pull little stunts. "We were playing in Wigan once, and the promoter hadn't told us that the date was part of a one-day folk festival and that we were playing the evening segment. The result of this was we couldn't gain access to the hall until about 7pm to soundcheck, so we had a free afternoon on our hands. This wound Ralph up a bit, as he's nervous before a gig at the best of times.

"So I suggested we both go up the road and see Wigan Athletic play a Third Division game, and that's the standard Ralph's used to, as he's a Fulham supporter. It's a freezing afternoon, so midway through the first half I go and get us a couple of Bovrils. This guy comes to me and says 'That bloke you're with – is that Ralph McTell?' I say yes it is. 'What, from *Tickle On The Tum* on the telly?' I say yes it is. He says 'If only we'd known! At half-time we're giving the annual Christmas gifts to the kids from local children's homes and it would have been great to have had him give them the presents." I said, 'He'll do it.' So I get back to our seats with the Bovril and say nothing.

"The half-time whistle goes and there's an announcement on the tannoy that goes 'Ladies and gentlemen, shortly we will be presenting the annual children's Christmas gifts on the pitch – and a special celebrity, Ralph McTell from *Tickle On The Tum* and who wrote "Streets Of London", will be presenting them'. He turns to me and says 'How did they know I was here?' I say 'I haven't a clue, Ralph.' And of course he was lumbered!"

An area where McDonagh achieved success was in Germany, where acoustic music was enjoying a fair degree of popularity and McTell had always been popular. In 1991, he was invited to tour with Donovan, who himself was enjoying a comeback in the UK via a chart hit with Happy Mondays. They toured under the banner of 'Donovan meets Ralph McTell',

Ralph McTell

Sunday 11th November

7.30 p.m.

The ALBERT HALLS
VICTORIA SQUARE, BOLTON BL1 1RU

Tickets: £6.00
(Concessions: £5.00)

TEL: (0204) 364333

Ralph getting the better reviews and being invited back for more dates on his own. John Jones has two particular memories of those tours.

"We were in Salzburg, Austria, and the weather was horrendous. Our next gig was in Berlin at the Quasimodo Club, and because of the travelling distance the next day, we decided to skip bed and get an early start. I decided it was too far for Ralph to go by car, so the plan was for him to fly on ahead, taking the equipment with him in case something went wrong, and we'd follow on by car. We left at 4.30am and, after problems at customs, were on the Berlin transit road. After driving through thick snow with only one stop we were in Berlin at 6pm, but there was no sign of Ralph. We go to the hotel but he's not there either.

"Back at the club, everything is set up waiting. At 10pm, I phone Pan-Am, but for security reasons they won't give me any details on if he'd made the flight. I'm panicking, bearing in mind that his arrival time was supposed to be 3pm! Meanwhile at the club we have a party of autograph hunters waiting for Ralph. Evidently the Germans play this sort of game, collecting autographs to swap, and they take it very seriously; they're all standing outside in the snow and it's turned 10.30pm. There's a big queue by now and I say to the club's Italian owner 'If Ralph isn't here soon, we're going to have to cancel and refund everybody.'

"Just then, Ralph appears and says 'Don't speak to me. It's been an effing disaster.' I say 'All right. Let's get you in the club and get some hot coffee down you.' Ralph's completely shot: 'Whatever you do, don't make me go straight onstage. I'm knackered!' he says. He had all the equipment cases and I got everything in. Meanwhile, all the autograph hunters are there and I say 'Can you do these now?' to him. 'Is there no peace?' he shouts.

"It turns out his plane had to return to Nuremberg airport because of the bad weather, then he transferred to another flight to Frankfurt and he's going backwards and forwards in the air. Once in Berlin, he manages to find the only taxi driver who didn't know where the club was!"

Ralph himself supplies a table-turning postscript to the tale. "Once the queue of autograph hunters had gone, Jonah disappeared into the toilet. I followed a minute later with a piece of paper on which was written '*Ein Autograph bitte?*' ('Can I have your signature, please?') and slipped it under the door..." It was a trick worthy of the arch-joker himself.

Concert ticket for the joint German tour.

STREETS OF LONDON

The gig went ahead, McTell rewarding the audience's patience with a set that stretched into the early hours. However, in 1991 a sad event would hit the touring party. 'Jonah' Jones again: "On the tour with Donovan, we had a new driver. This can be a problem, as you don't know who you're getting or what they'll be like, but the chap we had, George, was absolutely wonderful. He was one of the nicest, gentlest people you could ever meet. When he wasn't road managing, he worked in an old people's home. He wanted to get off the road as he was going to get married and he'd recently written a murder thriller which was going to be published, so he was really happy.

"On the tour, Ralph developed back trouble and was really struggling. Though it was George's day off, he ran Ralph around to try and find a chiropractor to help sort him out. He really went beyond the call of duty. Eventually, Ralph got sorted out so that he could do the gig and George took us to Hamburg airport. The next we heard was he'd been involved in a head-on collision returning from the airport and was killed. We were back over the next week for a few more dates and we went to see George's mother with Donovan. There we found this very sad lady surrounded by all her photos of George on her table. She couldn't really understand us too well. That incident really cut us all up in a big way."

Chapter
19
The Boy With A Note

Inspiration can come in strange ways. The writer's block from which McTell had been suffering had been giving him great cause for concern, as he revealed when interviewed in 1988 by Ian A Anderson for *Folk Roots* magazine. "I'm worried about not writing, having written a hundred and something songs for those TV shows. I don't dash things off, I've never been able to do that, and I've always been deeply envious of people who can do that. I've not written anything of substance for two years."

Things were to change in a way that was totally unexpected: while visiting a friend's house for dinner one evening, McTell noticed a copy of Constantine Fitzgibbon's biography of Welsh poet Dylan Thomas lying on a table. He found the book extremely interesting, to the point where he found he could not put down…apart from when he dropped it into the bath while reading it there! When he went out to buy a copy to replace it, he found that he had purchased another book on the poet, with a similar cover illustration. Reading that book as well, ideas began to take shape.

Gradually, this reawakening to the work of Dylan Thomas began to strike a chord. It wasn't as if he had never come across him before: indeed, back in the 1960s when McTell was hanging out with the beatniks in Poole, his poetry seemed to be everywhere and was a massive influence on the American Beat Poets of the 1950s like Lawrence Ferlinghetti and Allen Ginsberg. Thomas's widely acclaimed reading tours of America in the 1950s had undoubtedly revolutionised his audiences' perception of poetry, since it was Thomas's belief that verse should be performed live, and freed from the page.

Reading about his life, McTell absorbed information on Dylan Thomas's art and his human failings, and ideas slowly evolved over the next few years that would become the most ambitious project that McTell would undertake in his entire career. Martin Allcock: "I remember being in the Half Moon with Ralph one night, and asking him if he had any new songs that Fairport could use. He said to me rather worryingly that he hadn't written anything for a couple of years. I was shocked at this, as I had always thought that he was 'McTell: The Unstoppable Writing Machine.' Then in early March 1990, he phoned me and asked me to do a session with him at Raezor Studio in Wandsworth for two days, as he had nine new songs he wanted to demo.

"I went down and Ralph ran through the songs one by one. I wrote them down in my own hieroglyphic way and the following day we manhandled my MIDI rack into the studio and started work. Either Ralph put down a version by himself, vocal

P. W. PRODUCTIONS LTD PRESENT

DYLAN THOMAS
RETURN JOURNEY

"SPELL-BINDING"
THE TIMES

"IMMACULATE ...
IRRESISTIBLE'
DAILY EXPRESS

"SPLENDID'
WALL ST JOURNAL

"MAGNIFICENT"
VARIETY

WITH
BOB KINGDOM

DIRECTED BY
ANTHONY HOPKINS

Monday **13 APRIL** - Saturday **2 MAY** 1992

EMLYN WILLIAMS THEATRE

THEATR *clwyd*

BOX OFFICE MOLD (0352) 755114

Handbill for Bob Kingdom show.

and either guitar or piano, and then I'd overdub my bits, or I would provide a fairly advanced backing track of sequenced drums, rough piano chords and bass that he could play to. Ralph would then do his bits and I'd re-do the other instruments. I was given free rein at all times and the arrangements were all mine. The demos were really great, and I was very pleased with them."

What was it about Dylan Thomas that restarted McTell's creativity? Certainly, there were many things in Thomas's life that had also happened to McTell and other solo artists he knew: drinking to provide confidence and companionship, the loneliness of travel, the whole solo performer trip. All his human failings endeared him to McTell, who began to develop a real empathy for this character whom many disliked and who was totally hopeless as a human being.

As actor Michael Elphick confirmed, "He was obviously still remembered from his days in Soho. I was in a pub there one day, and somebody asked me what I was working on. When I told them I was involved in a project on the life of Dylan Thomas, they replied 'Oh, *that* little shit.'"

McTell confirmed the story: "Some while before, I had read a book called *Soho In The '50s* by Daniel Farson, which included only one reference to Dylan Thomas, whom he mentions meeting in a bar on his way to America; he noticed that Farson had a magazine with him with which contained a short story by Raymond Chandler. As Dylan's favourite reading was pulp detective fiction, this gave me the idea to write a story about him, using a gumshoe who's always on Dylan's trail, making notes on him as he follows him around. So the narrative poem was where it all started."

McTell finished the poem, realising that it might well form the basis of an album if he could write a few songs to tie in. In fact, he ended up with nine, which gave him the confidence to progress the idea a stage further. Suddenly, he found that this writing project was providing poetic titles for songs from the lines he was writing. Things were starting to move at a decent pace.

After McTell had recorded demos with Allcock, Mick McDonagh contacted head of BBC Radio 2 Frances Line. As a result, she commissioned 'The Boy With A Note' as a project for radio. However, McTell was not as pleased as he had expected with the resulting BBC production (subtitled 'An Evocation of the Life of Dylan Thomas in Words And Music'). He had originally wanted to narrate the radio version himself, but McDonagh, with one eye on selling the work to a major label, felt it would be better if someone else performed the narrative parts.

Many of those he approached showed a genuine interest, including Anthony Hopkins, but eventually, the part of narrating a piece McTell had written in the style of Dylan Thomas went to Bob Kingdom, who was touring with the widely acclaimed one-man show, *Dylan Thomas: Return Journey* (directed by Anthony Hopkins), while character actor Michael Elphick was given the role of the private eye on Thomas's trail, his highly recognisable gruff voice making him eminently suitable for the role.

However, for the version which was released on record, McTell felt that Elphick had been given insufficient time to acquaint himself with the words, and as a consequence failed to grasp certain elements of the script. As Elphick was not available to re-record his part, Ralph decided to attempt it himself.

Much debate ensued regarding who would play the part of Caitlin. BBC producer John Langridge put forward the name of Maggie Reilly, a more than capable session singer who'd found limited fame fronting Scots band Cado Belle before working with such high-profile names as Mike Oldfield. There was, however, a case for employing an Irish singer, and three well-known names were approached in turn to fulfil the role.

The first, Mary Black, was amenable, but happened to be touring Japan at the time so had to decline. The next name on the list, Dolores Keane, made it as far as England, but had to fulfil a prior live engagement on the evening of the recording date and adverse weather conditions meant she had to return to Ireland without setting foot in the studio. A tape was then sent to Mary Coughlan, who liked it and agreed to do it. She flew in, but for several reasons the recording session proved abortive.

The spotlight then fell by default on Maggie Reilly, the original name in the frame. Unphased by all the controversy, she stepped into the breach and, in McTell's words, "did a wonderful job" supplying lead and backing vocals alongside a band consisting of Martin Allcock, Andy Findon (saxophone), Graham Preskett (piano, violin) and Dave Mattacks (percussion).

Showing enormous maturity and autobiographical in places, 'The Boy With A Note' should dispel any doubts people may have about McTell being one of this country's major songwriters. Its theme is about deception and asks whether art is a deception – which is where it starts, with a deception about being excused a games lesson at school. A later deception relates to passing oneself off as somebody else, which is something all young men are prone to do, and which McTell did in his efforts to impress the opposite sex and, more importantly, to mask his insecurities.

Subsequent songs on the album deal with Thomas's deceptions and unfaithfulness to Caitlin later in life. McTell: "If someone says 'Oh, that was magic', it implies a trick to me. My analysis of Dylan was that later on, he wondered if what he was doing was a deception. He would refuse to discuss his poems and discouraged probing about deep meanings in what he wrote."

Apart from his artistic work, Dylan Thomas is also remembered for his legendary drinking, even though he only drank beer. Born in Swansea in 1914, he had his first poems published when he was just ten years old. In the spring of 1936, he was in London and, while drinking in the Wheatsheaf public house in Rathbone Place, met Caitlin Macnamara, the woman who later became his wife. Born in Hammersmith in West London, she was indeed a fiery character. The couple married in Penzance the following year, and in 1938, moved to Laugharne in Wales. Their stormy relationship continued until Thomas's death in New York in 1953 at the age of 39.

STREETS OF LONDON

Dylan Thomas the poet was an enormous influence on poetry and remains so to this day, yet his private life was almost that of the typical artiste. He was irresponsible, unfaithful and guilt-ridden, and money slipped through his hands like water. His endless search for perfection often led him to rewrite finished works. He was protective of his work, and took criticism very personally.

McTell regarded Thomas as almost a contemporary pop star who adopted an image and became 'The Poet'. The insecurities he lived through and his relationship with Caitlin became the core of 'The Boy With A Note', and, as mentioned earlier, allowed McTell to draw comparisons between his and the poet's life (but not his art) at appropriate points. 'The Irish Girl' can be likened to Winifred May's view of her son marrying Nanna all those years ago. Here was a mother's concern that her son, who had no real prospects and was a professional singer, had taken a young wife who was a stranger in a new land with a young son, and was living in a caravan. That young wife would have to fulfil the roles of a mother, lover, nurse and psychiatrist. How were they going to live?

'Slip-Shod Tap-Room Dance', with its quirky melody line, perfectly captures Dylan Thomas in Soho, searching for both liquid sustenance and companionship and impressing the town lads as he had when he was younger with his drinking, smoking and bragging. Now he was a man, he could do it in Soho but he had no money left. Here McTell was able to revisit his own sorties into London's West End during the 1960s where, unknown to him on his own quest for learning, he was on Thomas's trail. There are fine images of the poet staggering from pub to pub.

Oxford Street is a river tonight
But he must cross it once more. Soho.
Plus the perfect image of a drunk:
In a Slip-Shod Tap-Room Dance
Tubes rumbling not so very far to go
Took six matches to light one cigarette
Just another night in old Soho.
('Slip-Shod Tap-Room Dance', 1992)

The published letters that Dylan wrote Caitlin are poetry in their own right, yet can be interpreted as being full of self-pity and are largely guilt-ridden. McTell draws upon these works in two songs: 'Miss You Most Of All' shows Thomas's guilt about the affair he had while he was in America and how he asked Caitlin for forgiveness. There are shades of a resignation about these things, the promise of 'things will be different when I get home.' In a similar vein, 'Wonderful Country' (originally titled 'A Proposition Of Propositions') is an admission that, despite being amazed by America, there is still a deep longing to return to a simpler way of life and the security of a relationship. Here McTell echoes his own sentiments about being a solo artist away on tour, recalling his first visit to America in 1971. It is a subject he had written about before in 'If I Don't Get Home', a song that could easily have appeared on 'The Boy With A Note'.

'Conundrum Of Time' goes deeply into the relationship between Dylan and Caitlin. It has been said that Caitlin was not capable of coping with her husband, whereas a stronger-willed woman might well have. They would fight and she would strike him. She had been hopeful that she could make it as a dancer, yet with her thick-set build that was always highly unlikely. In 'Conundrum Of Time', McTell describes the games they played with each other, and the times when Caitlin would join Thomas in long drinking sessions out of her sheer inability to do anything else.

At his local hostelry, Brown's Hotel, they hold a truce before returning home and continuing with their conflict. There is a lovely line in the song where, after they arrive home, they both "tumble upstairs", while across the estuary from their house in Laugharne, a ship "in distress sends up flares." Trouble lies ahead…

'Caitlin's Dream (Summer Birds Are Leaving)' is McTell's attempt to portray Caitlin having a premonition about her husband's impending demise, and includes her views on how he has changed from a humble Welsh poet to a man "enrobed like Valentino's sheik."

She is annoyed that, in his letters to her, all he tells her is that they adore him and sit at his feet (his audiences listened to him in quite informal settings) as his poetry went over the heads – both literally and metaphorically – of these uncultured Americans in their barren wasteland.

Hareemed girls lay languidly
On carpets at your feet
And with each word a tiny pearl
Tripped from your lips, and fell
On desert ground, it rained today
The children all are very well.
('Caitlin's Dream', 1992)

Their relationship is about to end: its whole spirit is being slowly taken away from Caitlin and she senses it. Each verse ends with Caitlin returning to her own mundane existence in Wales: "Children well, friends at the pub ask about you, bills are piling up. Please send some money." She follows her dream through, and the sheik's tent becomes the oxygen tent containing the dying Dylan when she eventually sees him next.

The whole euphemism for the tent is interesting. Thomas was on his fourth American tour when, after a drinking bout in New York's Greenwich Village, he sank into an alcoholic coma. When the news reached Caitlin, she went to New York and when she arrived at the hospital was refused admission as Dylan's mistress, Liz Reitell, was there. When she eventually did see him, she went crazy and had to be hospitalised herself.

Ralph with author Chris Hockenhull in Southport, 1990.

The earlier narration, 'These Soho Streets', refers to "The smashed crucifix and bruised fists", which happened at the hospital when Caitlin tore the cross off the wall and threw it on the ground. She had lost him and felt cheated. On the voyage back across the Atlantic bringing his body home, she went down into the ship's hold and found some of the crew playing cards on his coffin as he is 'Cradled In The Rocking Boat', which is the final piece on the record. For further reading, *The Last Days Of Dylan Thomas* by Rob Gittins (Futura, 1986) is recommended.

'No Grown Man's Land' is another narrative, this time read by Nerys Hughes, with whom he had worked some years before on *Alphabet Zoo*. In Welsh, the name Dylan means "the son of the sea waves", and this leads to many references to water on the record. The image of water pulling one away can be related to Thomas's yearning for somewhere bigger and better as a platform than standing by 'the house on the shore', and where he saw the Atlantic at his feet was the estuary flowing to the Atlantic that ran all the way to America. 'No Grown Man's Land' is suggesting that when we see clouds reflected on the water's surface, the world really begins underneath what we can see. Therefore, there really *is* "another world below the sky reflected in pools amongst the rocks."

Nerys Hughes was an excellent choice, as she was familiar with Thomas's work and has played nearly every female role in *Under Milk Wood* during her career. McTell is full of praise for her contribution: "She is a wonderful reader and was so encouraging. She told me that, when she was listening to the demos, she just kept shouting out aloud and was constantly telling me what I'd written was wonderful. She completely understood 'No Grown Man's Land' the first time, and she read it beautifully. Nerys even contributed the full stops and commas, as I'm hopeless at punctuation."

In relation to this theme of water, when writing the early parts of 'The Boy With A Note', McTell remembered a comment made to him by a Welsh schoolmaster many years previously about how it can be "better to be a small fish in a big pool." A goldfish removed from a bowl and placed in a pond will grow bigger. Remove it from the pond and place it in a lake, and it will grow even bigger. The other narrative – 'The Certain Tide', read this time by Bob Kingdom – uses the image of a fish denied the space it needs ramming the walls of its tank.

It refers to Thomas feeling trapped, a prisoner in his hotel room as a result of his fame, and for once he is staring reality in the face. He is finally beginning to realise his mistakes, but the inevitable end is nigh, and it is too late to turn back. Perhaps he realises that if he had stayed in that pond in Wales, life would be a lot easier. Bob Kingdom does a superb job both in parodying Thomas's speaking voice and getting exactly the right intonation which McTell intended in the prose.

> *God, I feel captured like a sea minnow*
> *In a sandboy's bucket*
> *Release me to the sea*
> *I could be prey to bigger fish*
> *I am only small fry*
> *But if detained here at your pleasure*
> *I will surely die.*
> **('The Certain Tide', 1992)**

Caitlin Thomas eventually found happiness in the years following her husband's Dylan's death. She met a Sicilian, Guiseppe Fazio, and they had a son when she was aged 49. After years living in Italy, she died in Catania after a long illness in August 1994 aged 81. She had told her son of her wish that, upon her death, she be taken back to Laugharne and buried next to Dylan. After years of feeling cheated by his death, she was eventually reunited with him.

'The Boy With A Note' stands up to serious analysis as McTell's most important piece of work. It was a most ambitious project to undertake at a time in his career when his audiences were dwindling and record-company interest was nil. The project cost a lot, much of it contributed by the BBC, but the depth of time and effort that McTell invested into it should be commended. The only minor criticism is that he dispensed with Michael Elphick in the role of the detective for the album release. While McTell has an excellent speaking voice, Elphick provided authenticity to the role of the gumshoe, thus separating the narratives from McTell's songs, while on the album they seem to blend together too much.

Praise is due to Graham Preskett's superbly sympathetic orchestral arrangements, which add so much to the texture of the work, and it is to his credit that, while they are striking, they are also unobtrusive throughout. As usual with McTell, 'The Boy With A Note' received little in the way of in-depth press coverage, either for the BBC broadcast or for the album. A pleasing (albeit brief) review in *Q* magazine suggested that the release should perhaps trigger a reappraisal of McTell's work, while a review in *Gold* called it "a delightful mixture of spoken passages interspersed with songs in McTell's simple, traditional style."

Of the radio broadcast, Russell Twisk in *The Observer* noted "Anybody who has sat through *Les Misérables* or *Miss Saigon* will be inured to amplified banalities and find this collection full of insight." Due to this paucity of media coverage, the release largely sank without trace, which must have been an enormous disappointment to its writer, although it is still being discovered by new listeners. Nevertheless, 'The Boy With A Note' is arguably Ralph McTell's greatest achievement and a most fitting project to coincide with the 25th anniversary of his career as a professional performer.

Chapter
20 *A Silver Celebration*

1992 was the 25th anniversary of the release of McTell's first recording. This should have been the year when everything fell into place, and once again his artistic talents would bring him the credibility he so richly deserved. Certainly, after the writer's block of the late 1980s/early 1990s, there had been hopes that everything would return to comparative normality, and that new songs would be written and recorded. For, while 'The Boy With A Note' was the most ambitious piece of work he had attempted and produced in his career, it was not a commercial success, and was perhaps too specialist in its subject-matter for mass appeal.

To mark the anniversary, McDonagh had set up a gruelling schedule of concert dates amounting to 48 shows in just 54 days as the first instalment of a two-part Silver Celebration Tour, commencing in Hayes on 4 March and concluding at Eastbourne on 26 April. As well as 'The Boy With A Note', a CD retrospective of his career titled 'Silver Celebration' was also released.

With the tour approaching, McDonagh set about getting McTell as much media coverage as possible. While he succeeded to some extent, it was nevertheless the usual loyal Middle of the Road radio presenters who invited McTell to their shows to talk about his 25 years as a performer and writer, and such coverage wasn't really likely to break new ground and reach new listeners. Or *would* it?

One of the radio interviews was on BBC Radio 2's early-evening show, whose presenter John Dunn introduced his subject as follows: "My guest here this evening is Ralph McTell. But McTell isn't your real name, is it?" The response "My real name is Ralph May" almost sent a car in Hampshire careering off the road. Driving the car was someone who had not seen McTell since before he'd joined the army all those years ago. "I couldn't get home quickly enough to tell my wife, Terri," said one-time Croydon gang leader Vernon Burford. "When I got in, I ran into the room and said 'I've found him…I *knew* I would. I've found Ralph'. She had to calm me down.

"I must admit to not being up on the music scene, but I was really excited that I had found one of the missing members of our gang. And he was quite famous too. I sent a note to the BBC and they wrote back informing me that Ralph was soon doing a concert at the Royal Festival Hall, so I booked Terri and myself tickets. When I collected them before the show, there was a note with them inviting us backstage afterwards, but even then I still wasn't convinced it was him. But as soon as he came out on stage and I saw that smile…I knew it really *was* Ralph May."

Despite the number of concerts scheduled for the tour, McTell was apparently

content to continue at this pace, as he told John Tobler in an interview for *Folk Roots*: "I want to keep on going, because I'm enjoying it more than ever before. I feel confident about what I am doing, so I'm looking at special projects now and then to break up the solo touring thing." As a live performer, the Silver Celebration tour showed McTell at a new peak of his ability to entertain audiences in his own unique way for two hours at a time night after night.

Great care had been taken to structure the sets so that they contained the best of his writing over that 25-year period, and that meant revisiting some songs (though McTell performed the classic 'Red And Gold' only on the first six nights). His support act, Huw and Tony Williams, were not only humorous but had also written fine original songs of their own, and they proved to be the perfect foil for McTell's own performances.

Also celebrating 25 years together in 1992 were Fairport Convention, who invited McTell to share the stage as one of their guests at their annual festival at Cropredy in August of that year. For this special show, McTell, backed by Fairport, chose to perform two songs, 'Polly On The Shore' and 'Iron Lion', as a tribute to the late Trevor Lucas, who had originally sung them during his time in Fairport. "Trevor really impressed me," explained McTell. "He had an attitude that said just because we love acoustic music and the tradition doesn't mean we can't enjoy the rock'n'roll lifestyle. He dressed up when hardly any of us bothered to dress up, and he bought a big car. Trevor and I had actually planned to record an album together, as our voices were compatible, but sadly it was not to be."

Meanwhile, the summer of 1992 also brought major disagreements behind the scenes resulting in a far from celebratory mood. While on the surface the Silver Celebration tour appeared a success, McTell and Mick McDonagh were having what can be described a frank exchange of views which resulted in yet another management break-up. McTell went into the second part of the tour without a manager and, despite now having to finance it himself, managed on occasion to surpass the standards of the March/April shows. On the road, McTell was once again joined by 'Jonah' Jones, whose usual japes helped keep McTell's mind off the disastrous administrative aspects of his career. "When you're on the road, it's always difficult to get good food regularly, and anybody who knows Ralph knows he likes his food. When travelling, Ralph always gets engrossed in the arts sections of the quality newspapers, and at times it's difficult to get his attention. He gets very nervous as he approaches the venue for the next gig, so I would throw in the odd remark to see if he was listening.

"I'd suddenly say out loud 'How the hell do they do *that*?', and Ralph would look up and say 'Do what?', so I'd say 'I've just seen a sign that says "Soup of the day, liver and bacon, onions, boiled potatoes, carrots and peas, suet pudding and custard for 99p." And Ralph would immediately be interested because, like me, he's a war baby and loves a bargain.

Annual Cropredy beermat!

He'd put the papers down and want to know where this place was, and I'd say 'About a mile back'. Ralph would suddenly be paying attention, and ask 'Why didn't you say anything?' I'm dying to laugh, as there never was any such sign, and I'd go 'Couldn't stop, Ralph. Double yellow lines!'

"He'd be totally sold on the idea of stopping for food, and he'd make us pull up at the next available eating place which, nine times out of ten, would be a real duffer and expensive, too. But he'd fall for that one three or four times each tour. I used that same stunt when I was touring with the Fureys, and they fell for it too!"

With Wizz Jones at the Half Moon, Putney, at a charity gig for old friend Pete Berryman, 1993.

The end of 1992 was somewhat reminiscent of 1975, after the 'hit'. McTell should have been going into the next phase of his career with renewed optimism and enthusiasm after a successful year's work celebrating 25 years as an artist of international renown. Instead, he was back to square one without management and with no record contract to speak of. Sure, he could always continue to release his recordings on his own Leola label, but doing it himself was not the same as having a label investing time and money promoting future releases and maintaining a credible profile for him.

Thankfully, this time McTell was a lot stronger and wiser, and able to deal with this latest setback without running away confused from the situation as he had in 1975, but the absence of a 'father figure' remained a void in his life as once again he needed someone to confide in and guide him through a sticky patch.

Since then, however, that role has been undertaken by someone who is physically inappropriate, but temperamentally perfect: Nanna is not just a wife, but someone from whom he can seek advice. Since she came to England as an expectant mother in the winter of 1966, Nanna May has had a lot to deal with, and it is a true testimony to her strength and devotion to Ralph that she has kept home and raised four children often single-handed while McTell's career has taken him far away.

For many years, she has "run the ship" above and beyond the call of duty in such a way that she is almost an informal manager to him as well as a supportive wife through many difficult times. Danny Thompson: "What do I consider to be Ralph's greatest achievement? Without doubt, it has to be marrying Nanna. How she's kept things afloat at home down the years I'll never know. When I think of Ralph and Nanna, I always see this scenario in my mind. He's sitting there with his head in *Auto Trader* magazine, trying to find another of his famous 'bargains', she's there going through the kids' school reports and asking him what school is best for them to go to next.

"As she asks him this, he's looking out of the window trying to come up with the next line of a new song. And the amazing thing is that it all pulls together. He writes the song, gets a bargain deal on a new car and the kids get the right education. Ralph and Nanna together are a wonderful combination. She's always been at his side when he's needed her, in good and bad times."

Following a period of intensive writing, McTell was finally in a position to start demo-ing some new songs. Martin Allcock was once again involved, and a week was spent at Dave Pegg's Woodworm Studios at the beginning of March which produced positive results and gave McTell something tangible to proceed with. Clearly the fact that he was at last writing again was a weight off his shoulders, and all that was now required was to find new management and a suitable record deal.

But if another indication were needed to illustrate his more positive frame of mind, it came in a most unlikely form – one sufficiently newsworthy to be reported in the British national press. After nearly 40 years, Ralph McTell announced to the world that he had stopped smoking!

"I have always tried to take care of myself," he said, "and am pleased to say that I've stuck at it down the years despite the unhealthy lifestyle one leads being on the road so much. Stopping smoking was, I suppose, a natural progression and, having reached my 50th year, was something that I needed to do. The odd thing was that Albert, my pet African Grey parrot, had a lot to do with it. I bought him shortly after the last tour I did with the Everly Brothers, and he's been a great pal ever since.

"Parrots mimic all sorts of sounds, and when he seemingly developed a nasty sounding cough, I was obviously quite concerned about him. However, it turned out that Albert was in perfect health: the cough he appeared to have was the smoker's cough I wasn't aware I had. There was little else I could do but own up and give up smoking."

With Joan Woollard unveiling a plaque in 1993 in memory of the late Ken Woollard, founder of the Cambridge Folk Festivals.

Despite the main attention being focussed on recording the new songs he had written, there were several live appearances during 1994. He performed at two memorial concerts, both of which were inevitably tinged with sadness. One was for Brenda Wootton, who had been such an encouragement in those early days in Cornwall: a concert was staged in Penzance, where McTell performed along with John the Fish, 'Whispering' Mick Bennett and Michael Chapman. Later in the summer, he appeared at the Royal Albert Hall alongside Christy Moore and Loudon Wainwright III in a tribute to Ken Woollard, the instigator of the world-famous Cambridge Folk Festival.

On a happier note, one of his new songs was aired on prime-time television that summer. Long-time friend Billy Connolly had toured his home country with a BBC film crew in tow, and the result was titled *Billy Connolly's World Tour Of Scotland*. The theme music was 'The Islands', a song McTell had demoed earlier in the year, and the series was such a success that it won a BAFTA award in 1995. McTell meanwhile had been working with other musicians with a view to performing with them at a couple of festivals during the summer. His friend Alun Davies led a tight little band known as the Good Men in the Jungle, and they became an ideal backing unit for McTell, proving he was perfectly capable of presenting a fuller sound on stage.

In 1994, the Cambridge Folk Festival was celebrating its 30th year with a star-studded bill, featuring Mary Black and Joan Baez. McTell was asked to close the festival on the Sunday evening after performing his own set the previous evening. Also on the bill was legendary Texas singer-songwriter Carolyn Hester, who took the opportunity to watch McTell perform for the first time in 23 years: "I stood by the side of the stage and took in his whole set. He was absolutely *amazing*. His guitar playing continues to knock me out and his voice just seems to get better with age. The version of 'Streets Of London' that night brought tears to my eyes, and the whole crowd singing it along with him is a memory I will always have of that festival."

For the closing finale, the Good Men in the Jungle were augmented by Martin Allcock and Frank Gallagher from Mary Black's band. While no new original material was performed, there were a number of impressive cover versions including Neil Young's 'Dance Dance Dance', 'Save The Last Dance For Me' and a rousing version of Woody Guthrie's 'Do Re Mi', before Mary Black joined in on 'Will The Circle Be Unbroken' to end an eventful festival that would surely have made the late Ken Woollard proud.

McTell hit the road again in September for his eighth tour of Australia, also performing in Hong Kong and New Zealand, before returning to the UK for a series of shows in November and early December. The schedule culminated with a performance at the Paul Robeson Theatre in London where the Good Men in the Jungle appeared to back him – a surprise present from Nanna on his 50th birthday!

Chapter
21 *Telling Yesterday's News*

Any mention of the name of Ralph McTell is almost inevitably coupled with 'Streets Of London' in virtually the same breath. As mentioned earlier, the idea of researching McTell's life and career was intended to demonstrate that there was an awful lot more to the man than merely that one song. Nevertheless, the song has almost had a life of its own and as a result, it deserves special scrutiny and investigation, both into its origins and into its creator's feelings about it now, some 30 years later.

It is also important to note that the title of this book was changed at its subject's request (and against its author's recommendation) precisely because it is far and away his best-known composition, although everyone involved with the book feels he has written numerous songs which are artistically superior.

McTell first started working on the song when he was in Paris in 1966, although it was some time before it became the version we know: "It was just a tune initially. I put a few chords together, but nothing really happened, then I got C, G, A minor, E minor, F and C and when I got that sequence, it became a tune almost immediately.

"What particularly pleased me was that the bass line was there from the start, so basically, it almost wrote itself. The verse stayed with me for some time, but the middle eight came quite a while later. At that time, I was playing a lot with Gary Peterson, who played quite complicated stuff – better than I could manage, so when I got that tune together, I was most pleased with the way it turned out."

As a young man on the streets of Paris, McTell saw sights that moved him considerably. The winter of 1966 was colder there than usual, and the people who lived out on the streets naturally suffered most. One image in particular caught McTell's attention:

The sleeve of the German release.

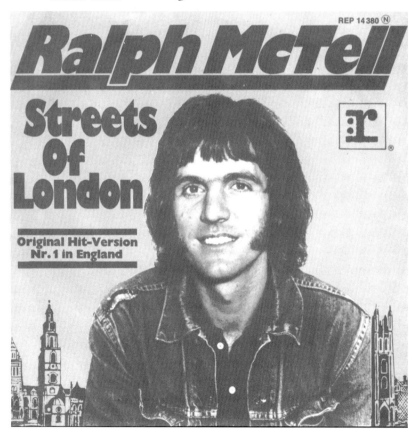

REP 14380 Ⓝ

Ralph McTell

Streets Of London

Original Hit-Version Nr. 1 in England

"There were a lot of guys living rough, and I can vividly remember them sleeping over the hot-air gratings to try and keep warm. They used to sleep with their boots under their heads so that no-one could steal them whilst they were asleep. Their shoes were their most valuable possession."

Eventually, the sights and scenes of Paris gave McTell the idea of lyrics to complement the melody he had conceived. However, using other images from earlier in his life, the basis of the song shifted from the poor people of Paris to those in his native London.

> *Have you seen the old man*
> *In the closed down market*
> *Kicking up the papers*
> *With his worn out shoes?*
> *In his eyes you see no pride*
> *And held loosely at his side*
> *Yesterday's paper telling*
> *Yesterday's news.*

"I used images from my childhood of Surrey Street market in Croydon. There was this one guy who used to go around after the market had closed for the day looking for fruit and vegetables that had fallen off the stall on to the floor. He wasn't at all embarrassed, and used to kick around the waste paper, almost pretending to be unconcerned. What struck me was that he appeared to be most uninhibited in his scavenging.

"Another childhood image was when I used to go by the Tower of London, which was such a scene of activity and amusement for me as a child. There one could find all sorts of fellows doing magic tricks, which always fascinated me, and stunts like jumping barefoot on broken glass.

"There were a lot of vagrant types around there, and they would always be carrying newspapers. This wasn't because they were interested in what was going on in the world, but the newspapers served as their undergarments and insulation against the cold when they slept rough. They would roll up sheets of paper and stuff them down their trouser legs and arms. It was cheaper and easier for them to change papers than change and wash their clothes."

> *Have you seen the old girl*
> *Who walks the streets of London*
> *Dirt in her hair*
> *And her clothes in rags?*
> *She's no time for talkin'*
> *She just keeps right on walkin'*
> *Carrying her home*
> *In two carrier bags.*

A much later experience, when McTell was in his late teens, formed the background to the second verse. On his way home from one of his jaunts up to London's West End, he came across a lone woman moving towards him: "She was one of the bag ladies. She was shuffling towards me with all these bags that obviously contained her worldly possessions. It always struck me as odd that the men never seemed to carry very much with them, if at all, but the women did for some reason. I looked around and there was no-one else on the street. As she came towards me, I

Streets Of London

Words and Music by
RALPH McTELL

20p
Essex Music
International Ltd.

felt in my pockets and gathered what loose change I had with me. As she passed, I didn't say anything but dropped the coins into one of her bags and carried on walking past.

"I'd only walked a few feet when I heard her shout, and I turned around. She'd put her bags down, removed the coins from them and hurled them back at me, yelling 'I don't want your effing money' and other abuse. It startled me. I had meant it as a simple act of kindness – I'd never patronise these people. In the first verse, I included the line 'In his eyes you see no pride', but she *did* have her pride. This woman obviously wanted her independence and not charity."

In the all night café
At a quarter past eleven
Same old man
Sitting there on his own
Looking at the world
Over the rim of his tea-cup
Each tea lasts an hour
And he wanders home alone.

One of the popular features of the West End in the mid-1960s were the cafes, especially those which stayed open all-night, as McTell remembered: "There was one in particular called 'Mick's' in Fleet Street that I had in mind when I wrote this verse. It had a lot of customers who simply had nowhere else to go, and even those who did have a home were lonely; the cafe gave them something to see with people coming and going, which eased their loneliness. The tea-cup is their horizon line for all they have in the world. The line 'Looking at the world over the rim of his tea-cup' is to say that he can't see anything in the world beyond the rim of the cup that he holds."

Have you seen the old man
Outside the seaman's mission
Memory fading with
The medal ribbons that he wears?
In our winter city
The rain cries a little pity
For one more forgotten hero
And a world that doesn't care.

The final verse was written separately, several months' distant from the rest of the song, and again it reverts to more memories from childhood: "At the bottom of Factory Lane was a hostel occupied by all sorts of men: labourers, drop-outs, some who were quite disturbed, and so on. This one old guy was a First World War veteran, and he used to wear slippers all the time along with a homburg and an old army greatcoat with his army medals on. As a young boy, he used to frighten me when I saw him.

"He lived out his last days there at the hostel. I can vividly remember the scars on his neck and with his medals I saw him as some sort of forgotten hero who was fodder for the army. When I came to writing the verse, calling it the 'working men's hostel' didn't work. I remembered a seaman's mission in Whitechapel, so I used that."

> *So how can you tell me*
> *You're lonely*
> *And say for you*
> *That the sun don't shine?*
> *Let me take you by the hand*
> *And lead you through*
> *The streets of London*
> *I'll show you something*
> *To make you change your mind.*

"After I'd written the verses, I still felt a need to resolve the whole thing. On the chords side of things, the E minor against the F came to me and the whole thing then fell into place. All along I had wanted to write something for my mate Tubs, and that's who it was written for."

As already mentioned, the song has had a career of its own and is known throughout the world, even if the name of its creator may not be. It was interesting to find, as the book neared completion, that there was a message on the Internet from someone in America who knew some of the words but wanted information on the song's title and the name of its composer!

It has been recorded on countless occasions by the most diverse range of artists – yet, while it is a song of great feeling and is another illustration of McTell's compassion, it pales in comparison with many others he has written during the last 30 years. However, it is a song many teachers cite as one of the first pieces any budding acoustic guitar-player wants to master. It made the name of Ralph McTell comparatively familiar in the early part of his career, long before the public at large got to hear him perform the definitive version. Today, he gratefully admits "I'm just glad it was me who wrote it."

However, there has been more than one occasion during his career when he has fallen out of love with the song, none more so than when it charted in 1974 and elevated him to the status of 'pop star'. Which of his own performances of the song does he consider the most memorable?

"I guess it was the 1968 Cambridge Folk Festival. I really didn't have any idea how well my career was going in those days, because the interest in me hadn't really hit home. I felt it had died a death the first time I ever performed it in public – there was this split-second silence at the end that seemed an eternity. I suppose it transports people somewhere as they hear it, and at Cambridge, the whole crowd sang along with it, which was totally unexpected; I felt a lump in my throat. Martin Carthy came up to me as I came off stage and couldn't believe the impact the song had made. I was stunned."

In America in 1971, McTell appeared on the *David Frost Show* in New York. After he had performed 'Streets Of London', another of the show's guests called into

his dressing room: "Mel Tormé popped in to see me, and he said 'That song you did – did you write that song, young man? That's such a beautiful song.' I was really pleased that an artist of his stature should say such a thing. It meant a lot to me."

One particular incident helped bring the song to prominence in the late 1960s. McTell performed it on a session for the BBC *Country Meets Folk* radio programme, which was broadcast live from a studio in London, and afterwards was blissfully unaware that, at Broadcasting House, the switchboard was literally jammed with callers wanting to know who had performed the song that had just been aired.

It has been covered hundreds of times by a whole range of performers who have left their mark on it in some way – but which versions had left an impression upon its composer?

"I've always felt it works best when it's performed by young singers, as it's a young person's song. I don't have a particular favourite version – all I ask is that it is done with a degree of sincerity. I was particularly fond of Mary Hopkin's version, and most recently Sinead O'Connor's performance was most pleasing. I felt that Glen Campbell added something to it when he did it, as well as again being pleased that an artist of his stature had liked it enough to perform it.

"Although I've never heard her version, I believe Aretha Franklin has done it, which would have been nice to hear. As regards the Anti-Nowhere League's version, it wasn't subtle and I don't think there was too much sincerity about it, but it was meant to shock, which was what punk was all about, and it has to be viewed in that context.

"There's one version that *does* stand out that I heard played live: some years ago, I was asked by promoter Derek Block to drop in to see Harry Belafonte perform in London. He followed a version of Woody Guthrie's 'Pastures Of Plenty' with 'Streets Of London', and his was a version where he literally talked the lyrics, and he did it beautifully. I was most pleased that he'd put it back-to-back with a song by my great hero, so that'll do for me.

"I am immensely proud of the song. It is certainly not the best song I've ever written, but if you seek to touch hearts and move people, then it succeeds from that point of view."

McTell's opinion that 'Streets Of London' is far from the best song he has ever written is shared by this biographer, who believes it has remained in his live repertoire at the expense of better material. However, he confirms that the song has saved particular shows

With Prince Edward during a walk in aid of the London homeless, 1992.

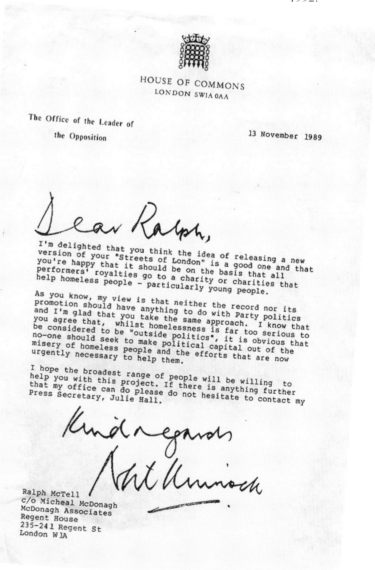

HOUSE OF COMMONS
LONDON SW1A 0AA

The Office of the Leader of
the Opposition

13 November 1989

Dear Ralph,

I'm delighted that you think the idea of releasing a new version of your "Streets of London" is a good one and that you're happy that it should be on the basis that all performers' royalties go to a charity or charities that help homeless people – particularly young people.

As you know, my view is that neither the record nor its promotion should have anything to do with Party politics and I'm glad that you take the same approach. I know that you agree that, whilst homelessness is far too serious to be considered to be "outside politics", it is obvious that no-one should seek to make political capital out of the misery of homeless people and the efforts that are now urgently necessary to help them.

I hope the broadest range of people will be willing to help you with this project. If there is anything further that my office can do please do not hesitate to contact my Press Secretary, Julie Hall.

Kind regards

Neil Kinnock

Ralph McTell
c/o Micheal McDonagh
McDonagh Associates
Regent House
235-241 Regent St
London W1A

when things have not been going well, and conceivably his insecurity may have been responsible for him continuing to do the song for so long. (Editor's note: when asked whether he wasn't bored rigid by having to perform his hits every night onstage for his entire career, one of the Everly Brothers justified it by saying that if he went to see, for example, Little Richard, playing live, and didn't hear 'Good Golly Miss Molly', he would feel somewhat short-changed.)

It should be remembered that Ralph fought very hard with both Warner Brothers and Bruce May over the song appearing on his seventh album, and was also unhappy that the album was titled 'Streets'. No doubt he felt trapped by the song, and raised concerns that re-releasing it as a single was a financially-motivated venture. However, in defence of his management and record label, nobody could have ever envisaged just how successful the reissue was going to be, and the period after the song became a hit vividly illustrates McTell's discomfort with the whole business.

When considering 'Streets Of London', another more recent composition should also be mentioned, as it is linked with the former song and confirms McTell's social awareness, to which he has stayed true throughout his career. On his 1995 album, 'Sand In Your Shoes', 'Care In The Community' again revisits the sentiments expressed in 'Streets Of London', highlighting the lack of compassion for the less fortunate who, as a result of government policy, are given less attention, allowed out on to the streets and forced to survive as part of the very community with which they find it difficult to cope.

Launched in 1993, the Care In The Community programme is, in principle, a reasonably good idea, with people living with and looking after their own, and offering real personal support. Unfortunately, the strong message of the Thatcher years was very much that one should look after Number One, and get as much out of life as fast as possible in a competitive world. The more recent song is written against a backdrop of closed hospitals and the disappearance of centres where qualified staff can offer real support, as a consequence of which the Care In The Community programme merely shoves unstable souls back into a community that is unable to cope, doesn't know what to do and is afraid.

> *There's a man riding the tube train*
> *He's got voices in his head*
> *One voice says get off at your stop*
> *But he might get on instead*
> *Another voice tells him it's time*
> *Be ready to take a life*
> *Another voice tells him he'll know when;*
> *In his pocket he handles a knife.*

McTell claims that he was not aiming to write a sequel to his best-known song: "When Nanna first read through the lyrics, she asked me 'Is this a new version of "Streets Of London"?', which I hadn't thought about. The song is basically about the way this country treats its less fortunate. It's a euphemism for abandonment and an attempt to say 'Enough'. I made a direct reference to the incident where a guy with a mental illness killed somebody on the London Underground.

"Also there is the whole issue of drug abuse, which is completely out of hand. These are all real people out there, just like the characters in 'Streets Of London', and people feel so threatened that in London, office staff are bussed to their place of work from the stations so that they don't have to run the gauntlet of the beggars and vagrants who live on the streets near the office blocks."

Slowly a young girl comes down
From what she's had to do
To feel cradled in somebody's arms
Fixed for an hour or two
You see she's helping herself
Providing for what she needs
The community cares for itself, it seems
It don't affect you or me.

Cleverly, McTell plays on the term 'care in the community' to get his message across – now it's the 'community (who had) better take care'. Also, it was a brave move to arrange the song not as a guitar and vocal item, as one might expect for a song with such a serious message, but with a jaunty traditional jazz backing which, on the surface, seems ill-suited to such a song, but works wonderfully well. 'Care In The Community' is another illustration of the power and depth of concern which inspires the songs of Ralph McTell, a quality many more people should recognise.

Chapter
22
Sand In Your Shoes

On 28 January 1995, McTell was invited by Iris Bentley to attend a memorial service at Croydon cemetery where a new headstone was laid on Derek's grave bearing the inscription 'A victim of British justice.' Along with various dignitaries, including Labour leader (now Prime Minister) Tony Blair as well as fellow Croydon boy Wizz Jones, McTell was able once again to lend his support to a cause which has stayed with him throughout his life. In the chapel he performed his song about Bentley, which, he confessed, was "one of the most difficult things I have ever had to do. I could feel my own emotions almost getting to me so I just sang and played louder and somehow got through it."

The spring found him once again touring Australia to the usual positive response. Three years on, 'The Boy With A Note' appeared to gain him even greater popularity, almost as if it had only just been released. Throughout the years, Australia has given McTell a far more respectful hearing than his own country, and the tour was such a success that there were immediate plans for him to return in 1996.

The Dylan Thomas work was recognised in Thomas's own land in March 1995, when McTell was invited to perform six of the songs at the Year of Literature Festival in Swansea. He also recorded a haunting duet with Jacqui McShee for her first solo album, the song a traditional item oddly enough titled 'Factory Girl'. His contribution to the song showed how he had improved as a vocalist through the years, and helped make it one of the standout tracks on a very fine album.

"It was Gerry Conway who suggested getting Ralph in to do the duet," revealed McShee. "I thought he made a superb contribution, offering a great deal to the song. Shortly after the release of the record, we did a gig and Ralph came along to do 'Factory Girl' with me. There I am, not very tall, and there's six foot plus Ralph at his mic. It was a real contrast. He was really nervous, as usual, saying 'What do I do with my hands?' He's not used to appearing on stage without his guitar."

A brief tour of the UK followed his return from Australia – but though the shows were somewhat run of the mill, largely consisting of the usual in terms of the set list, there was one exception. Midway through the tour, McTell introduced one newly recorded composition, 'Peppers And Tomatoes', into his set. The reaction was immediate to a song that displayed a power and topical feel that had been missing from his shows for many years. Audiences let him know their approval – or perhaps they were letting it be known that they were pleased to hear something they hadn't heard before!

More new songs were aired in public in August, as McTell and the Good Men in the Jungle took the stage at the Sidmouth Festival, where they gave 'Seeds Of Heaven' its first live performance in front of a crowd of 4,000. The rest of the summer was spent away from the concert stage as the final touches to the new record were added, and once it was finished negotiations continued to obtain a deal for its release. A long association with German-based concert promoter Michael Bisping resulted in the announcement that he was to be McTell's full-time manager. It was felt that his personal belief in Ralph could stem the business problems of recent years, allowing McTell to concentrate on the creative side of his career.

Ralph and Iris Bentley

Meanwhile, the London-based Castle Communications label had acquired the rights to the defunct Transatlantic label, thus controlling McTell's earliest albums, and Bisping's first move was to ensure that the artist's first 'song-based' album in eight years was released by the label that had given him his start. Titled 'Sand In Your Shoes', it was released in early October. The circle had been completed.

Some of the songs that make up 'Sand In Your Shoes' were among the strongest he has ever put on record. They show the maturity of a man in his early fifties, and demonstrated that he was comfortable with his age and the roads he had taken, enabling him to write from varying angles about a wide range of subjects. One thinks back to Alan O'Leary's frustration with McTell in the 1980s when, on trying to cajole him into writing songs with a topical feel, Ralph would say such things were only "for young men to write about." It was as if he had ridden the writer's block, waiting until he felt himself to be at an age where he could make comments, knowing full well what he was talking about.

This is true of a number of the songs on the album. The title track was inspired by a comment Bruce May had made to his brother many years before, as McTell explained: "I've always thought there was an insanity about older blokes trying to get off with a young girl and actually believing for a time it's going to work out. This happened to someone I knew who went to California. When he came home, Bruce said 'He's still got a bit of sand in his shoes. He'll wake up.'

"The sand in your shoes is either a bit of grit between your toes, that irritates you because it's something that's unresolved, or something that gives you a pleasant warm holiday feeling. It's non-specific, about refusing to grow up, staying young or accepting your past."

'The Enemy Within (The Band)' is both a lament for the loss of one of Britain's natural industries and a look back to the Thatcher era and the 1984 miners' strike. It

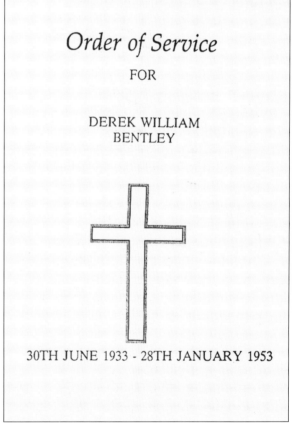

Order of Service

FOR

DEREK WILLIAM
BENTLEY

30TH JUNE 1933 - 28TH JANUARY 1953

was Margaret Thatcher who dubbed the striking miners "the enemy within", which was a damning indictment of those who had fuelled the country's industries for generations. In the north of England, communities, now rapidly declining, were based around the collieries and the colliery band was a focal point of those communities.

As the pits closed, the only link with past generations of mining families were those bands, and many continued after the pits closed. However, slowly but surely, the bands started to become fewer. The instruments were sold off and all links with the past began to crumble and fade away like the industry itself.

> *I've spent months now the music's gone*
> *Gazing at the mine*
> *The rust that creeps across the plant*
> *Like a dullness in the mind*
> *The gates are closed, the shops are shut*
> *Our very jobs they stole*
> *The bandroom's just a shell that keeps*
> *An echo of our soul.*
> **('The Enemy Within', 1993)**

'Fear Of Flying' was inspired by a comment made by comedian Kenneth Williams, who likened life to a bus ride where people get on and off before the journey's end. It is a poignant description of life's journey and gave McTell a chance to remember friends who had stepped off the bus before reaching its destination, while giving thanks that he was still on board.

> *The last time someone got off the bus*
> *I never realised how long we'd spend*
> *Looking at empty seats in front of us*
> *It's a long old road that has no bend.*
> **('Fear Of Flying', 1995)**

Another song reflected religion, a constant theme throughout McTell's life, and a present-day view is heard in 'Jesus Wept', the longest and most powerful lyric on this or possibly any other album in his career: "Religion has stayed with me all my life without me being what I would describe as a religious person. All young men realise that what they believe in has been perverted and ruined, and that's so true of Christianity in every aspect."

There are many varying views of many aspects of religion within the song. The doubts about the miracles of water to wine, raising the dead: "the biggest miracle was that everyone believed it"; and of religious conflict: "in his dream he saw the crusade and all wars that would follow declared in his name." Also, there is a comment on situations like Ulster and Bosnia:

Ralph at Guildford Folk Festival, 1994.

> *Then he saw his houses burning*
> *On both sides of the border*
> *Saw the guiltless suffer*
> *With the guilty and the rest*
> *And when they called his name*
> *And he knew he couldn't help them*
> *That's why Jesus wept.*
> **('Jesus Wept', 1995)**

Winifred May told the story of Ralph as a small boy looking

at the figure of Jesus on the cross and asking her why, if he was a good person, people had done
that to him. It's a question
echoed in certain lines
of the song:

> *Was he supposed to bear it*
> *Like a man or like a God?*
> *Would tears show a weakness*
> *Or a strength by their effect?*
> *Would they be viewed as compassion*
> *Or failure and self pity?*
> *And that's why Jesus wept.*

One of the most intriguing songs is the opener, 'Tous Les Animaux Sont Tristes': "The chorus is in French, but it's actually from a Greek play, and the translation of the Greek was 'all animals are sad after making love.' I've seen animals mate, and afterwards there is distraction, and I've expanded the idea. Making love involves a climax and a subsequent anti-climax, which I equate with the young chap who's never satisfied. Also there is the phenomenon of men who are successful, raise their children and families, remain married and have plenty of money, yet they are so sad and depressed.

"From the little knowledge I have of him, I felt this was the case about Aristotle Onassis, the 'Arri' in the song. He got his boat, got more boats, he was still sad, he had his family but he wasn't happy, because he needed more. Like lots of wealthy men, he believed he could acquire happiness, and almost 'acquired' an artistic talent like Maria Callas because he hadn't anything else to do with his money.

"I think what happened to poor Callas, 'the small brown bird', was that she relieved the ache and the emptiness in his life, but in the end it wasn't enough, and the 'silver arrow' is a metaphor for money and neglect. He metaphorically killed her, and then his darkness returned and he was still alone, so basically, as he couldn't get himself enough power, he married the widow of the most powerful man in the world."

'Peppers And Tomatoes' is the hardest-driving song on the album, showing the full vocal power of which McTell is capable, no doubt helped by his recent work with a live band, helped on by Martin Allcock's guitar and drums from Gerry Conway. The idea of long-established roots growing side by side in the same soil for centuries, then being ripped apart forever by conflict, echoed the nightly images seen on television screens throughout the world, showing the civil war in Bosnia and its tragic consequences. The powerful sound of the song fitted its equally powerful message.

> *This little patch of dirt*
> *This little pile of stones*
> *I can wash the dust from off my face*
> *But this earth is in my bones.*
> **('Peppers And Tomatoes', 1993)**

The excellent production of 'Sand In Your Shoes' owes an enormous debt to Martin Allcock who provided a more sympathetic ear in the studio for McTell than anyone in recent years; hopefully, the pair will work together again. As well as being

STREETS OF LONDON

With Fairport Convention at Deddington Church, Oxon, on 23 April 1994.

an incredibly talented musician, Allcock has a natural ability to sense the right way for songs to develop from an early stage. He has fond memories of his work on this album.

"Some of the songs on there really blew me away as soon as I heard them. 'Still In Dreams' is a perfect example – he'd done about two takes of it and then went for a third. The hairs stood up on my head and arms. Mark Tucker (the engineer) and I looked at each other, and we both burst into tears at the same time. 'We'll take it,' says I. Mark came up with the rolling reverb effect, and it was complete. 'Peppers And Tomatoes' is a very powerful song and I wanted it to be very hard. I needn't have worried with Peggy and Gerry, although we'd tried it about five times and it was late in the day, last song and people's concentration was slipping.

"Peggy said 'Right, everybody. PUB! NOW!' We went for a pint and went straight back and got it first take. We were back in the pub within 20 minutes, and the regulars thought we were taking the piss, but I was a very happy producer. Top marks to Mr Pegg! (Whistle and fiddle player) Frank Gallagher was a little 'relaxed' when he came up to do his bits, but he played great on it eventually.

"'The Case Of Otto Schwarzkopf' is very moving. Ralph trusted me with this song, and I'm very proud of how it came out. He gave me a co-writing credit because I did the arrangement and it wasn't a complete song when he presented it, so I just dived in, keys blazing. The released version was a third re-recording. 'The Islands' meant a lot to me as well. I got very angry when the (trawler) *Braer* went down off Sumburgh Head. I have lived and worked in Shetland, and it was my birthday when the boat came a cropper in 1993. I was moved to write something about it, but having the songwriting talent of a vole, I frustratedly rang Ralph and asked him to write something about it. He came up with a cracker and I wrote the big instrumental bits.

"Chris Leslie is really good on that song – when Peggy heard it, I knew it would end up on (Fairport's) 'Jewel In the Crown', which came out first. I was careful about not nicking Ralph's version, which I still had in the computer. On 'An Irish Blessing', I used the same Uillean pipe sample that I used on Robert Plant's album, 'The Fate Of Nations', and 'Sand In Your Shoes' is actually one of my favourite songs of all time.

"'The Band' just didn't work when it was in my hands, and I was glad to hand it over to Graham Preskett – using the Mevagissey Male Choir was a masterstroke on Ralph's part. However, there were a couple of things on the album I felt indifferent about; 'Daddy's Whistling Home' I think is too long, though I like the basic gist, and 'Care In The Community' I find overlong. I was very busy when that one was being done, so I passed it over with a couple of others to Graham Preskett. They finished up very different to the rest of the album.

"If I'd had complete control, I would have left that track off the record and instead used 'Rue de la Montagne Saint Genevieve'; although that's an old song, I don't understand why it was left off at all! But we had some good laughs making the album, and I was really pleased it was eventually released."

One of the most dramatic songs McTell has ever written, 'The Case Of Otto Schwarzkopf' was inspired by a poem by an Israeli scholar named Schmuel Huppert, who as a child had been imprisoned in the Nazi concentration camp in Belsen during the Second World War. McTell was visibly moved by the poem, which he showed the author in the summer of 1993, and wanted to do something with such a powerful piece of writing but was unsure precisely what.

The scene then changes to Woodworm Studios, where he was working on demos with Martin Allcock in March 1994. Climbing the stairs to the control room, a haunting melody on piano could be heard – and, having attended the screening of Spielberg's *Schindler's List* the previous evening, it seemed almost like listening to the moving score that John Williams had composed for the movie. McTell looked shocked at my comparison between the film score and what could be heard: "What he's playing is that song about the holocaust I told you I was working on," he said. "You've got it absolutely right" was my response.

> *In winter 1944*
> *The German order came*
> *Take what you think you'll need*
> *You're moving East*
> *And don't make any fuss*
> *Just leave everything to us*
> *Twenty kilos or just one suitcase each.*
> **('The Case Of Otto Schwarzkopf', 1994)**

Schwarzkopf, who came from Prague, was imprisoned at Theresienstadt which, according to the Nazis, was one of their landscaped and comfortable 'model camps' – a ruse to hide the awful truth from those who entered its gates. His suitcase is exhibited at the holocaust museum.

> *The case of Otto Schwarzkopf*
> *Has made its way without him*
> *To Jerusalem in anger, guilt and sorrow*
> *Pray humanity can hear*
> *What it cannot see through tears*
> *The cry of yesterday before tomorrow.*

There is a wonderful moment in the song when Allcock's piano perfectly captures that mid-European feel of sadness and despair and slowly gathers momentum, perfectly illustrating the moving train taking its cargo of suffering towards a final indignity.

> *Reference your trip/A.L.L. 1/*
> *Cattle trucks as per specification*
> *The livestock rule allows*
> *Thirty pigs or seven cows*
> *One hundred and twenty Jews*
> *For transportation.*

The final song on the album, 'An Irish Blessing', is an appropriate ending to what is the most satisfying batch of songs that McTell has assembled in his entire career. As previously mentioned, many show the maturity he has attained during 30 years as a writer, and, more directly, as a father. 'An Irish Blessing' portrays a man seeing his children moving away to develop their own identities and lives, and is a progression from the sentiments expressed in 'Love Grows', which suggests that if you have love and compassion you can spread it around.

Now, as those same loved ones move on, the love and compassion is as strong as ever, but now has to be given from a distance.

> *And now it's me who has to learn*
> *To let you make your way alone*
> *To try not to direct each turn*
> *Your triumphs and mistakes your own*
> *Your path will be different from mine*
> *Tricks of my trade no use to you*
> *To others and yourself be kind*
> *Your suffering will hurt me too.*
> **('An Irish Blessing', 1994)**

This song gives McTell another chance to show his affinity to the traditions of Ireland. It was therefore most apt that he has received recognition from *Irish World* for his contribution to Irish culture throughout his career. Christy Moore: "The Irish have a thing in them where they recognise a kindred spirit, and can spot if it's genuine. They have an uncanny knack of making them one of their own, wherever they may originate from. A perfect illustration of this is how they bonded to Jack Charlton and his success with the Irish national football team.

"Ralph is recognised as having that same kindred spirit. I can guarantee that somewhere in Ireland, on any day of the week, someone will be playing 'From Clare To Here'. They may not all be able to tell you who wrote it, but that, to them, is a true Irish song."

'Sand In Your Shoes' was reviewed in the UK music press soon after release as a sound, if not spectacular, release that still showed McTell to be an above average writer. This may not seem a big deal, but in the past, McTell's records, especially those released on Mays, have seemed to fall to the bottom of list of records which should be reviewed and have only received brief write-ups some time after the event. While it was not suggested that there was a significant shift in his status, it was nevertheless pleasing that the album was reviewed on time and fairly positively into the bargain.

At the end of 1995, McTell played a short tour of the East Coast of America, where he was greeted as enthusiastically as ever by a growing hard-core audience who, by their reaction to him, have seen too little of him down the years. However, his records were still not easy to find, a situation that needs to be corrected not just on the other side of the Atlantic but in the UK. It seems a strange oversight that such albums as 'Not Till Tomorrow', 'Easy' and 'Right Side Up', to name just three, are unavailable.

In an age of CD anthologies and retrospective boxed sets, where artists and their labels make so much of their early work available to the public, this illustrates an area where McTell or whoever is managing him should swiftly sort out the contractual problems of back catalogue and make these releases available before it's too late. It is, sadly, another example of where McTell's career has suffered some lack of foresight and needs someone with the care of, for example, John Tobler who showed with his 1994 re-release of 'Slide Away The Screen' on Road Goes On Forever Records how such re-issues should be undertaken.

So as this story reached its conclusion, McTell's second live album, 'Songs For Six Strings', was released in the autumn of 1996. It is a pleasing selection that, in comparison with 'Ralph Albert And Sydney', shows the way McTell and his earlier songs have matured over the past 30 years. A more adventurous idea might have been to introduce a series of previously unreleased songs into his repertoire and record some dates with this release in mind, but this is a minor gripe – and it was most pleasing to discover a live version of 'Red And Gold' had at last been found intact.

Which is where we end this particular version of the story of Ralph McTell's life and the work he has produced. This version? It is to be hoped that there will be a lot more of the unique and personal vignettes of life which he writes so well, and, against the backdrop of 'Sand In Your Shoes', it is by no means impossible that his best writing is still to come.

It has always been my belief that McTell could and should have been a far bigger act in terms of public acceptance than he has become. It is also my belief that he has underachieved, although this can be set against a constantly unsteady relationship with managers and the feeling that McTell never really wanted to become any bigger – a view shared by his erstwhile producer, Tony Visconti.

"He's got a built-in level of success which is very clearly recognisable, and which he doesn't want to exceed, because he's rooted in a certain area of London where he's been going to his local pub for 15 years or something, and he'd rather forsake success and stay at home if it takes him too far from the pub. When he re-recorded 'Streets Of London' and got a big hit, that supplied him with a three-storey house within walking distance of that pub, and he's a very happy man. I wish more people would realise that life can be that simple, because people who want enormous success have to give up all sorts of things." This is probably the most accurate description of McTell yet!

In the spring of 1997, there was a further change of management when Steve Brown, Billy Connolly's manager, expressed interest in

With Carolyn Hester, a fellow singer and confirmed McTell fan.

handling McTell throughout the remainder of a year which would mark his 30th anniversary as a recording artist. Meanwhile, Michael Bisping would continue to look after his European affairs.

It is probably something to do with the 'ordinary bloke' persona in which most people categorise him that has prevented McTell's elevation to a deserved position among the best writers and players, but this is something Christy Moore is keen to dismiss: "Forget that myth. Ordinary blokes do not make records of the calibre of Ralph McTell or sell out the Royal Albert Hall. If that was the case, everybody would be doing it and they are not. Ralph is a writer of some power – and that should not be forgotten."

The purpose behind writing this story was to try to juxtapose the life and the work, demonstrating that this wonderful songwriter didn't simply appear from nowhere and that his songs possess an extraordinary depth. My analysis of many of his songs are simply my own opinions, with which some readers may disagree and hopefully form their own. In order to do that, they must search for McTell's records, which contain some of the most crafted songs of the last 50 years. The real story of Ralph McTell is all there.

It was recently said that Richard Thompson should be looked upon as one of Britain's 'national treasures.' If that is so, then Ralph McTell is this land's undiscovered gem. The final word should go to Christy Moore: "When Ralph McTell walks out on a stage, he brings just two things with him. His incredible talent and his humanity through his work."

Ralph and Nanna on their 25th Anniversary, as photographed by their son Sam. Despite being featured in Hello *magazine, they are still together!*

Chapter 23
Discography

SINGLES

Nanna's Song/Eight Frames A Second
EMI.
Released 1968.

Summer Come Along/Girl On A Bicycle
Transatlantic BIGT125.
Released 1969.

Kew Gardens/Father Forgive Them
Transatlantic BIGT131.
Released 1970.

Spiral Staircase/Terminus
Transatlantic BIGT134.
Released 1970.

First And Last Man/In Some Way I Loved You
Famous G & W FAM105.
Released 1971.

Teacher Teacher/Truckin' Little Baby
Famous G & W FAM 111.
Released 1972.

When I Was A Cowboy/Small Voice Calling
Reprise K14214.
Released 1972.

Zimmerman Blues/First Song
Reprise K14225.
Released 1972.

Take It Easy/Sweet Mystery
Reprise.
Released 1974.

Streets Of London/Summer Lightning
Reprise K14380.
Released December 1974.

El Progresso/Grande Affaire
Warner Bros K16537.
Released 1975.

Let Me Down Easy/Would I Lie To You
Warner Bros K16633.
Released 1975.

Dreams Of You/Sweet Forgiveness
Warner Bros K16843.
Released December 1975.

Weather The Storm/First Song
Warner Bros.
Released 1976.

Naomi/Tequila Sunset
Warner Bros K16884.
Released February 1977.

Maginot Waltz/Winnie's Rag/Streets Of London/Sweet Mystery
Warner Bros K17008.
Released August 1977.

Heroes And Villains/Sweet Girl On My Mind
Warner Bros K17274.
Released 1978.

Love Grows/Banjo Man
Warner Bros K17304.
Released January 1979.

From Clare To Here/Promises
Warner Bros K17584.
Released 1979.

England/Grey Sea Strand
Mays Records ING1.
Released 1981.
(Reissued June 1982 on EMI 5315.)

I Fall To Pieces/I'm Not A Rock
Mays Records ING2.
Released November 1982.

Kenny The Kangaroo EP
Kenny The Kangaroo/Holly The Hedgehog/
Camilla The Camel/Nellie The Newt
Mays Records ING3.
Released December 1982.

Kenny The Kangaroo/The Parrot Song
Mays Records ING4.
Released May 1983.

Stranger To The Season/Mr Connaughton
Mays Records ING7.
Released October 1983.

Wind In The Willows/Open Road
Red Bus RBUS 94.
Released May 1984.

The Winner's Song/Geordie's On The Road
Mays Records ING11.
Released November 1984.

I Like Rubbish/Five Balloons
Mays Records.
Released 1986.

The Things You Wish Yourself/Keeping The Night At Bay
Mays Records ING14.
Released 1986.

Bridge Of Sighs/Blind Arthur Goes To Adelaide (Adelaide Rag)
Mays Records ING15.
Released 1987.

ALBUMS

Eight Frames A Second
Transatlantic Records TRA165.
Released 1968.
Nanna's Song – The Mermaid And The Seagull – Hesitation
Blues – Are You Receiving Me? – Morning Dew –
Sleepytime Blues – Eight Frames A Second – Willoughby's
Farm – Louise – Blind Blake's Rag – I'm Sorry I Must Leave
– Too Tight – Granny Takes A Trip

Spiral Staircase
Transatlantic Records TRA177.
Released 1968 (re-released on Wooded Hill HILL CD5
in 1996).
Streets Of London – Mrs Adlam's Angels – Wino And The
Mouse – England 1914 – Last Train And Ride – The
Fairground – Spiral Staircase – Kind Hearted Woman Blues –
Bright And Beautiful Things – Daddy's Here – Rizraklaru –
(My) Baby Keeps Staying Out All Night Long – Terminus

My Side Of Your Window
Transatlantic Records TRA209.
Released 1969.
Michael In The Garden – Clown – Girl On A Bicycle –
Father Forgive Them – All Things Change – I've Thought
About It – Factory Girl – Blues In More Than 12 Bars –
Kew Gardens – Wait Until The Snow – Silver Birch &
Weeping Willow

Ralph McTell Revisited
Transatlantic Records TRA222.
Released 1970.
Spiral Staircase – Michael In The Garden – Last Train And
Ride – Kew Gardens – The Fairground – Streets Of London
– Factory Girl – Bright And Beautiful Things – Father
Forgive Them – Clown – Terminus

You Well Meaning Brought Me Here
Famous SFMA5753.
Released 1971 (re-released as 'Ralph McTell 1971-72' on
Mays Records TG001A in 1982 and 'The Ferryman'
TPG001 in 1987).
Genesis 1 Verse 20 – First And Last Man – In Some Way I
Loved You – Lay Your Money Down – Old Brown Dog –
Pick Up A Gun – You Well Meaning Brought Me Here –
Chalkdust – The Ballad Of Dancing Doreen – Claudia –
The Ferryman

Not Till Tomorrow
Reprise K44210.
Released November 1972.
Zimmerman Blues – First Song – When I Was A Cowboy –
Nettle Wine – Sylvia – Birdman – Barges – Standing Down
In New York Town – Another Rain Has Fallen – This Time
Of Night – Gypsy

Easy
Reprise K54013.
Released March 1974.
Take It Easy – Maddy Dances – Maginot Waltz – Sweet
Mystery – Stuff No More – Run Johnny Run – ZigZag Line
– Let Me Down Easy – Would I Lie To You – Summer
Lightning

Streets
Warner Bros K56105.
Released March 1975 (re-released on Leola Music
TPGCD 12 in April 1995 with track variations).
Streets Of London – You Make Me Feel Good – Grande
Affaire – Seeds Of Heaven – El Progresso – Red Apple Juice
– Heron Song – Pity The Boy – Interest On The Loan –
Jenny Taylor/Je n'etais La – Lunar Lullaby

Right Side Up
Warner Bros K56296.
Released November 1976 (re-released as 'Weather The
Storm' on Mays Records TG002 in 1982).
San Diego Serenade – Naomi – Tequila Sunset – Weather
The Storm – River Rising – From Clare To Here –
Chairman And The Little Man – Country Boys – Slow
Burning Companion – Nightmares – May You Never

Ralph, Albert And Sydney
Warner Bros K56399.
Released August 1977 (re-released on Mays Records
TG003 in 1982).
First Song – Grande Affaire – Big Tree – Michael In The
Garden – Dry Bone Rag – Zimmerman Blues – Maginot
Waltz – Five Knuckle Shuffle – When I Was A Cowboy –
Let Me Down Easy – Naomi – Sylvia – Streets Of London –
Winnie's Rag – Waltzing Matilda

Slide Away The Screen
Warner Bros K56599.
Released April 1979 (re-released as 'Love Grows' on Mays
Records TG004 in 1982 and 'Slide Away The Screen And
Other Stories' on Road Goes On Forever RGFCD 021 in
September 1994 with track variations).
Love Grows – One Heart – Gold In California – Van Nuys
(Cruise Night) – London Apprentice – Traces – Heroes &
Villains – Harry (Don't Go) – Autumn – Promises – White
Dress – Save The Last Dance For Me

Water Of Dreams
Mays Records TG005
Released 1982.
Got To Be With You – Please Don't Haunt Me – I'm Not A
Rock – Hands Of Joseph – Pykey Boy – Bentley And Craig
– Water Of Dreams – Affairs Of The Heart – Cold On The
Stones – I Want You – Geordie's On The Road – Song For
Martin

Songs From Alphabet Zoo
Mays Records TG007.
Released 1983.
Kenny The Kangaroo – Fergus The Frog – Peter The Parrot
– Yuri The Yak – Holly The Hedgehog – Tammy The
Tortoise – Sally The Seal – Ollie The Otter – Victor The
Vulture – Nellie The Newt – Gordon The Goat – Wagstaff
The Woodpecker – Quentin The Quail – Unwin The
Unicorn

Best Of Alphabet Zoo
Music For Pleasure MFP4156741.
Released September 1984.
Zoo Zoo Zoo – Albert The Albatross – Fergus The Frog –
Gordon The Goat – Holly The Hedgehog – Impala Song –
Kenny The Kangaroo – Maurice The Mole – Nigel The
Nightingale – Ollie The Otter – Peter The Parrot – Sally
The Seal – Tammy The Tortoise – Victor The Vulture –
X-ray Fish – Yuri The Yak – Zoe The Zebra

At The End Of A Perfect Day
Telstar Records 2263.
Released December 1985.
Streets Of London – Scarborough Fair – You've Got A
Friend – Penny Lane – The Lamplighter (England 1914) –
The Last Farewell – Sailing – Beautiful Dreamer –
Homeward Bound – Scarlet Ribbons – I'll Have To Say I
Love You In A Song – Morning Has Broken – Weather The
Storm – Those Were The Days – Barges – England

Tickle On The Tum
Mays Records TPG008.
Released November 1986.
I Like Rubbish – Freddie The Fireman – I Love My Bicycle – Chicken Chicken Banjo – Freckles And Spots – Five Balloons – Holding Hands – Keeping The Night At Bay – Tap Tap Tap With The Hammer – The Counting Song – Dora The Driver – Buzz Buzz Buzz (The Fly Song) – Connie Capers On Patrol – Bessie's Washboard Blues – Come On You Rovers – The Things You Wish Yourself

Tickle On The Tum – Stories and Songs
St Michael 1361/5606
I Love My Bicycle – Dora The Driver – Connie Capers On Patrol – Dr Dimple – Teacher's Lost Voice – Rowland Crust (NB: Only Ralph McTell's contributions listed – this release also features stories from the series read by others.)

Bridge Of Sighs
Mays Records TPG009.
Released January 1987.
Throw Out A Line And Dream – Mr Connaughton – The Girl From The Hiring Fair – Choux Fleur – Something The Matter with Mary – Bridge Of Sighs – The Setting – Little Actress – Bad Girl – Holiday Romance – Dreams Of You – Words I Couldn't Say

Blue Skies Black Heroes
Leola Records TPG010.
Released May 1988.
Truckin L'il Babe – Coalman Blues – Fables Ain't Nothing But Doggone Lies – Drybone Shuffle – Louis Collins – Love In Vain – Can't Be Satisfied – Corrine What Makes You Treat Me So – Statesboro Blues – Arthur Blake – Kind Hearted Woman – Untrue Blues – Early This Morning – Working On The Railroad – Leah's Favourite – I Bid You Goodnight

Affairs Of The Heart
Castle CCSCD219.
Released October 1989.
First Song – Promises – Tequila Sunset – You Make Me Feel Good – River Rising – Naomi – Affairs Of The Heart – Would I Lie To You – Choux Fleur – Words I Couldn't Say – Summer Lightning – Nanna's Song – White Dress – Seeds Of Heaven – Let Me Down Easy – Traces – Terminus – Heron Song – Grande Affaire – If I Don't Get Home – Love Grows – Dreams Of You – One Heart

Stealin' Back
Essential Records ESSCD137.
Released December 1990.
I'm Going To Germany – Sugar Babe – Prison Wall Blues – Hesitation Blues – Weeping Willow – When You've Got A Good Friend – Candy Man – When Did You Leave Heaven – Stealin' – That'll Do Babe – Black Girl – Sweet Petulie – Nobody Knows You When You're Down And Out – Lovin' I Crave – Dying Crapshooters Blues – This'll Bring You Back

Silver Celebration
Castle CCSCD329.
Released March 1992 (re-released as 'The Songs Of Ralph McTell' on Red House Records RHR CD 86 in US, 1996).
Summer Girls – The Girl From The Hiring Fair – Barges – Michael In The Garden – Tequila Sunset – Bridge Of Sighs – Song For Martin – Throw Out A Line And Dream – The Setting – From Clare To Here – Mr Connaughton – Hands Of Joseph – Stranger To The Seasons – Weather The Storm – The Ferryman – Streets Of London

The Boy With A Note
Leola Music TPGCD11.
Released MONTH 1992.
Overture (Son Of The Sea Wave) – Introductory Narration..Meet The Detective – Summer Girls: Narration..The Slim Lover – Irish Girl ; Narration.The Fitzroy – Slip Shot Tap Room Dance (Soho So What) – Narration..These Soho Streets – Narration..No Grown Man's Land – Narration..Reprieve of Home (Laugharne) – Conundrum Of Time (Shouldn't You Be Dancing) – Milk For One (Storm In A Teacup) – Narration: Leaving For The States – Wonderful Country (A Proposition Of Prepositions) – Caitlin's Dream (Summer Birds Are Leaving) – Narration: The Certain Tide – Narration: Continuing Investigations – Get Me A Doctor – Narration: The Tunnels "Never End" in Sight – I Miss You Most Of All – Narration: Naked In The Station – Cradled In The Rocking Boat

The Complete Alphabet Zoo
Road Goes On Forever RGFCD016.
Released January 1994 (partially released originally on 'Songs From Alphabet Zoo' in 1983).
Albert Ross The Albatross – Boris The Bat – Camilla The Camel – Digger The Dog – Edna The Elephant – Fergus The Frog – Gordon The Goat – Holly The Hedgehog – Impala Song – Jake The Jackdaw – Kenny The Kangaroo – Laurence The Lion – Maurice The Mole – Nigel The Nightingale – Nellie The Newt – Ollie The Otter – Peter The Parrot – Quentin The Quail – The Rabbit Song – Sally The Seal – Tammy The Tortoise – Unwin The Unicorn – Victor The Vulture – Wagstaff The Woodpecker – X-Ray Fish – Yuri The Yak – Zoe The Zebra

Sand In Your Shoes
Transatlantic TRACD119.
Released October 1995.
Tous Les Animaux Sont Tristes – The Islands – Fear Of Flying – Care In The Community – I Don't Think About You – The Enemy Within – Sand In Your Shoes – Jesus Wept – After Rain – Peppers And Tomatoes – The Case Of Otto Schwarzkopf – Daddy's Whistling Home – Still In Dreams – An Irish Blessing

Songs For Six Strings Volume 2
Leola Music OLA15B2CD.
Released 1996.
Gypsy – Mrs Adlam's Angels – Mermaid And The Seagull – Lovin' I Crave – Factory Girl – From Clare To Here – Red And Gold – Summer Girls – Fingerbuster – Near Enough – The Slipshot Taproom Dance – Old Brown Dog – The Girl From The Hiring Fair – The Setting – First And Last Man – Affairs Of The Heart – When Did You Leave Heaven – Great Dreams Of Heaven
(NB: This album is titled 'Vol 2' as McTell's first live album, 'Ralph Albert And Sydney' will be released for the first time on CD in 1997 as 'Vol 1'.)

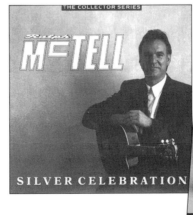

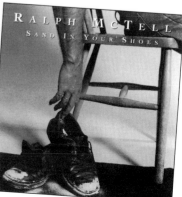

STREETS OF LONDON

APPEARANCES ON
OTHER ARTISTS' RECORDINGS

COB – Clive's Own Band
The Spirit Of Love
CBS 69010.
Released 1971.
McTell contributes guitar to the title track

Mary Hopkin
Earth Song – Ocean Song
Apple Records SAPCOR21.
Released 1971.
McTell contributes guitar

John Kongos
Kongos
Fly Records HIFLY7.
Released January 1972.
McTell contributes acoustic guitar to 'Tomorrow I'll Go'

Harvey Andrews
Writer
Cube HIFLY 10.
Released 1972.
Hey Sandy – In The Darkness – Boothferry Bridge – Gift Of
A Brand New Day – Soldier – Anna (My Love): Borne On
The Breeze – Martha – When I Am Old One Day – Soap
Opera
McTell on acoustic guitar

Tom Paxton
Peace Will Come
Reprise Records K44182.
Released July 1972.
McTell on acoustic guitar

Fairport Convention
Rosie
Island Records ILPS 9208.
Released 1973.
McTell contributes acoustic guitar to 'Me With You'

Tom Paxton
New Songs For Old Friends
Reprise Records K44237.
Released 1973.
Recorded live before an invited audience at the Marquee
Club in London. McTell contributes guitar, vocals and
harmonica on all tracks. (Two tracks 'Silent Night' and
'When Princes Meet' were recorded at Marquee Studios with
McTell playing guitar.)

Bert Jansch
Moonshine
Reprise K44225.
Released February 1973.
McTell contributes harmonica to 'Brought With The Rain'

Lynsey De Paul
Lynsey Sings
MAM Records MAME 3002.
Released 1974.
McTell contributes acoustic guitar to 'Storm In A Teacup'
and 'Crossword Puzzle'

Various Artists
Just Guitars
CBS Records 25946.
Released 1983.
Clown – Anji (McTell & Bert Jansch) – Mr Connaughton –
Song For Martin (McTell & John Williams) – Streets Of
London (McTell & John Williams)
This album was recorded at the Barbican Centre, London, on
18 December 1982, at a benefit concert for the Samaritans

The GPs
Saturday Rolling Around
Woodworm Records WRC 014.
Released May 1992 (reissued on HTD Records HTDCD53
in March 1996).
Saturday Rolling Around – Steel Guitar Rag – Zimmerman
Blues – Together Again – Pretty Boy Floyd – Love Grows –
I'm So Lonesome I Could Cry – Penitentiary Bound – Don't
Do It – Going Going Gone – Red Apple Juice – Honky
Tonk Blues – I'm The One You Need – Cut Across Shorty –
Great Balls Of Fire
Recorded at Fairport Convention's annual reunion festival at
Broughton Castle, Oxfordshire, in August 1981. As well as
lead vocals, McTell plays rhythm guitar, harmonica and bass
guitar (on the opening track)

Phil Coulter
Words And Music
Four Seasons Music FSCD007.
Released July 1992.
McTell co-wrote words and music to 'I Loved The Ground'

Fairport Convention
25th Anniversary Concert
Woodworm Records WRDCD 022.
Released 1993.
'Polly On The Shore'
This album was recorded at Cropredy, Oxfordshire, on 15
August 1992

Cilla Black
Through The Years
Columbia 474 650 1
Released September 1993.
McTell contributes guitar to 'Streets Of London'

Various Artists
**Out On the Rolling Sea – A Tribute To The Music of
Joseph Spence**
Hokey Pokey Records HPR 20042.
Released 1994.
A newly-recorded version of 'Stealin'' for this charity album.

Show Of Hands
Beat About The Bush
Isis Records CD IS05.
Released March 1994.
McTell contributes vocals and harmonica to 'The Hook Of
Love' and 'Cars'

Paul Millns
Against The Tide
Hypertension Records HYCD 200 138.
Released January 1995.
McTell contributes acoustic guitar to 'When Love Comes
Along' and 'Don't Wait Too Long'

Billy Connolly
Musical Tour Of Scotland
Tickety-Boo Records 529816-2.
The Islands – Will Ye Go (Wild Mountain Thyme) – Flower
Of Scotland
(This album also features instrumental versions of 'The
Islands' and 'Barges')

McShee, Conway & Cozens
About Thyme
GJS Records GJSCD 012.
Released July 1995.
McTell duets with Jacqui McShee on 'Factory Girl'

Wizz Jones
The Legendary Me
Village Thing VTS4.
McTell contributes harmonium and electric guitar

Billy Connolly
Single of unknown title
McTell on tracks 'Song To', 'Heartbeat' and 'You're The
Ointment In My Fly'